Envision It! | Visual Skills Handbook

Author's Purpose

Cause and Effect

Compare and Contrast

Draw Conclusions

Fact and Opinion

Generalize

Graphic Sources

Literary Elements

Main Idea and Details

Sequence

EI•1

Author's Purpose

An author writes for many purposes, some of which are to inform, to entertain, to persuade, or to express feelings or a mood. An author may have more than one purpose for writing.

Cause and Effect

An effect is something that happens. A cause is why that thing happens. An effect sometimes has more than one cause. A cause sometimes has more than one effect. Clue words such as *because*, *as a result*, *therefore*, and *so that* can signal causes and effects.

Cause

Effect

Compare and Contrast

To compare and contrast is to look for similarities and differences in things. Clue words such as *like* or *as* show similarities. Clue words such as *but* or *unlike* show differences.

Draw Conclusions

When we draw conclusions, we make sensible decisions or form reasonable opinions after thinking about the facts and details in what we are reading.

Fact and Opinion

A fact is something that can be proved. Facts are based on evidence. Opinions express ideas and are based on the interpretation of evidence.

Generalize

To generalize is to make a broad statement or rule that applies to many examples.

Graphic Sources

A graphic source shows information in a way that the reader can see.

Table

A table is a box, square, or rectangle that contains information in rows and columns.

ANIMAL	FOOT-PRINT	#
		3
		10
		6
		12
		9

Bar Graph

A bar graph uses horizontal and vertical lines to compare information.

NUMBER OF ANIMALS OBSERVED

Map

A map is a drawing of a place that shows where something is or where something happened.

Diagram

A diagram is a drawing, usually with parts that are labeled.

Literary Elements

A Day at the Beach

Understanding a story requires knowing the four main parts of a story: character, setting, plot, and theme.

Setting - the time and place in which a story happens

Character - a person or animal in a story

Plot - the pattern of events in a story

Climax

Rising Action

Conflict

Solution

Theme - the big idea of a story

Main Idea and Details

Main idea is the most important idea about a topic. For example, it takes a lot of people to put on a big rock concert.

Details are smaller pieces of information that support the main idea. Musicians, technicians, and fans are all part of the rock concert experience.

Sequence

Sequence refers to the order that events happen.
We use sequence when we list the steps in a process.

Envision It! | Visual Strategies Handbook

Background Knowledge

Background knowledge is what you already know about a topic based on your reading and personal experience. Make connections to people, places, and things from the real world. Use background knowledge before, during, and after reading.

To use background knowledge

- with fiction, preview the title, author's name, and illustrations
- with nonfiction, preview chapter titles, headings, graphics, and captions
- think about what you already know
- think about your own experiences

Let's Think About Reading!

When I use background knowledge, I ask myself
- Does this character remind me of someone?
- How is this story or text similar to others I have read?
- What else do I already know about this genre or topic?

Important Ideas

Important ideas are essential ideas and supporting details in a nonfiction selection. Important ideas include information and facts that provide clues to the author's purpose.

To identify important ideas
- read all titles, headings, and captions
- look for words in italics, boldface print, or bulleted lists
- look for signal words and phrases: *for example, most important,* and others
- use photographs, illustrations, or other graphic sources
- note how the text is organized—cause and effect, problem and solution, question and answer, or other ways

Let's Think About Reading!

When I identify important ideas, I ask myself
- What information is included in bold, italics, or some other special lettering?
- What details support important ideas?
- Are there signal words and phrases?
- What do illustrations, photos, diagrams, and charts show?
- How is the text organized?
- Why did the author write this?

Inferring

When we **infer** we use background knowledge with clues in the text to come up with our own ideas about what the author is trying to present.

To infer
- identify what you already know
- combine what you know with text clues to come up with your own ideas

Let's Think About Reading!

When I infer, I ask myself
- What do I already know?
- Which text clues are important?
- What is the author trying to present?

Monitor and Clarify

We **monitor** comprehension to check our understanding of what we've read. We **clarify** to find out why we haven't understood what we've read and to fix up problems.

To monitor and clarify
- use background knowledge
- try different strategies: ask questions, reread, or use text features and illustrations

Hmmm. This part about the pyramids is difficult to understand. I'll slow down and reread to clarify.

Let's Think About Reading!

When I monitor and clarify, I ask myself
- Do I understand what I'm reading?
- What doesn't make sense?
- What strategies can I use?

Predict and Set Purpose

We **predict** to tell what might happen next in a story or article. The prediction is based on what has already happened. We **set a purpose** to guide our reading.

To predict and set a purpose
- preview the title and the author's name
- preview any illustrations or graphics
- identify why you're reading
- use what you already know to make predictions
- check and change your predictions based on new information

Let's Think About Reading!

When I predict and set a purpose, I ask myself
- What do I already know?
- What do I think will happen?
- What is my purpose for reading?

Questioning

Questioning is asking good questions about important text information. Questioning takes place before, during, and after reading.

To question
- read with a question in mind
- stop, think, and record your questions as you read
- make notes when you find information
- check your understanding and ask questions to clarify

Let's Think About Reading!

When I question, I ask myself
- Have I asked a good question with a question word?
- What questions help me make sense of my reading?
- What does the author mean?

Story Structure

Story structure is the arrangement of a story from beginning to end. Most stories involve a conflict and a resolution. You can use this information to summarize a story.

To identify story structure
- note the conflict, or problem, at the beginning of a story
- track the rising action as the conflict builds in the middle
- recognize the climax when the characters face the conflict
- identify how the conflict gets resolved and the story ends

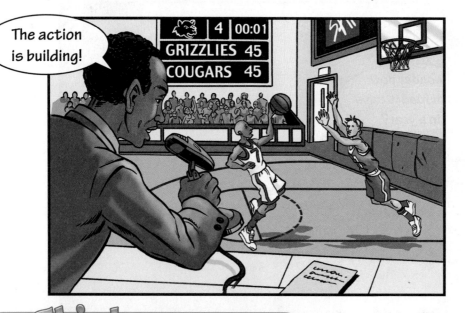

The action is building!

Let's Think About Reading!

When I identify story structure, I ask myself
- What are the characters' goals?
- What is the story's conflict?
- How does the conflict build throughout the story?
- How is the conflict resolved in the end?

Summarize

We **summarize,** or retell, to check our understanding of what we've read. A summary is a brief statement—no more than a few sentences.

To summarize fiction
- tell what happens in the story
- think about the characters and their goals, the setting, and the plot

To summarize nonfiction
- tell the main idea, leaving out supporting details
- think about text structure and how the selection is organized

Let's Think About Reading!

When I summarize, I ask myself
- What is the story or selection about?
- In fiction, what are the characters' goals? Are they successful?
- In nonfiction, how is the information organized?

Text Structure

We use **text structure** to look for the way the author has organized the text; for example, cause and effect, problem and solution, sequence, or compare and contrast. Analyze text structure before, during, and after reading to locate information.

To identify text structure
- before reading: preview titles, headings, and illustrations
- make predictions
- during reading: ask questions, identify the structure, and notice the organization
- after reading: recall the organization and summarize the text

Let's Think About Reading!

When I identify text structure, I ask myself
- What clues do titles, headings, and illustrations provide?
- How is information organized?
- How does the organization help my understanding?

Visualize

We **visualize** to form pictures in our minds as we read. This helps us monitor our comprehension.

To visualize

- combine what you already know with details from the text to make pictures in your mind
- use all of your senses to put yourself in the story or text

Let's **Think** About **Reading!**

When I visualize, I ask myself
- What do I already know?
- Which details create pictures in my mind?
- How can my senses put me in the story or text?

Program Authors

Peter Afflerbach

Camille Blachowicz

Candy Dawson Boyd

Elena Izquierdo

Connie Juel

Edward Kame'enui

Donald Leu

Jeanne R. Paratore

P. David Pearson

Sam Sebesta

Deborah Simmons

Alfred Tatum

Sharon Vaughn

Susan Watts-Taffe

Karen Kring Wixson

 Glenview, Illinois • Boston, Massachusetts • Chandler, Arizona • Upper Saddle River, New Jersey

We dedicate Reading Street to
Peter Jovanovich.

His wisdom, courage,
and passion for education
are an inspiration to us all.

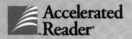

About the Cover Artist

Mark Fredrickson was born in the Upper Peninsula of Michigan, in a little town on Lake Superior. As a child, he loved to draw and paint everything he saw around him. He moved to the big city to become a famous illustrator so that later he could afford to move back to the Upper Peninsula, to a little town on Lake Superior. He has won numerous awards for his paintings, including a gold medal from the Society of Illustrators. He works from his home, a log cabin in the woods.

ISBN-13: 978-0-328-45569-0
ISBN-10:   0-328-45569-5
4 5 6 7 8 9 10 V042 14 13 12 11

CC1

Dear Reader,

Are you enjoying your trip down *Scott Foresman Reading Street?* Get ready for more reading adventures. This book is about explorers and adventurers, different kinds of resources, and the ways that one culture affects another. You will read about people who have gone first in their fields, such as Jane Goodall, the Buffalo Soldiers, and Thomas Alva Edison.

You will read about a boy who learns what makes some senior citizens tick, about Cesar Chavez and his struggles and triumphs, and about a town that was blown away by a tornado and decided to rebuild green. You will meet memorable characters who live and have lived all over the world, from the Aztecs to Don Quixote to brave immigrants in the United States.

At each intersection, you will learn something new and be able to practice what you learned before.

So buckle up and enjoy the rest of the journey!

Sincerely,
The Authors

Unit 4 Contents

EXPLORERS, PIONEERS, AND DISCOVERERS

How have those who've gone first influenced those who've gone after?

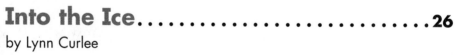

Week 2

Week 3

Unit 4 Contents

Week 6

Unit 4

Envision It! A Comprehension Handbook

RESOURCES

What are resources and why are they important to us?

Week 2

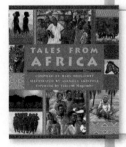

Week 3

Unit 5 Contents

Week 6

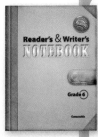

Unit 5

Envision It! A Comprehension Handbook

**Envision It! Visual Skills
Handbook EI•1–EI•13**

**Envision It! Visual Strategies
Handbook EI•15–EI•25**

Words! Vocabulary Handbook W•1–W•15

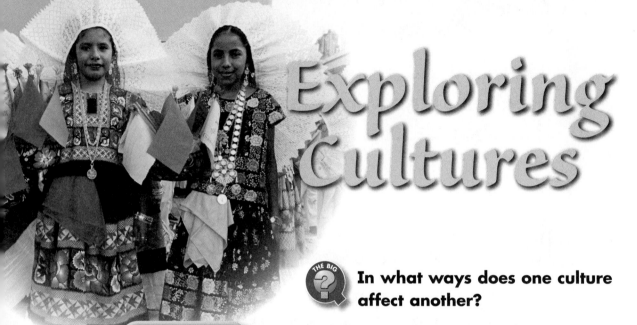

Exploring Cultures

In what ways does one culture affect another?

Week 1

Let's Think About Reading!

classic historical fiction • social studies

retold and adapted by Eric A. Kimmel

textbook entry • social studies

from *Scott Foresman Social Studies: The World*

Week 2

expository text • social studies

expository text • social studies

Week 3

realistic fiction • social studies

expository text • social studies

Unit 6 Contents

Envision It! A Comprehension Handbook

Don Leu
The Internet Guy

Right before our eyes, the nature of reading and learning is changing. The Internet and other technologies create new opportunities, new solutions, and new literacies. New reading comprehension skills are required online. They are increasingly important to our students and our society.

Those of us on the Reading Street team are here to help you on this new, and very exciting, journey.

See It!

- Big Question Video

- Concept Talk Video

- Envision It! Animations

- eReaders

Hear It!

- eSelections

- Grammar Jammer

- Vocabulary Activities

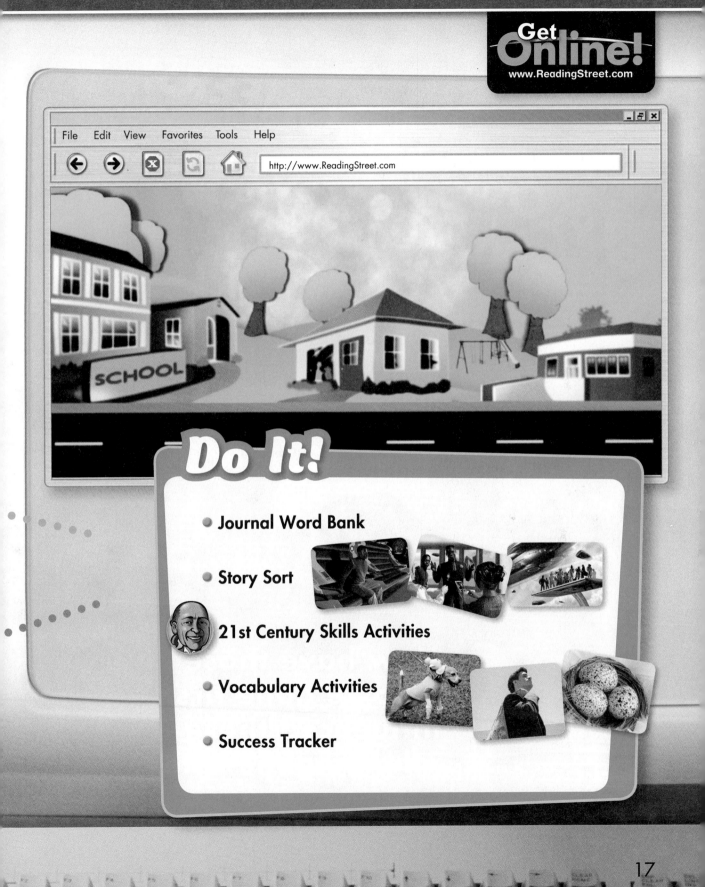

File   Edit   View   Favorites   Tools   Help

http://www.ReadingStreet.com

Do It!

- Journal Word Bank
- Story Sort
- 21st Century Skills Activities
- Vocabulary Activities
- Success Tracker

EXPLORERS, PIONEERS, AND DISCOVERERS

How have those
who've gone first
influenced those
who've gone after?

Objectives
● Listen to and interpret a speaker's message and ask questions. ● Identify the main ideas and supporting ideas in the speaker's message.

Oral Vocabulary

Let's Talk About

Exploration

● Share what you know about the Arctic or Antarctic.

● Ask questions about weather and climate conditions at either the North or the South Pole.

● Express opinions about why you think some people want to explore extreme places.

READING STREET ONLINE
BIG QUESTION VIDEO
www.ReadingStreet.com

20

You've learned
1 5 0
Amazing Words
so far this year!

21

Objectives
● Analyze how the organization of a text, such as cause-and-effect, affects the way ideas are related.
● Identify effects and their causes.
● Summarize the main ideas and supporting details in a text.

Envision It! | Skill Strategy

Skill

Strategy

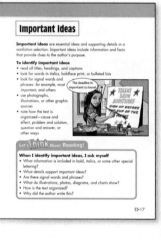

Comprehension Skill

🎯 Cause and Effect

- A cause is what makes something happen. An effect is something that happens as a result of a cause. To find a cause, ask yourself, "Why did this happen?" To find an effect, ask yourself, "What happened because of this?"

- Clue words such as *because, so,* and *due to* can help you spot cause-and-effect relationships.

- Make a graphic organizer like the one below to note cause-and-effect relationships as you read "The Arctic."

| **Cause** what makes something happen | → | **Effect** what happened |

Comprehension Strategy

🎯 Important Ideas

Important ideas in a nonfiction text are often set off in different typefaces, with signal words, or by the use of other text features, such as capital letters, that can guide the reader to better understanding.

THE ARCTIC

THE ARCTIC is located on the northernmost part of Earth. It is often considered to lie north of the "tree line," which marks where trees cannot grow because of frigid year-round temperatures. This area includes Greenland as well as parts of Alaska, Canada, Europe, and Siberia. It also includes the Arctic Ocean and, of course, the North Pole.

Ice and snow cover two-fifths of arctic land year-round, while the rest of the land has grasses and shrubs. Ice covers more than half the Arctic Ocean all the time. This mass of jagged ice is called pack ice.

THERE ARE LARGE temperature differences throughout the Arctic. Due to Earth's tilt, the sun's rays do not even reach the northern Arctic during the winter. Yet the coldest arctic temperatures are not at the North Pole. That's because the North Pole is located on the Arctic Ocean pack ice. Water—even as ice—slowly takes in heat during the summer. It slowly gives it off during the winter. The most extreme temperatures, then, occur on the land in northern Canada, Alaska, and Siberia.

On the pack ice, winter air is still and dry. Most of the water is already frozen. In fact, more snow falls in New York City!

Skill Clue words such as *due to* help you spot cause-and-effect relationships. Why don't the sun's rays reach the northern Arctic in winter?

Skill Why aren't the coldest temperatures at the North Pole?

Strategy What are the most important ideas in this article? Summarize the article to state its most important ideas.

Your Turn!

⏸ Need a Review? See the *Envision It! Handbook* for help with cause and effect and important ideas.

Let's Think About...

▶ Ready to Try It? Use what you've learned about cause and effect as you read *Into the Ice*.

23

Envision It! | Words to Know

insulated

isolation

provisions

conquer

destiny

expedition

navigator

verify

Vocabulary Strategy for
🎯 Unfamiliar Words

Context Clues When you come across a word that is unfamiliar, the author may have provided clues that can help you figure out its meaning. Look at the context, or the words and sentences around the unfamiliar word, for help.

Choose one of the Words to Know and follow these steps.

1. Reread the sentence in which the unfamiliar word appears.

2. Look for a specific clue in the words near the unfamiliar word.

3. If there isn't one, think about the overall meaning of the sentence. Does that give you a clue?

4. If you need more help, read the sentences near the unfamiliar word. They may contain clues or additional information that suggest the word's meaning.

5. Determine a meaning for the word based on any clues you have found. Try your meaning in the sentence. Does it make sense?

Read "Exploring the Unknown." Use context clues to help you figure out the meanings of any unfamiliar words.

Words to Write Reread "Exploring the Unknown." What frontier would you like to explore? Write about your expedition. Use as many words from the Words to Know list as you can.

Exploring the Unknown

There have always been people determined to conquer the unexplored corners of the world. Whether they have battled their way to the top of the Earth, the bottom of the ocean, or the silence of the moon, explorers feel it is their destiny to be the first.

They plan, organize, and outfit each expedition. To improve their odds of surviving, they take along food, clothing, transportation, and tools. They gather everything they think they will need to protect them from the cold or the heat and the extremes of nature. However, for all their provisions and planning, explorers are not insulated against the dangers of the unknown or of isolation.

The navigator may be able to tell explorers exactly where they stand. Yet he or she can never verify that the group will make it safely there and back. Think of a little knot of people standing on Mars sometime in the future. Will they have reached their goal?

Your Turn!

⏸ **Need a Review?** For help using context clues to determine the meanings of unfamiliar words, see *Words!*

Let's Think About...

▷ **Ready to Try It?** Read *Into the Ice* on pp. 26–39.

Genre

Narrative nonfiction often recounts a series of events. Look for a number of related events as you read.

INTO THE ICE
The Story of Arctic Exploration

by Lynn Curlee

Question of the Week
What drives people to explore harsh climates and dangerous places?

Let's **Think** About **Reading!**

Fridtjof Nansen and the Fram

The great pioneer in the search for the North Pole was a brilliant young Norwegian scientist named Fridtjof Nansen. Also an athlete, outdoorsman, artist, and poet, Nansen wrote of the strange atmospheric effect called the *northern lights,* "The aurora borealis shakes over the vault of heaven its veil of glittering silver—changing now to yellow, now to green, now to red. . . . It shimmers in tongues of flame . . . until the whole melts away in the moonlight . . . like the sigh of a departing spirit."

In 1888, at the age of twenty-six, Nansen organized his first expedition—a trek across Greenland on skis, a feat never before accomplished. Dropped off by ship on the uninhabited east coast, Nansen and five companions had no choice but to ski westward to civilization, carrying only the provisions required for the one-way journey.

This kind of bold yet calculated risk-taking was typical of Nansen. He carefully planned every detail, even designing his own equipment. He also knew how to improvise off the land, adopting Inuit methods such as the use of dog sledges, kayaks, and snow houses.

After the Greenland trek, Nansen became interested in the idea of *polar drift.* In 1884, in the ice near Greenland, some debris was found from the *Jeannette,* a ship crushed in the ice off Siberia in 1881. There was only one possible explanation: the ice and debris had drifted around the entire Arctic Ocean. Nansen had a breathtaking proposal: he would sail a ship directly into the ice pack off Siberia, deliberately let it be frozen in, and drift with the ice across the top of the world, penetrating the heart of the Arctic.

Nansen's small ship, the *Fram* (*Onward* in Norwegian), was specially designed with a hull that would ride up over the crushing ice and living spaces insulated with cork and felt. Fully provisioned with scientific equipment and supplies for five years, the *Fram* had workshops, a smithy, and even a windmill for electricity. On June 24, 1893, the *Fram* sailed from Norway. By September 25, Nansen and his crew of twelve were frozen fast in the polar ice pack off Siberia.

Let's **Think** About...

How does the author tell Nansen's story so that it is easy to follow and understand?
Text Structure

29

As they drifted slowly northward, the expedition settled into a routine of scientific observation. The ship was so comfortable that by the end of the second winter Nansen was restless and bored. Now only 360 miles from the North Pole, Nansen decided to strike out over the ice.

In the arctic dawn of mid-March 1895, Nansen set out with one companion, Hjalmar Johansen, three sledges of provisions, twenty-eight dogs, and two kayaks. As in Greenland, there could be no turning back—this time their home base was drifting. For three weeks they struggled northward, maneuvering the sledges over jumbled fields and immense ridges of broken ice. By early April they were still 225 miles from the Pole, and the drifting ice was carrying them south almost as quickly as they could push north. Provisions were also running low, so they reluctantly headed for the nearest land, three hundred miles to the south. As the weeks passed and the sun rose higher, the broken surface of the ice pack became slushy, then treacherous as lanes of water called *leads* opened and

Let's **Think** About...

How do the author's words let the reader feel a sense of moving across the Arctic?

Text Structure

• *The* Fram *drifts in the Arctic night.*

closed between the ice floes. It took four months to reach land. After provisions ran out, the men survived by hunting seals in the open leads and by feeding the weak dogs to the stronger ones.

Nansen and Johansen finally found a remote island. With no hope of rescue, the two men prepared for the winter, building a tiny hut and butchering walrus and bears for a supply of meat and warm furs. They survived the winter in isolation, burning greasy blubber for heat and light and growing fat on the diet of oily meat. When the ice broke up in the spring, Nansen and Johansen set out in their kayaks. On June 13, 1896—one year and four months after leaving the *Fram*—they were picked up by an English expedition. Two months later the *Fram* and its crew broke free of the ice in the ocean east of Greenland, more than a thousand miles from their starting point. The scientific expedition was a triumphant success, and Nansen and Johansen had gone farther north than anyone had before.

Let's **Think** About...

How does the illustration on this page help to convey the isolation Nansen and Johansen must've felt?

🔟 **Important Ideas**

Let's **Think** About...

Why do you think the earliest North Pole explorers came from northern European countries?
Inferring

Now the race to the North Pole was on. Another daring attempt was made the very next year—a flight to the Pole in a balloon. Salomon Andrée was a Swedish engineer with experience in aeronautics and an interest in the Arctic. He had built a large hydrogen-filled balloon with a passenger gondola designed to hold three men, four months of supplies, sledges, and a small boat.

The Ornen *comes down on the ice.*

Developed more than one hundred years earlier, balloons were still the only means of flight in the 1890s. As transportation they have serious limitations: first, they cannot be steered; and second, they are sensitive to temperature changes. Andrée tried to solve the first problem with a complicated system of sails and drag lines. He completely ignored the second problem, and the result was disastrous.

In midsummer 1897 the *Ornen* (*Eagle* in Swedish) lifted off from Spitsbergen, an island north of Norway. As they sailed northward Andrée wrote in his journal, "The rattling of the drag lines in the snow and the flapping of the sails are the only sound, except for the whining of the wind." As the balloon was alternately heated by the sun and cooled by freezing fog, the precious gas that kept them aloft leaked away. By the third day the *Ornen* was down on the ice, two hundred miles from land. In the Arctic summer at the edge of the ice pack, Andrée and his two companions faced a terrifying world of slushy, grinding floes and open leads; it took them three months to struggle to the nearest island. But inexperienced and unprepared, they were unable to survive the winter. We know what happened only because thirty-three years later their frozen remains were found, along with Andrée's journal and another eerie relic—undeveloped images of the doomed expedition that were still in their camera.

PHYSICALLY, THE NORTH Pole is nothing more than a theoretical point on the Earth's surface—but reaching it came to symbolize mankind's mastery of the entire planet—and a landmark human achievement. An American naval engineer desperately wanted to be the first explorer to stand on the North Pole. Robert E. Peary first entered the Arctic in 1886. For twenty years he mounted expeditions to northwest Greenland, looking for the best route north. Peary was not particularly interested in scientific discovery or mapping. He had one goal: the glory of being first. Over the years, Peary came to believe that it was his destiny to conquer the North Pole.

Let's Think About...

What might a person's desire to be first at something say about that person? **Background Knowledge**

33

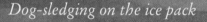

Dog-sledging on the ice pack

Vain and arrogant, Robert Peary ran his expeditions like a military campaign. His chief lieutenant was his personal assistant, Matthew Henson, a man of African descent. This was unusual at the turn of the century, but then, Peary was unconventional in many ways. He also took his wife on some of his early expeditions. Josephine Peary was the first white woman in the High Arctic, and she gave birth to their daughter while on expedition. Inuit came from miles around to see the newborn blond "snowbaby."

As an explorer, Peary was innovative, taking ideas from everyone and improving on them. But the Polar Inuit were the key to his success. Inuit women made his furs, and Inuit men used their own dogs to pull his sledges. They built his snowhouses on the trail and hunted for his meat in exchange for metal tools and other material goods. On one occasion Peary pushed himself so relentlessly that his feet froze. When his fur boots were removed, several of his toes snapped off. As soon as the stumps healed, he was back on the trail.

Let's **Think** About...

What do the two paragraphs on this page suggest about Robert E. Peary as a person?
Inferring

In 1906 Peary made a full-scale assault upon the North Pole. His plan was to take a ship as far north as possible, winter over in Greenland or the Canadian Islands, then strike out for the Pole in late February, before the ice pack started breaking up. The Arctic did not cooperate, however. When only a hundred miles out on the ice pack, the expedition was delayed several days by a broad lead, then a blizzard kept them camp-bound for another week. Supplies dwindled, and the disappointed Peary had to settle for a new farthest-north record, 175 miles from the Pole.

After another appeal to the men who financed his expeditions, Peary sailed from New York in July 1908 in the *Roosevelt,* named for Theodore Roosevelt, then President of the United States and the explorer's most enthusiastic supporter. Peary was fifty-two years old, and he knew that this was his last expedition.

Let's Think About...

What major problems faced Peary and his team in their 1906 attempt to reach the North Pole?
● Important Ideas

Let's **Think** About...

Why is one of Peary's fellow explorers holding an American flag in this illustration?
Inferring

36

Peary claims the North Pole.

But Peary was not the only explorer in the Arctic in 1908. There was also Dr. Frederick A. Cook, a veteran of both the Arctic and the Antarctic, which was just then being explored. Cook had been the physician on one of Peary's earlier expeditions. Always jealous and overbearing, Peary had refused to allow Cook to publish an article about his experiences and they had quarreled. Now the doctor was rumored to be thinking about his own attempt on the North Pole. Peary dismissed the rumors; he considered Cook an amateur, not in the same league as himself.

On March 1, 1909, Peary stood on the frozen shore of the Arctic Ocean and faced north. With him were 23 men, 19 sledges, and 133 dogs. For the next month Matt Henson led out in front, breaking trail, while Peary rode a sledge in the rear, supervising the troops. Other sledges traveled back and forth relaying tons of supplies northward, provisions for the return trip that were stored in snowhouses strung out over almost five hundred miles of floating, shifting ice. Everything had been carefully calculated, down to the sacrificing of weak dogs to feed the strong.

For the final dash to the Pole, Peary took only Henson and three Inuit. The entry in his diary for April 6, 1909, reads, "The Pole at last!!! The prize of 3 centuries, my dream & ambition for 23 years. MINE at last."

Or was it?

PEARY CAME HOME to the stunning news that Dr. Cook had already returned, claiming to have reached the North Pole on April 21, 1908, a year before Peary. In the investigations that followed, Peary accused Cook of lying, and it was demonstrated that Cook had lied once before when he claimed to have climbed Mt. McKinley in Alaska, North America's highest peak. Lacking documentation or witnesses, except for two Inuit companions who said they were never out of sight of land, Cook's claim to have reached the Pole was officially rejected.

Let's Think About...

How does the author introduce the explorer Dr. Cook so that you know he will be a rival to Peary?
Text Structure

37

Then, incredibly, Peary was also unable to completely verify his own claim. The careful explorer was a sloppy navigator, and from his solar observations and daily journal it was impossible to say that he had stood at the Pole. Henson and the Inuit were unable to take solar readings, so it was Peary's word against Cook's. Commander Robert E. Peary was finally given the credit and made a rear-admiral, but his great prize was tarnished, and he died an embittered man. As for Cook, he vowed until his dying day that he had reached the North Pole. In recent years, historical researchers have determined that neither man actually stepped foot on the northernmost point of the globe.

THE CLASSIC ERA of Arctic exploration ended with Peary. Attention then shifted to the Antarctic and to the South Pole, which Roald Amundsen reached in 1911. Three years later the world was at war and most exploration was postponed. When it resumed in the 1920s the world was a different place. Balloons were no longer the only means of flight, and several attempts were made to fly to the North Pole in small airplanes.

For many years Richard E. Byrd was given credit for the first successful flight, but his claim is now disputed. In 1926 Roald Amundsen flew across the entire Arctic Ocean in an Italian dirigible piloted by its designer, Umberto Nobile. The first person to stand at the North Pole, whose claim is undisputed, is Joseph Fletcher, a United States Air Force pilot who landed there in 1952. Arctic flights are great achievements, but they are achievements of technology, somehow different

Let's Think About...

What are three reasons Arctic exploration ended after Peary's expedition?

 Important Ideas

from crossing nearly five hundred miles of shifting ice by dog sledge and then returning. Although many people have now stood at the North Pole, no one has ever completed Peary's journey without being resupplied by plane or airlifted out.

Let's **Think** About...

What is your final impression of the explorers' efforts to be the first to reach the North Pole?
◉ **Important Ideas**

This map shows the routes of various Arctic explorers.

Objectives
• Provide evidence from the text to demonstrate understanding.
• Read independently for a sustained period of time and paraphrase the reading.

Envision It! | Retell

Think Critically

1. Compare Robert Peary to another real-life adventurer you have read about. Describe how the adventurers' goals and obstacles were alike and different. **Text to Text**

2. This author gives you a bit of information about the personalities of two of the explorers. How does he help you get to know Nansen and Peary? **Think Like an Author**

3. What caused Fridtjof Nansen and Hjalmar Johansen to leave the *Fram* when they were 360 miles away from the North Pole and frozen in the polar ice? What were some of the effects of this adventure? **Cause and Effect**

4. What information from the selection helps you form an opinion about Salomon Andrée's attempt to reach the North Pole in a balloon? **Important Ideas**

5. **Look Back and Write** Beyond personal fame, why would explorers have attempted to reach the North Pole? Look back at page 33 to find the author's answer. Write it in your own words. Then write a paragraph about whether that reason is still important today. Provide evidence to support your answer.

TEST PRACTICE | Extended Response

Meet the Author

LYNN CURLEE

Lynn Curlee is a studio painter who exhibits his work in galleries and who along the way became a book creator. "With my second book," he says, "I began writing myself and started the series of nonfiction informational picture books which continues to this day." Many of Mr. Curlee's books are about monuments, such as the five in Washington, D.C., that are featured in *Capital.* He says, "I have had the rare privilege and honor of making books about some of the most important and iconic monuments of our American heritage." Mr. Curlee lives in New York State.

Other books by Lynn Curlee:
Liberty **and** ***Capital***

Use the Reading Log in the *Reader's and Writer's Notebook* to record your independent reading.

41

Let's Write It!

Key Features of a Narrative Poem

● tells a story through poetry

● lines have rhythm or rhyme

● may appeal to reader's emotions

READING STREET ONLINE
GRAMMAR JAMMER
www.ReadingStreet.com

Narrative Poem

A **narrative poem** tells a story. Its lines are arranged to show rhythm, and may rhyme. The student model on the next page is an example of a narrative poem.

Writing Prompt Write a narrative poem about a place in nature you know about.

Writer's Checklist

Remember, you should . . .

☑ have your poem tell a story.

☑ choose words that create strong images in the reader's mind.

☑ try to have rhythm, or a pattern of stress or beats.

☑ use figurative language, such as similes and metaphors.

The Jewel

The lake was a carpet of blue
With sunlight that looked fresh and new.
The grass was like a blanket of green,
And **we** all gazed with awe at the scene.

My friend lost **her** ring near the shore.
And **she** knew **it** would be a true chore
for **us** to search high and search low,
but **we** helped our friend dash to and fro.

The ring had belonged to **her** aunt,
Who had given this gift with a chant:
"Do not lose this jewel, dear niece;
For this jewel will bring **you** true peace."

I bent low, to feel around in the sand,
until I found **her** ring — shining bright in my hand!

**Writing Trait
Voice** Similes
and metaphors
add color to
the writer's
description.

Genre
A **narrative
poem** tells
a story in
rhythmic lines.

**Subject
and object
pronouns** are
used correctly.

Conventions

Subject and Object Pronouns

Remember Subject pronouns are used as the subject of a
sentence: *I, you, she, he, we, they.* **Object pronouns** are used as a
direct object, indirect object, or object of a preposition: *me, her, him,
it, us, you, them.*

43

Social Studies in Reading

Genre
Procedural Text

- Procedural text tells the reader how to do something, from beginning to end.

- Procedural text gives directions, or steps, to follow.

- A how-to article is an example of procedural text.

- In procedural text, illustrations and captions help the reader understand what to do.

- Read "How to Survive in Antarctica" and look for information that could help you build a snow shelter if you ever needed one.

How to Survive in

Antarctica

written and photographed
by Lucy Jane Bledsoe

Let's **Think** About...

What assumption does the author make about her readers and their interests?
Procedural Text

This is a snow shelter that the author (facing page) built and used in Antarctica.

Most likely, you'll have a berth on a ship, a room in a dorm, or a heavy-duty tent to house you in Antarctica. But in case of an emergency, knowing how to make a quick shelter is an essential survival skill.

The beauty of snow caves is that they are very warm. No matter how cold the air gets, snow is always 32 degrees Fahrenheit (zero degrees Centigrade), so a snow cave is always at least that warm. In a good, tightly constructed snow cave, a person's body heat can warm it up even more.

There are many kinds of snow shelters. Some are more elaborate than others. Here are instructions for building two very easy kinds. For the first one, you will need only a shovel. For the second, you will need a shovel and a snow saw.

Let's Think About...

How does dividing the text into sequenced steps help you understand the directions?
Procedural Text

The Mound

Step 1 Throw all your gear, including duffels, sleep kits, buckets—whatever you have—into a big pile. Be sure to keep your shovel out!

Step 2 Shovel lots of snow onto your pile of gear.

Step 3 When your gear is completely buried, climb up on the mound and stamp the snow solid. Then, pile more snow on and stamp it again.

Step 4 Dig a tunnel into your gear. Beginning a few feet away from the mound, dig down and forward, so that the tunnel will come out under your mound of gear.

Step 5 Pull your gear, piece by piece, out of the tunnel.

Step 6 Scoot into the tunnel yourself. There is your snow shelter!

These kinds of shelters are very quick to construct and hold up quite well. However, they don't work if you are one person traveling alone without much gear. In that case, the fastest snow shelter to build is a trench.

The Trench

Step 1 Dig a trench in the snow a few feet longer than your height and at least two feet deep.

Step 2 Use a snow saw to cut blocks of snow. The number of blocks you need depends on the size of your trench.

Step 3 Place the blocks of snow across the top of your trench. If possible, create a "cathedral ceiling" by tipping two blocks against each other.

Step 4 Pack snow in all the cracks between the blocks of snow.

Step 5 Place a final block of snow next to the entrance to your trench. Climb in and pull the "door" block as tightly against the entrance as you can. Don't worry if you haven't completely filled in every crack— you need some air vents to breathe!

Let's Think About...

What tools would you need to carry if you were about to build a snow shelter?
Procedural Text

Let's Think About...

Reading Across Texts If the explorers in *Into the Ice* had read "How to Survive in Antarctica" before heading to the North Pole, how might their trips have differed?

Writing Across Texts Write a set of directions for survival that would help any explorers.

Vocabulary

Unfamiliar Words

Context Clues Recall that you can use nearby words and phrases as clues to help you understand the meaning of an unfamiliar word. If the nearby words do not provide a definition for the unfamiliar word, look to nearby sentences.

Practice It! Use an encyclopedia in the classroom or media center to find three words that you do not understand. Using context clues, try to figure out the meaning of each new word. Remember to look for prefixes and suffixes that may give you more clues. If you can't figure out a word, use a dictionary.

Fluency

Appropriate Phrasing

When you read aloud, group related words together to make them sound the way they would sound in natural speech. Follow the cues of punctuation to guide you. A comma signals a pause; a dash or semicolon or colon means a longer pause; and a period or other end mark means a stop.

Practice It! With a partner, practice reading aloud the last three paragraphs on page 29 of *Into the Ice*. How can you use appropriate phrasing to group together related words? Give your partner feedback.

Listening and Speaking

When you participate in a listening and speaking activity, always take turns.

Analyze Media

When you analyze media, you may compare how a movie, television documentary, magazine, and book treat the same topic.

Practice It! In a small group, discuss television shows or movies you have seen about polar exploration. Note the kinds of images they presented, and compare those images to information you may have found in books or magazines. Present your findings to the class.

Tips

Listening . . .

- Face the speakers.
- Listen attentively and take notes.
- Think of your own experiences as you listen.

Speaking . . .

- Take turns speaking.
- Stay on the topic you chose to speak about.

Teamwork . . .

- Acknowledge others' ideas.
- Ask classmates to share their ideas about media they have experience with on the topic of polar exploration.

Objectives
● Listen to and interpret a speaker's message and ask questions.
● Identify the main ideas and supporting ideas in the speaker's message.

Oral Vocabulary

Let's Talk About

Animal Research

● Share what you know about animal behavior.

● Express opinions about what makes animal research responsible.

● Ask questions about why animal research may be necessary.

READING STREET ONLINE
CONCEPT TALK VIDEO
www.ReadingStreet.com

51

Objectives
- Identify the author's purpose.
- Draw conclusions about the text and evaluate how well the author achieves his or her purpose. • Analyze how the organization of a text affects the way ideas are related.

Skill

Strategy

Comprehension Skill

Author's Purpose

- Authors usually write to persuade, inform, express ideas or feelings, or entertain.

- As you preview a selection, try to predict the author's purpose. After reading, ask yourself if the author met that purpose.

- Use a graphic organizer like the one below in order to determine the author's main purpose in writing "Jane Goodall's Career."

Before Reading Preview to decide purpose. Set reading pace.

↓

During Reading Look for clues to purpose.

↓

After Reading Ask if purpose was met and how.

Comprehension Strategy

Text Structure

Text structure is how a piece of nonfiction is organized. Types of nonfiction text structure are compare and contrast, cause and effect, sequence, and problem and solution. Sometimes titles and headings as well as bold-faced words and other features are used to organize information for the reader.

Jane Goodall's Career

Jane Goodall is known worldwide for studying chimpanzees. As a child she became interested in how animals behaved. She left school at age 18 and eventually traveled to Africa, where in 1960 she started a camp in the Gombe Stream Game Reserve. From there she could carefully research the chimpanzees that lived in the region.

Goodall and her family lived in Gombe until 1975. Over the years Goodall discovered many surprising facts about chimpanzees. For example, she learned that chimpanzees are omnivores. This means that they eat both plants and animals. Before her discovery most scientists believed that chimpanzees were vegetarians, or plant eaters. Goodall also discovered that chimpanzees are capable of making and using their own tools, using twigs and the like.

Goodall wrote several fascinating books about her research with chimpanzees. In 1971 she told about her first years at Gombe in the book *In the Shadow of Man.* Later, in 1986, she wrote all she had learned about chimpanzee behavior in *The Chimpanzees of Gombe.*

Skill How do the title and first paragraph help you predict the main purpose of the article?

Skill Do you think the author's purpose in this paragraph is to entertain, give information, or persuade?

Strategy What text structure do you think the author uses to organize information?

Your Turn!

⏸ **Need a Review?** See the *Envision It! Handbook* for help with author's purpose and text structure.

▶ **Ready to Try It?** Use what you've learned about author's purpose as you read *The Chimpanzees I Love.*

53

Envision It! | Words to Know

captive

companionship

sanctuaries

BIRD SANCTUARY KEEP OUT

existence

ordeal

primitive

stimulating

Vocabulary Strategy for
🎯 Unknown Words

Dictionary/Glossary When you come across a word you do not know, first see if you can use context clues to figure out the meaning. If that doesn't work, use a dictionary or glossary for help.

Choose one of the Words to Know and follow these steps.

1. Look in the back of your book for the glossary.

2. Find the entry for the word. The entries in both glossaries and dictionaries are listed in alphabetical order.

3. Use the pronunciation key to pronounce the word.

4. Read all the meanings given for the word.

5. Choose the meaning that makes sense in your sentence. If you need more information, use a dictionary as well.

Read "Zoos Then and Now" on page 55. Look for context clues to help you figure out the meanings of unknown words before you turn to the glossary or a dictionary.

Words to Write Look ahead at the pictures in *The Chimpanzees I Love*. Choose one to write about. Use as many words from the Words to Know list as you can.

Zoos Then and Now

The first zoos existed to entertain people, who came to see strange, wild animals from around the world. Hardly anyone thought about the health and happiness of these captive animals. For the most part, they were kept in small cages. Little was known about them, so no one knew what they needed for food or homes. Zoo life was nothing like their existence in the wild. Being shut in a tiny space and looking at metal and concrete all day was surely an ordeal.

Today, zoos are very different from those early, primitive places. Zoos today try hard to make life interesting and "normal" for their animals. The best zoos provide environments like those the animals would have in the wild. They offer many stimulating objects to keep the animals from getting bored. Animals are grouped in ways that make sure they have companionship. One aim is to set up family groups so babies can be born, helping endangered species increase their numbers. Zoos have become important to the survival of many animals. They are both sanctuaries and places of learning. They offer a safe place for animals to live and opportunities for people to understand the Earth's creatures.

Your Turn!

⏸ **Need a Review?** For help using a dictionary/glossary to determine the meanings of unknown words, see *Words!*

▶ **Ready to Try It?** Read *The Chimpanzees I Love* on pp. 56–69.

The Chimpanzees I Love

Saving Their World and Ours

by Jane Goodall

Question of the Week
Why is it important to study animals responsibly?

57

The Mind of the Chimpanzee

ANIMALS ARE much smarter than scientists used to think. I was told at school (fifty years ago) that only human beings have personalities, can think and reason, feel pain, or have emotions. Luckily, as a child, I had spent hours learning about animal behavior from my dog, Rusty—so I knew none of that was true!

The more we have learned about chimpanzees, the clearer it is that they have brains very like ours and can, in fact, do many things that we used to think only humans could do. I've described how the Gombe chimps use grass stems and twigs to fish termites from their nests. The chimps also use long, smooth sticks to catch vicious, biting army ants. They use crumpled leaves to soak up water from hollows in trees that they cannot reach with their lips, then suck the homemade sponge. They wipe dirt from their bodies with leaf napkins. They use stout sticks to open up holes in trees to get at birds' nests or honey, and as clubs to intimidate one another or other animals. They pick up and throw rocks as missiles. In other parts of Africa, chimps have different tool-using behaviors. For instance, in West Africa and parts of Central Africa, they use two stones, a hammer and an anvil, to crack open nuts. It seems that infant chimps learn these behaviors by watching the adults, and then imitating and practicing what they have seen. So the chimps have their own primitive culture.

Many scientists are finding out more about the chimpanzee mind from tests in captive situations. For example, chimps will go and find sticks to pull in food that has been placed outside the cage, beyond their reach. They can join two short sticks together to make one long tool. They have excellent memories—after eleven years' separation, a female named Washoe recognized the two humans who had brought her up. A chimp can plan what he or she is going to do. Often I've watched a chimp wake up, scratch

"How many times I have wished that I could look out onto the world through the eyes, with the mind, of a chimpanzee. One such minute would be worth a lifetime of research."

Chimpanzees can communicate by means of calls, gestures, postures, and facial expressions.

Ai has been learning language skills at Kyoto University since 1978. Her infant, Ayumu, will learn to stack blocks.

himself slowly, gaze around in different directions, then suddenly get up, walk over to a clump of grass, carefully select a stem, trim it, and then travel quite a long way to a termite mound that was out of sight when he made his tool.

Chimpanzees can be taught to do many of the things that we do, such as riding bicycles and sewing. Some love to draw or paint. Chimps can also recognize themselves in mirrors. But they cannot learn to speak words because their vocal cords are different. Two scientists, the Hayeses, brought up a little chimp named Vicky and tried to teach her to talk. After eight years she could only say four words, and only people who knew her could understand even those.

The Gardners had another idea. They got an infant chimpanzee, named her Washoe, and began teaching her American Sign Language (ASL) as used by deaf people. Then other infant chimps were taught this language. Chimps can learn three hundred signs or more. They can also invent signs. The chimp Lucy, wanting a Brazil nut but not knowing its name, used two signs she knew and asked for a "rock berry." A fizzy soda became "listen drink," a duck on a pond, "water bird," and a piece of celery, "pipe food." Washoe's adopted son learned fifty-eight signs from Washoe and three other signing chimps by the time he was eight years old. He was never taught these signs by humans. Other chimps have been taught computer "languages" and can punch out quite complicated sentences. These experiments have taught us, and continue to teach us, more and more about the chimpanzee mind.

These two young chimps are good friends.

Fifi is a very good mother. Here she is with offspring Ferdinand, Faustino, and Fanni.

Chimpanzees in Captivity

UNFORTUNATELY chimpanzees, so like us in many ways, are often very badly treated in many captive situations. Chimpanzees were first brought to Europe from Africa in the middle of the seventeenth century. People were amazed by these humanlike creatures. They dressed them up and taught them tricks.

Since then we have often treated chimpanzees like slaves, shooting their mothers in Africa, shipping them around the world, caging them in zoos, training them to perform in movies and circuses and advertisements, selling them as pets, and imprisoning them in medical research laboratories. Some chimps become famous. J. Fred Muggs starred on TV's *Today* show for years and was known by millions of viewers. What they didn't know was that whenever J. Fred Muggs got too big and strong for the show, he was replaced by a younger one.

A young male called Ham was sent up into space. He was shot up in a Mercury Redstone rocket in January 1961, and because he survived the ordeal (he was terrified), it was decided that it was safe for the first human astronauts. Ham was taught his routine by receiving an electric shock every time he pressed the wrong button. Often circus chimps are taught, right at the start of their training, that instant obedience is the way to avoid a beating. The beatings are given when the trainer and chimp are on their own, so no one sees. It is the same for other animals—and for many of those used in movies and other forms of entertainment.

Infant chimpanzees are adorable and, for the first two or three years, are gentle and easy to handle. People buy them and treat them like human children. But as they grow older they become more and more difficult. They are, after all, chimpanzees, and they want to behave like chimpanzees. They resent discipline. They can—and do—bite. And by the time they are six years old they are already as strong as a human male. What will happen to them then? Zoos don't want them, for they have not been able to learn chimpanzee social behavior and they do not mix well with others of their kind. Often they end up in medical research labs.

It is because their bodies are so like ours that scientists use chimps to try to find out more about human diseases and how to cure and prevent them. Chimpanzees can be infected with almost all human diseases. Hundreds have been used (with no success) in AIDS research. The virus stays alive in their blood, but they do not show the symptoms. It is very unfair that, even though chimpanzees are being used to try to help humans, they are almost never given decent places to live.

Zoos are improving gradually, but thousands of chimpanzees around the world spend their lives in barren cement-floored cages with nothing to do.

Jou-Jou has been caged alone in a Congolese zoo. He reaches to touch me, desperate for contact.

Hundreds of them are shut up in 5' x 5' x 7' bare, steel-barred prisons, all alone, bored, and uncomfortable. Measure out this space and imagine having to live in it your whole life. (Many closets are much bigger!)

I shall never forget the first time I looked into the eyes of an adult male chimpanzee in one of these labs. For more than ten years he had been living in his tiny prison. The sides, floor, and ceiling were made of thick steel bars. There was a car tire on the floor. His name, I read on the door, was JoJo. He lived at the end of a row of five cages, lined up along a bare wall. Opposite were five more cages. At either end of the room was a metal door. There was no window. JoJo could not touch any of his fellow prisoners—only the ends of his fingers fit between the bars. He had been born in an African forest, and for the first couple of years he lived in a world of greens and browns, leaves and vines, butterflies and birds. Always his mother had been close to comfort him, until the day when she was shot and he was snatched from her dead or dying body. The young chimpanzee was shipped away from his forest world to the cold, bleak existence of a North American research lab. JoJo was not angry, just grateful that I had stopped by him. He groomed my fingers, where the ridges of my cuticles showed through the surgical gloves I had to wear. Then he looked into my eyes and with one gentle finger reached to touch the tear that rolled down into my mask.

JoJo and I touch through the bars of his prison cage in a research lab.

La Vieille spent years alone in a Congolese zoo. We were able to move her to our Tchimpounga sanctuary and introduce her to other chimpanzees.

"Chimpanzees are more like us than any other living beings."

In the United States, several hundred chimpanzees have been declared "surplus"—they are no longer needed for medical research. Animal welfare groups are trying to raise the money to build them sanctuaries, so that they can end their lives with grass and trees, sunshine and companionship. Some lucky ones—including JoJo—have already been freed from their laboratory prisons. Many others are waiting.

Zoos are getting better, but there are still many chimps in small concrete and metal cages with no soft ground and nothing to occupy them. Good zoos keep their chimpanzees in groups and provide them with all kinds of stimulating things to do, different things each day, so that they don't get bored. Many zoos now have artificial termite mounds. Chimps use sticks or straws to poke into holes for honey or other foods. These innovations make a world of difference.

Protecting the Chimpanzees

CHIMPANZEES live in the forested areas of west and central Africa. In some places, where there is a lot of rain, these are thick tropical rain forests. In other places there are strips of dense forest along the rivers, with woodland and even open grassland in between. The chimpanzees usually cross open ground in groups, traveling without stopping until they reach the safety of the trees again. Chimpanzees can survive in quite dry areas, but there they have very big home ranges, for they must travel widely to get food. Like the other African great apes, the gorillas and bonobos, they are disappearing very fast. One hundred years ago we think there were about 2 million chimpanzees in Africa; now there may be no more than 150,000. They are already extinct in four of the twenty-five countries where they once lived. There are more chimpanzees in the great

Congo basin than anywhere else—but that is where they are disappearing the fastest. They are disappearing for various reasons:

1 All over Africa, their forest homes are being destroyed as human populations grow and need even more land for their crops and for their homes, and even more wood for making charcoal or for firewood.

2 In many places chimpanzees are caught in snares set for bush-pigs or antelopes. Snares were once made of vines, but now hunters use wire cable. Often the chimps are strong enough to break the wire, but they cannot get the noose off. Some die; others lose a hand or a foot, after months of agony.

3 There are still dealers who are trying to smuggle chimpanzees out of Africa for the live-animal trade. Mothers are shot so that hunters can steal their infants for entertainment or medical research. Many individuals die in the forest (including adult males who rush to the rescue and are shot) in order for one infant to reach its destination alive. The dealers pay the hunters only a few dollars while they themselves can sell an infant chimp for $2,000 or more.

4 The greatest threat to chimpanzees in the great Congo basin is commercial hunting for food. Local tribes, like the Pygmies, have lived in harmony with the forest and its animals for hundreds of years. Now logging companies have made roads deep into the heart of the last remaining forests. Hunters ride the trucks to the end of the road and shoot everything—chimps, gorillas, bonobos, elephants, antelopes—even quite small birds. The meat is smoked or even loaded fresh onto the trucks and taken for sale in the big towns. The trouble is that so many people living there prefer the taste of meat from wild animals, and they will pay more for it than for that from domestic animals. If this trade (known as the "bushmeat" trade) cannot be stopped, there will soon be no animals left.

There are many people and organizations trying to help protect chimpanzees and their forests, but the problems are very hard to solve. Most of the people destroying the forests are very poor. They can't afford to buy food from elsewhere, so they cut down more trees for

"Every individual has a role to play. Every individual makes a difference. And we have a choice: What sort of difference do we want to make?"

Fanni gazes down at Fax.

their farms and shoot or snare more animals for food. Because the soil needs the shelter of the trees in the tropics, the people are soon struggling to survive in a desertlike place. So they cut down more trees. And the bushmeat trade has become a very big money-making operation, with many high-up government officials involved. We shall not give up until solutions have been found.

Chimpanzee Facts

- A fully grown male chimpanzee at Gombe is about 4 feet tall and weighs up to 115 pounds. The female is about as tall, but she is lighter, seldom weighing more than 85 pounds.
- In west and central Africa the chimpanzees are a little bigger and heavier. Often they are heavier in captivity too, at least when they are well fed and given medicine. This is not surprising, as they have much less exercise than when they live in the wild.
- Chimpanzees in the wild seldom live longer than fifty years, though some captive individuals have lived more than sixty years.
- A female chimpanzee in the wild raises two to three offspring, on average. But she may raise as many as eight or nine.

Chimpanzee Habitats

Chimpanzees are found in twenty-one African countries, from the west coast of the continent to as far east as western Uganda, Rwanda, Burundi, and Tanzania. Chimps live in the greatest concentrations in the rain forest areas along the equator. Due to the fast-paced destruction of these rain forests, as well as other pressures, chimpanzees are considered an endangered species.

The Gombe Stream Research Center is located on the eastern shore of Lake Tanganyika, in Tanzania.

CHIMPANZEE RANGE

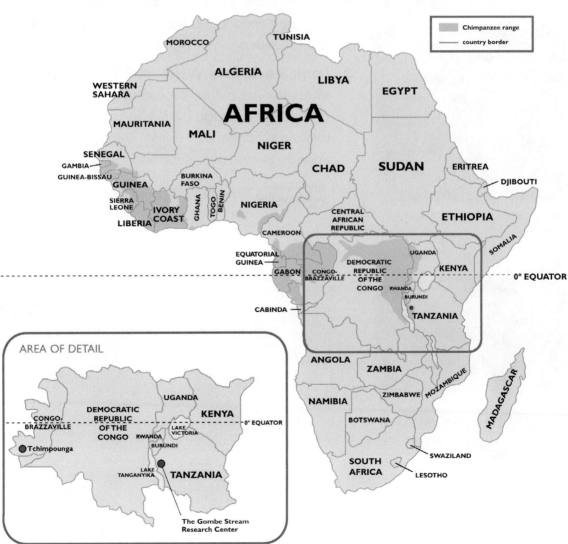

Objectives

• Provide evidence from the text to demonstrate understanding.
• Read independently for a sustained period of time and paraphrase the reading.

Envision It! | Retell

Think Critically

1. How can doing something about poverty in Africa help the chimpanzees? **Text to World**

2. Jane Goodall tells readers a great deal about chimpanzees. Why do you think she includes details about her work with chimpanzees as she tells her stories? **Think Like an Author**

3. Do you think the author's purpose in writing *The Chimpanzees I Love* was to inform, to persuade, to entertain, or to express an idea or feeling—or a combination of these purposes? Explain your answer. 🔄 **Author's Purpose**

4. Reread page 66. How does the text structure help you understand the reasons chimpanzees are disappearing? 🔄 **Text Structure**

5. **Look Back and Write** Look back at page 63 to review the author's meeting with JoJo. Then rewrite the passage from JoJo's point of view. Explain what he was doing, seeing, and feeling. Provide evidence to support your answer.

TEST PRACTICE | **Extended Response**

Meet the Author

Jane Goodall

Valerie Jane Morris Goodall loved animals of all kinds when she was a child in London, England. "Luckily," Dr. Goodall says, "I had a wonderful mother who encouraged my interest. She told me that if I worked hard, took advantage of opportunities, and never gave up, I would find a way." After visiting Tanzania and then returning to college for her degree, Dr. Goodall established the Gombe Stream Research Center in Tanzania, where her groundbreaking research included the discovery that chimpanzees, like humans, can make and use tools. She later founded the Jane Goodall Institute, a global leader in the effort to protect chimpanzees and their habitats. Today, through her lectures and books, Dr. Goodall is known around the world for her scientific research with chimpanzees and for her efforts to preserve the environment.

Other books by Jane Goodall: *The Chimpanzee Family Book* and *My Life with the Chimpanzees*

Use the Reading Log in the *Reader's and Writer's Notebook* to record your independent reading.

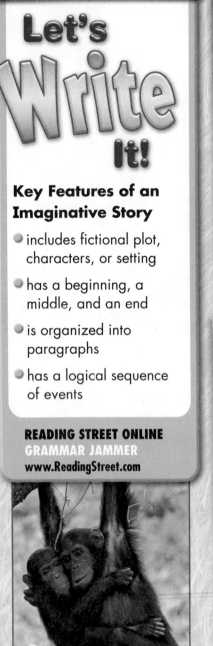

Let's Write It!

Key Features of an Imaginative Story

● includes fictional plot, characters, or setting

● has a beginning, a middle, and an end

● is organized into paragraphs

● has a logical sequence of events

READING STREET ONLINE
GRAMMAR JAMMER
www.ReadingStreet.com

Imaginative Story

An **imaginative story** tells a creative story using fictional characters or events. The student model on the next page is an example of an imaginative story.

Writing Prompt Think about an animal that interests you. Now write a story about that animal, complete with a beginning, a middle, and an end.

Writer's Checklist

Remember, you should . . .

✓ have a beginning, a middle, and an end.

✓ introduce the main character at the beginning of the story.

✓ include a problem or conflict that is solved at the end.

✓ write the events in logical sequence.

✓ use dialogue to make your story more lively and interesting.

The Moose Spelling Bee

Ruth the moose couldn't wait for the spelling bee. All the neighborhood moose were practicing their words, but Ruth thought she had a good chance to win. She had been playing spelling games with Granny Moose since she was just a small animal. At first, Granny would let Ruth win, but now Granny had to work hard to beat her.

The morning of the spelling bee, Ruth bounced out of bed. She was so excited, though, she didn't notice her toy pine cone on the floor. Ruth's hoof slipped on the toy and she fell and bumped her snout.

Ruth got up and carefully made her way to the mirror. Oh, no! She had knocked one of her teeth loose.

At breakfast, Granny knew something wasn't right.

"Granny Mooth," whimpered Ruth, "my tooth is looth."

"Oh, dear," said Granny. "But can you still spell?"

Ruth mused for a minute. "Of courth! C-o-u-r-s-e!"

Ruth smiled. She might have a hard time saying words out loud with her loose tooth, but she could still spell them!

Writing Trait Organization
The beginning of the story introduces the character and setting.

Genre
An **imaginative story** has made-up characters and events.

Pronouns and antecedents are used correctly.

Conventions

Pronouns and antecedents

Remember A **pronoun** takes the place of a noun or nouns. An **antecedent**, or referent, is the noun or nouns to which the pronoun refers. A pronoun and its antecedent must agree in number and gender.

Science in Reading

Genre
Expository Text

● Expository text tells and explains facts and information about the nature of people, animals, events, and things.

● Sometimes expository text includes stories that describe more than just facts.

● Graphics and other text features such as subheads help readers understand the text.

● Read "'Going Ape' over Language" and see how different text features help you understand what you are reading.

"Going Ape" over Language

by Natalie M. Rosinsky

Humans Talking with Apes?

Such conversations were once found only in fables or in science fiction like *Planet of the Apes*. But, since the 1960s, scientists have "gone ape" over other methods of interspecies communication.

Great apes physically cannot produce the consonants or some vowel sounds of human speech. So, instead of spoken language, researchers are using American Sign Language (ASL) and technology to teach human language to other primates.

A Chimpanzee Named Washoe

In 1966, Dr. Allen Gardner and his wife, Beatrix, began teaching ASL to a year-old female chimpanzee named Washoe. They taught Washoe by "cross-fostering" her—that is, treating her like a deaf human child. Washoe had a stimulating environment filled with toys and attentive human companions who used ASL to "discuss" daily activities. In those first years, one important topic of conversation was—of course—potty training! Dr. Roger Fouts, an early companion, and his wife, Debbi, have now spent more than 30 years with "Project Washoe." In 1992, the Foutses founded the Chimpanzee and Human Communication Institute at Central Washington University, where Washoe lives with an adoptive family of four other ASL-using chimpanzees.

Washoe is the most "talkative" member of this group, with an ASL vocabulary of 240 signs. She often "translates" spoken words she understands into ASL. Washoe signs correctly even when an object is out of sight—signaling "DOG," for example, whenever she hears canine barking. She also accurately puts together short "sentences"—signing "ROGER TICKLE WASHOE" when this is what has occurred. If she does not know the sign for an item, Washoe creatively yet logically "renames" it. She called her first candy bar a "CANDY BANANA"!

Yet emotion, not just logic, has filled some of Washoe's most memorable conversations with humans. Washoe had already had two unsuccessful pregnancies when she learned that a caregiver's baby had died. The chimpanzee looked groundward, then directly into the woman's eyes, and signed "CRY" while touching the woman's cheek just below her eye. Later that day, Washoe wouldn't let her caregiver go home without further consolation, signing "PLEASE PERSON HUG."

Let's Think About...

How does using capital letters for what Washoe says help your reading?
Expository Text

Let's Think About...

How do the section heads help you to better understand this article?
Expository Text

Researchers are also excited by the chimpanzees' use of ASL among themselves. Washoe, her adoptive son Loulis, and other family members have been videotaped having ASL conversations on their own about games, food, and "housecleaning." Birthday parties and holiday celebrations are other "hot" topics of conversation. The chimpanzees have even been observed "talking to themselves," much as a human might mutter under her breath. When Loulis mischievously ran away with one of her favorite magazines, an annoyed Washoe signed "BAD, BAD, BAD" to herself.

It is Loulis's use of ASL, though, that may be most significant. In a planned experiment, researchers avoided signing in Loulis's presence during his first five years. Yet Loulis—like deaf human children—learned ASL by watching and imitating his adoptive mother and other family members! Chimpanzees, it seems, not only can learn human language but also can transmit it to others.

Let's **Think** About...

How does the information in the sidebar add to the information in the main article?
Expository Text

"Aping Their Betters"?

Linguist Noam Chomsky insists that human beings are the only primates neurologically capable of language. Some other scientists, including MIT's Dr. Steven Pinker, share this view. They conclude that "Project Washoe" and similar research prove only that apes can be trained, and that they will imitate the behavior of trainers just for rewards or approval. These critics maintain that investigators, along with animal-rights activists, have misinterpreted the results of these research projects because they want to believe that apes can "talk."

But there are answers to these objections. The private signing done by chimpanzees is evidence that apes use language for more than rewards or approval. And the technology used to teach "Yerkish" to bonobos lessens the possibly questionable element of imitation in this and similar research. Furthermore, as Dr. Sue Savage-Rumbaugh notes, comprehension and visual cues between humans are themselves part of a broader definition of language. It may be unfair to define language for apes only in the narrowest sense. Lastly, current research into how apes communicate among themselves in the wild is reshaping our views of them. Geographically separated groups of bonobos have their own "dialects" of communicative gestures and sounds. And bonobos already may communicate symbolically among themselves, smashing plants and placing them at particular angles as "road signs."

A Gorilla Named Koko

Koko, a female lowland gorilla, began learning ASL in 1972, when she was one year old. Her teacher, Dr. Francine Patterson, provided her with a gorilla companion in 1976, when three-year-old Michael joined them at the official start of the Gorilla Foundation.

Koko has a working vocabulary of 1,000 signs and understands 2,000 spoken words. Michael—before his unexpected death in 2000—used 600 signs to communicate. Both gorillas, like Washoe, have shown creativity and logic in naming unknown objects. It was obvious to Koko that a face mask is an "EYE HAT," while Michael had no difficulty at all in titling his painting (yes, gorillas paint) of a bouquet of flowers "STINK GORILLA MORE"! Koko has even used ASL to "talk" herself out of trouble. When a teacher caught her eating a crayon, Koko signed "LIP" and pretended to be applying lipstick! Koko also likes to joke using ASL, calling herself an "ELEPHANT" after pointing to a long tube held out in front of her like that animal's trunk.

Koko has also used ASL to express sadness and some complex ideas. She mourned the death of her kitten, named All Ball, by repeatedly signing "SAD." When asked when gorillas die, Koko signed "TROUBLE OLD." When she was then asked what happens to gorillas after they die, Koko answered "COMFORTABLE HOLE." With Dr. Patterson as an interpreter, Koko has even participated in online, computerized "chats"!

Let's Think About...

Why do you think this article includes both sad and funny stories about Koko?
Expository Text

Dr. Sue Savage-Rumbaugh teaches Panibasha to speak using a complex sign language called Yerkish.

A Bonobo Named Kanzi

Kanzi, a male bonobo born in 1980, "speaks" a different human language than Washoe and Koko. He communicates in "Yerkish," a visual code invented by researchers at Georgia State University and the Yerkes Primate Research Center. Yerkish is a set of several hundred geometric symbols called "lexigrams," each representing a verb, noun, or adjective. These lexigrams are placed on an adapted computer keyboard, which bonobos learn to use while learning the meanings of the lexigrams. Kanzi communicates by computer! (Outdoors, Kanzi points to lexigrams on a carry-around tagboard.)

Kanzi, who also understands more than 1,000 spoken English words, first learned Yerkish by watching humans train his mother. Like a silent toddler who astonishes parents by first speaking in complete sentences, two-year-old Kanzi amazed researchers on the day he first "spoke" Yerkish by using most of the lexigrams taught to his mother. By the age of six, he had a Yerkish vocabulary of 200 lexigrams. According to Dr. Sue Savage-Rumbaugh, Kanzi and other bonobos construct logical sentences in Yerkish and even use the lexigram for "later" to discuss future activities.

Let's **Think** About...

What information about Kanzi, the bonobo, tells you that he is different from Koko, the gorilla?
Expository Text

Dr. Savage-Rumbaugh and an assistant teach sign language to a chimp.

Let's **Think** About...

Reading Across Texts After reading *The Chimpanzees I Love* and "'Going Ape' over Language," what are some surprising things you learned that apes can do?

Writing Across Texts Write about the most amazing thing you learned about chimpanzees from these two selections.

Objectives
- Use a dictionary or a glossary to locate information about words.
- Read aloud at an appropriate rate for the material. • Give an organized presentation that intends to persuade your audience. • Recognize exaggerated, contradictory, or misleading statements.

Let's
Learn
It!

READING STREET ONLINE
ONLINE STUDENT EDITION
www.ReadingStreet.com

Vocabulary

Unknown Words

Context Clues When you come across a word you do not know, first see if you can use context clues to figure out its meaning. If that doesn't work, consult a glossary or a dictionary, where you will find information about the word and how to pronounce it.

Practice It! Find the word *intimidate* in the sixth sentence of paragraph 2 on page 58 of *The Chimpanzees I Love*. If you did not know this word, what context clues help you to figure out its meaning? Next use a dictionary to find the pronunciation. Write down the word's definition, and then write your own sentence using the word.

Fluency

Rate

When you read aloud, remember to vary your speed according to ideas and mood in the text. For example, read more slowly when the mood is sad or serious or when the subject is difficult to understand. It is a good idea to slow your reading when you come across sentences with many facts and details.

Practice It! With your partner, practice reading paragraph 2 on page 60 of *The Chimpanzees I Love*. Practice changing your rate to match the text and the mood.

When you deliver a persuasive speech, be sure you have your facts straight.

Persuasive Speech

In a persuasive speech, the speaker tries to convince the audience to agree with what he or she says.

Practice It! Deliver a short persuasive speech about the treatment of animals used in research. Take a position and use facts from *The Chimpanzees I Love* or other sources you find. Your speech needs to state your position, give facts, and then restate your position.

Tips

Listening . . .

- Listen in order to form an opinion.
- Evaluate the speaker's persuasive techniques.
- Take notes so you can ask relevant questions.

Speaking . . .

- Support your opinions with details.
- Speak clearly and loudly enough to be heard.
- Maintain eye contact.

Teamwork . . .

- Discuss why you agree and disagree with others.

Objectives

● Listen to and interpret a speaker's message and ask questions. ● Identify the main ideas and supporting ideas in the speaker's message.

Oral Vocabulary

Let's Talk About

American Frontier

● Describe what you know about the American frontier.

● Share information about the different groups of people who lived on the frontier.

● Express ideas about a frontier where people can be pioneers today.

READING STREET ONLINE
CONCEPT TALK VIDEO
www.ReadingStreet.com

Objectives

● Analyze how the organization of a text, such as cause-and-effect, affects the way ideas are related.
● Understand and make inferences about a nonfiction text and provide evidence from the text to support understanding.

Envision It! | Skill Strategy

Skill

Strategy

Comprehension Skill

🎯 Cause and Effect

- A cause is what makes something happen. An effect is something that happens as a result of a cause. Several causes may lead to one effect.

- Clue words and phrases such as *consequently, as a result,* and *therefore* can help you spot cause-and-effect relationships. Sometimes, though, there are no clue words.

- Use a graphic organizer like the one below to organize causes and effects you find in "Goodbye, Jim Crow" on page 85.

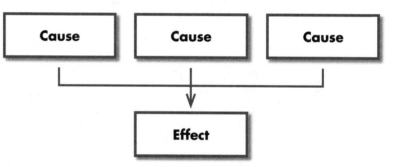

Comprehension Strategy

🎯 Inferring

Authors do not always tell you everything you need to know to understand what you are reading. You may need to add information you already know—your prior knowledge—in order to make inferences, or figure out what is happening in a text. Active readers infer about ideas and meanings to help them understand what they are reading.

READING STREET ONLINE
ENVISION IT! ANIMATIONS
www.ReadingStreet.com

GOODBYE, JIM CROW

It took many years for black people to receive full legal rights in the United States. The push for fair laws began after the Civil War ended.

• **Unfair Laws** Starting in 1865, a group of laws called black codes stopped blacks from having basic rights. Citizens in the northern part of the United States disagreed with these laws. This led to the Reconstruction laws, which got rid of the black codes. But soon new laws were passed that segregated, or separated, blacks from whites in many areas of everyday life. These were called the Jim Crow laws.

• **New Laws** In 1954, the United States Supreme Court ruled that it was not fair or lawful to have separate black and white schools. This helped the Civil Rights movement move forward with a strong, organized push to end segregation. In 1963, leaders of the movement staged a huge march in Washington, D.C., to speak out against racial discrimination.

President Kennedy could not get Congress to pass equal rights laws. After President Kennedy was assassinated, President Johnson got Congress to pass the Civil Rights Act of 1964, which ended legal segregation. Then, in 1965, Congress passed the Voting Rights Act. This led to a huge increase in the number of blacks registered to vote.

Strategy Use your ability to infer to answer this question: Why did the Civil Rights movement start *after* the Civil War ended?
a) Once the war ended, slaves were free.
b) There wasn't interest on the part of black people until then.
c) Before the war, discrimination was illegal.

Skill What caused the United States to pass the Reconstruction laws? Are there clue words?

Skill What was the long-term effect of the important 1954 Supreme Court decision?

Your Turn!

Need a Review? See the *Envision It! Handbook* for help with cause and effect and inferring.

Ready to Try It? Use what you've learned about cause and effect as you read *Black Frontiers*.

Envision It! | Words to Know

earthen

homesteaders

settlement

bondage

commissioned

encounter

Vocabulary Strategy for

Unfamiliar Words

Context Clues When you come across a word you do not know, check its context, or the words and sentences around the unfamiliar word. Often an author provides clues that suggest the word's meaning. When you encounter an unfamiliar word, follow these steps.

1. Reread the sentence in which the unfamiliar word appears. Look for a specific clue to the word's meaning.

2. Think about the overall meaning of the sentence.

3. Next read the sentences near the sentence with the unfamiliar word. They may contain enough information about the word and the subject to suggest the meaning of the unfamiliar word.

4. See if your meaning makes sense in the original sentence.

Read "Settling the West" on page 87. Use context clues to help you figure out the meanings of any unfamiliar words you may find.

Words to Write Reread "Settling the West." Study the photograph and write a description of it. Use words from the Words to Know list as you write.

SETTLING THE WEST

Settling in the American West took bravery and staying power. Men, women, and children traveled by boat or wagon, taking all their goods along. They never knew when they might encounter Native Americans. If the settlers did meet them, would these people be friendly or angry?

Once they chose a plot of land, the pioneers faced many difficulties. Homesteaders were pioneers who bought cheap public land and set up farms or ranches. In the grasslands, they often had to build makeshift earthen homes. They built with dirt or sod because wood was so scarce.

Over time, their numbers grew. In time, a settlement, or community in the wilderness, was established.

Battles between settlers and Native Americans continued in many places, as the Native Americans saw their land disappearing. There were losses on both sides. The U.S. government saw the land as its own. It commissioned officers and sent troops to battle the Native Americans. After many years of conflict and negotiating, Native Americans were mostly forced into the bondage of living on reservations. They no longer had the freedom to live as they once had.

Your Turn!

⏸ **Need a Review?** For help using context clues to determine the meanings of unfamiliar words, see *Words!*

▶ **Ready to Try It?** Read *Black Frontiers* on pp. 88–101.

Black Frontiers

by
Lillian Schlissel

Question of the Week
**What does it mean
to be a pioneer?**

89

Leaving the South

When the Civil War ended, men and women who had been slaves waited to see what freedom would bring. The land they farmed still belonged to the families who had once owned them, and because they had no money, former slaves were expected to pay back a share of their crops in exchange for seed, plows, and mules. They had to pay back a share of everything they raised for rent and food. These sharecroppers soon found they were perpetually in debt.

In 1879, a Louisiana sharecropper named John Lewis Solomon, his wife, and four children packed their belongings and started walking toward the Mississippi River. Along the riverbank they found other black families waiting for a chance to travel north. Some built rafts to carry them over the river's dangerous undertows and eddies. Others had money for passage, but riverboat captains would not let them on board. When a steamboat called the *Grand Tower* came close to shore, John Lewis Solomon called to the captain that he could pay his way. He said he had been a soldier in the Union Army. "I know my rights, and if you refuse to carry me on your boat, I will go to the United States Court and sue for damages." Solomon took a great risk, but the captain agreed to let him and his family board the steamboat.

Reaching Kansas, Solomon said, "This is free ground. Then I looked on the heavens, and I said, 'That is free and beautiful heaven.' Then I looked within my heart, and I said to myself, 'I wonder why I was never free before.'"

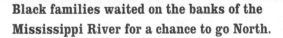

Black families waited on the banks of the Mississippi River for a chance to go North.

Black Homesteaders

omesteading was not easy for black or white settlers. Rocks, grass, and trees had to be cleared before crops could be planted. A farmer needed a horse, a mule, and a plow. He needed seed to plant and food for his family until the crops were ready to harvest. Most of all a pioneer needed a home.

In regions where there were trees, pioneers built log cabins. But in Kansas and Nebraska, there was only tall grass, as high as a man's shoulder. Pioneers learned that tough root systems under the grass held the dirt firmly, and sod could be cut like bricks and piled, layer upon layer, until it took the shape of a house. These homesteaders were called *sod busters,* and their homes were called *soddies.*

Sod homes could be warm and comfortable. Some were two stories high, with glass windows and chimneys. But in heavy rain, smaller sod houses leaked, and some families remembered being surprised by a snake slithering through a wall.

In North and South Dakota, where the land was rocky and winter temperatures fell to 30 degrees below zero, early pioneers burrowed into the ground and covered themselves with an earthen roof. They brought their small

A sod house

For pioneer families, homesteading was a desolate life.

animals into the house in the winter, while cows and goats huddled on the roof, warming themselves on the house that was under their feet.

During the first seasons in a new settlement, a pioneer woman might have no stove. She dug a hole in the ground and fed the fire with weeds, adding small rocks, like coals, to keep in the fire's heat. Buffalo chips, the droppings of buffalo, provided the fuel. When the great animals migrated across the land, women and children gathered chips for the family's cooking fires.

In the hot and dry climate of the Southwest, pioneers built homes with thick walls made of mud and straw. The mud walls, called *adobe,* kept the houses cool in the summer and warm in the winter. In desert regions, women learned from the Indians to brew teas out of wild grasses and to make soap and shampoo from the yucca plant.

In the early days of settlement, there were few black families homesteading. For them, loneliness was part of being a pioneer. But black pioneer families held on, and in sticking it out, they made the way easier for those who came after.

The Exodusters

Men and women who had been slaves read in the Bible about the ancient Israelites who were brought out of bondage and delivered into freedom. Benjamin Singleton, born a slave in Tennessee, was determined that he would bring his people to free soil if it was the last thing he ever did.

After the Civil War, Singleton visited Kansas and over a period of years, he and his friends managed to buy part of a Cherokee reservation. In 1877 they advertised for homesteaders to start an all-black community there. They hoped to attract two hundred families. Fliers promised that settlers who paid one dollar "in installments of 25 cents at a time or otherwise as may be desired" could be part of the new community. By 1879 an exodus of black families out of the Old South began, and before long there were eight hundred homesteaders in the new Kansas communities of Dunlap and Nicodemus. Benjamin Singleton said, "My people that I carried to Kansas came on our own resources. We have tried to make a people of ourselves. . . ." They were known as the Exodusters.

In the early days of the town the farmers in Nicodemus owned only three

Benjamin Singleton, founder of the black community of Dunlap, Kansas

94

horses. One man plowed with a milk cow, and others broke ground with shovels and spades. White farmers saw how hard their new neighbors worked and lent the new settlers a team of oxen and a plow. Black farmers planted their first crops and in time they prospered. By the turn of the century, there were about eight thousand black homesteaders in Nicodemus and Dunlap.

Handbills encouraged black families to move to Kansas. Notice the warning at the bottom of the flier.

Schoolhouse in Dunlap, Kansas. Pupil in foreground carries a sign that reads, "God Bless Our School."

95

The Shores family in front of their sod house near Westville, Custer County, Nebraska, 1887. The Shores became famous as musicians.

Some black settlers moved farther west to Nebraska and Oklahoma, where they built three new black communities—Taft, Langston, and Boley. George Washington Bush went all the way to Oregon Territory, where he introduced the first mower and reaper into the area around Puget Sound.

Of all the black communities, however, Nicodemus and Dunlap remained the most famous. Each year they celebrated the Fourth of July, and they had their own special holiday, Emancipation Day. On July 31 and August 1, a square mile of land was set aside as a carnival fairground. There were boxing matches and baseball

games. In 1907 the town formed one of the nation's first black baseball teams—the Nicodemus Blues. The Blues played black teams as far away as Texas, Nevada, and Louisiana. Satchel Paige, one of the greatest black pitchers in American baseball history, played ball in Nicodemus.

In 1976 Nicodemus was designated a National Historic Landmark. The town's history is being recorded and buildings restored. It marks the proud legacy of black homesteaders in America.

The Moses Speese family—neighbors of the Shores family—outside their sod house near Westville, Custer County, Nebraska

The Buffalo Soldiers

During the Civil War, nearly 180,000 black troops fought with the Union Army against the Confederacy, and more than 33,000 gave their lives to end slavery. After the war, General Ulysses S. Grant ordered Generals Philip Sheridan and William Tecumseh Sherman to organize regiments of black cavalry. These were designated the Ninth and Tenth Cavalry, each containing about a thousand men under the command of white commissioned officers—Colonel Edward Hatch for the Ninth and Colonel Benjamin Grierson for the Tenth. Two black regiments of infantry were organized, the Twenty-fourth and the Twenty-fifth. George Armstrong Custer refused to command black troops, but others accepted their tasks gladly.

Black troops who had been farmers, cooks, carpenters, and blacksmiths came from all parts of the country. The Army paid them thirteen dollars a month plus rations and sent them to the most desolate and dangerous frontier outposts, where they served under the harshest conditions with the oldest equipment. They fought Indian tribes few soldiers wished to encounter—the Cheyenne, Comanche, Kiowa, Apache, Ute, and Sioux.

Henry Flipper, first black graduate of West Point

It was the Indians who gave the black troops the name Buffalo Soldiers because their hair resembled the shaggy coats of the buffalo. The buffalo was sacred to the Indians, and the men of the Ninth and Tenth Cavalry and the Twenty-fourth and Twenty-fifth Infantry accepted the name as a badge of honor, and the buffalo became a prominent part of their regimental crest.

Thirteen men of the Buffalo Soldiers won the highest military award of the nation, the Congressional Medal of Honor.

Serving under harsh conditions, these Buffalo Soldiers of the Tenth Cavalry camped on Diamond Creek in New Mexico.

When all-black regiments were disbanded after World War II, almost one hundred years after they were organized, the Tenth Cavalry became the 510th Tank Battalion. But memories of frontier days were strong, and the 510th was redesignated the Tenth Cavalry in 1958 and stationed at Fort Knox, Kentucky.

A bronze statue in memory of the Ninth and Tenth Cavalry and the Twenty-fourth and Twenty-fifth Infantry was dedicated in 1992 at Fort Leavenworth, Kansas, to commemorate the courage of the Buffalo Soldiers and mark their place in American military history.

The Buffalo Soldiers helped to bring law and order to regions where ranchers fought with farmers, where Indian tribes warred with each other and with settlers, and where bandits threatened to overrun small towns. On rare occasions, settlers acknowledged their great debt to the black troops. When the Twenty-fifth was ordered to duty in the Spanish-American War, the people of Missoula, Montana, postponed Easter church services so that they could line up along the town's main street and wave goodbye to the black troops who had become their protectors and friends.

Over the years, that strange name, Buffalo Soldiers, became a prized possession of those black troops who left a legacy of courageous service in U.S. military history.

John Hanks Alexander, an African American graduate of West Point, class of 1887. He served among the respected Buffalo Soldiers during the Indian Wars.

Conclusion

I t would be wrong to suggest that the frontier was without prejudice. It had its share of violence and racial injustice. As settlements grew into cities, Jim Crow segregation laws confronted black settlers. But on those lonely, dangerous, and beautiful lands we call the frontier, black pioneers built new lives. Born into slavery, African Americans had the same dreams of freedom and independence as did all other Americans. Given the chance, they proved time and again that they possessed skills, initiative, and courage.

West of the Mississippi, between 1850 and 1900, there were some ten thousand African American exodusters, homesteaders, and sod busters. There were also four thousand miners, eight thousand wranglers and rodeo riders, and some five thousand Buffalo Soldiers. According to some historians, there were some eighty thousand African Americans doing whatever else the frontier demanded. They were trappers and mountain men, hotel keepers, and scouts. They were businessmen and women, teachers, and nurses.

And they were cowboys. From the Chisholm Trail to Hollywood, the American cowboy is a hero who walks tall. It is important to remember, then, that some of America's best cowboys and rodeo riders were black, and that some of our bravest pioneers were African Americans who lived and worked on America's western frontiers.

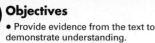

Objectives
• Provide evidence from the text to demonstrate understanding.
• Read independently for a sustained period of time and paraphrase the reading.

Envision It! | Retell

Think Critically

1. How might the post-Civil War years have been different for black frontierspeople if there had been little open land in the West? **Text to World**

2. To see why this author included old photographs, select one and study it for one full minute. Then cover it and report the scene as if you were there. **Think Like an Author**

3. The author tells us that the Indians gave the black troops the name Buffalo Soldiers because of their hair. How did the troops respond to this name given to them? **Cause and Effect**

4. How did adding your prior knowledge about America after the Civil War to the information in the text help you make inferences to better understand what you read? **Inferring**

5. **Look Back and Write** Who and where were the Exodusters? Did they succeed? Review pages 94–95. Provide evidence to support your answer.

   TEST PRACTICE Extended Response

Lillian Schlissel

Lillian Schlissel dedicated *Black Frontiers: A History of African American Heroes in the Old West* to her daughter and son, Rebecca and Daniel, and to her mother, Mae Fischer. About the book, Ms. Schlissel points out that "The black presence in the West is sometimes most powerfully expressed in old photographs." In addition to two books for young people, Ms. Schlissel has written several adult books about the frontier West. Her *Women's Diaries of the Westward Journey* received critical praise. The book is a collection of letters and diaries written by women traveling to California and Oregon between 1849 and 1870. Ms. Schlissel graduated from Brooklyn College, where she is a professor emerita, and she earned a doctorate from Yale University. She lives in New York City.

Other books about the West:
The Way West and *The Story of Women Who Shaped the West*

Use the Reading Log in the *Reader's and Writer's Notebook* to record your independent reading.

Objectives
● Write a description of a setting using sensory details. ● Understand how to incorporate one or more of the senses of smell, taste, touch, sound, and sight into a description. ● Use and understand possessive pronouns.

Let's Write It!

Key Features of a Description

● may tell more about a person, place, object, or event

● uses specific language to help readers visualize a scene

● may be written with first- or third-person narration.

READING STREET ONLINE
GRAMMAR JAMMER
www.ReadingStreet.com

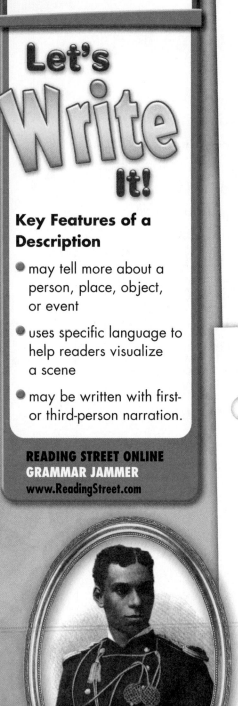

Description

A **description** offers vivid sensory details of a person, place, object, or event. The student model on the next page is an example of a description.

Writing Prompt The photographs in *Black Frontiers* show the setting of the selection in pictures. Think about a setting. Now write a detailed description of that setting.

Writer's Checklist

Remember, you should . . .

☑ write a description of a setting, such as a street in a small town, a favorite shop, or a secret room.

☑ use vivid details to help readers visualize what you describe.

☑ include one or more of the five senses as you write your description.

104

Sand and Waves

Sunlight played across the waves. It dotted the water like tiny bits of gold. I ran **my** hand across the rough grains of sand. Then I grabbed a handful of the grains and watched them trickle back to the beach. The sandy terrain stretched as far as the eye could see.

In an instant, a wave crashed to shore. I heard the whoosh of the water, and then the white tops of the wave melted back into the sea. A seagull cried out overhead and then it swooped down toward the beach.

As I walked toward **my** friends, the wet sand felt like soft, warm clay between **my** toes. There was no one else around. It felt like the whole beach was **ours**. I grabbed a bottle of cold juice from **our** cooler. It tasted like bits of orange dancing in **my** mouth.

Then the sun dipped behind a cloud, and a grumble of thunder rang out across the water. Lightning forked across the sky, so we headed for the car. It was time to leave **our** dreamy day behind.

Genre
A **description** uses sensory details to help the reader experience the setting.

Writing Trait Word Choice
Specific, vivid language adds depth to the description.

Possessive pronouns are used correctly.

Conventions

Possessive pronouns

Remember Possessive pronouns show ownership or possession. *My/mine, your/yours, her/hers, his, its, our/ours,* and *their/theirs* are all possessive pronouns. Do not use an apostrophe.

105

Objectives
● Examine features of poetry.
● Examine how poets use sound
effects to reinforce meaning in their
poems. ● Make connections between
and among texts.

Social Studies in Reading

Genre
Poetry

● Poems are carefully crafted compositions that are arranged in lines. The lines do not have to rhyme, but many poems have lines with a clear, regular rhythm.

● Poems have the ability to make readers feel deep emotions.

● Poets use their life experiences or views as they compose their poems.

● A poet might create new words or combinations of words to reflect a mood or image.

● Read these three poems by Langston Hughes. Which one is your favorite? Why?

Poems
by Langston Hughes

The Dream Keeper

Bring me all of your dreams,

You dreamers.

Bring me all of your

Heart melodies

That I may wrap them

In a blue cloud-cloth

Away from the too-rough fingers

Of the world.

Youth

We have tomorrow
Bright before us
Like a flame.

Yesterday
A night-gone thing,
A sun-down name.

And dawn-today
Broad arch above the
    road we came.

We march!

Dreams

Hold fast to dreams
For if dreams die
Life is a broken-winged bird
That cannot fly.

Hold fast to dreams
For when dreams go
Life is a barren field
Frozen with snow.

Let's **Think** About...

What are some examples of rhyme and rhythm that Hughes uses in these poems?
Poetry

Let's **Think** About...

Reading Across Texts What message do you think Langston Hughes would have for the black settlers of Nicodemus and Dunlap, or for young people today?

Writing Across Texts Write a message of hope for either group of people. Use lines from the poems if you wish.

107

Let's Learn It!

Vocabulary

Unfamiliar Words

Context Clues Words, phrases, and sentences around an unfamiliar word may give you clues to the word's meaning. Use these hints to help you figure out what an unfamiliar word means.

Practice It! Reread *Black Frontiers* and identify any unfamiliar words you find in the story. For each unfamiliar word, look at the surrounding words and sentences to find clues to the word's meaning. Make a list of words in the story whose meanings you figured out by using context clues.

Fluency

Accuracy

Reading accurately helps you to understand what you are reading. Slow down when you come to a word you don't recognize or when you see a sentence with complicated scientific terms or numbers ahead. Read these places carefully. Then read the sentence again at a normal rate.

Practice It! With a partner, practice reading pages 98 and 99 from *Black Frontiers*. Preview the words to make sure you understand and know how to pronounce them. Then read, alternating paragraphs with your partner. Give each other feedback.

108

Listening and Speaking

Use simple, direct language and action verbs in advertisements that you write.

Advertisement

An advertisement is an announcement that promotes a product, service, or event in order to sell it to people. Advertisers persuade customers to buy a product or service or to go to an event.

Practice It! With a partner, create an advertisement that intends to sell land in Kansas to black farmers in the South in the late 1870s. You may refer to pages 94–95 in *Black Frontiers*. Be sure you tell Exodusters why they should buy the land. Then present your ad to the class.

Tips

Listening . . .

- Listen for the ad's message.
- Ask questions to clarify the purpose of the ad.

Speaking . . .

- Make eye contact with your audience to communicate your ideas better.
- Use action verbs in your presentation of the ad.
- When you speak, use natural gestures.

Teamwork . . .

- Ask for and consider suggestions from others.

Objectives
● Listen to and interpret a speaker's message and ask questions. ● Identify the main ideas and supporting ideas in the speaker's message.

Oral Vocabulary

Let's Talk About

Other Worlds

- Share what you know about exploring above or beneath the Earth.

- Ask questions about the hazards deep-sea explorers face.

- Express ideas about the importance of exploring other worlds.

READING STREET ONLINE
CONCEPT TALK VIDEO
www.ReadingStreet.com

111

Objectives
● Explore, create ideas, and come to conclusions about descriptive writing and show proof from the text to support your conclusions.
● Set a purpose for reading a text based on what you hope to get from the text.

Envision It! | Skill Strategy

Skill

Strategy

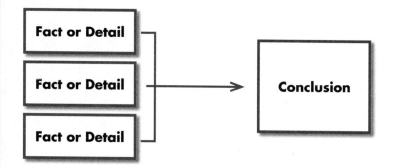

Envision It! Visual Strategies Handbook

Predict and Set Purpose

We **predict** to tell what might happen next in a story or article. The prediction is based on what has already happened. We **set a purpose** to guide our reading.

To predict and set a purpose
• preview the title and the author's name
• preview any illustrations or graphics
• identify why you're reading
• use what you already know to make predictions
• check and change your predictions based on new information

Let's Think About Reading!

When I predict and set a purpose, I ask myself
• What do I already know?
• What do I think will happen?
• What is my purpose for reading?

EI•20

Comprehension Skill

🔄 Draw Conclusions

• When you draw a conclusion, you form a reasonable opinion about what you have read. Use what you know about real life to help you draw conclusions.

• Be sure that there are enough facts and pieces of information in the text to support your conclusions.

• Make a graphic organizer like the one below to help you come to a valid conclusion as you read the letter from Lydia to Rachel on the next page.

Fact or Detail	
Fact or Detail	→ **Conclusion**
Fact or Detail	

Comprehension Strategy

🔄 Predict and Set Purpose

Good readers try to predict the kinds of facts or details they will find in the text. Doing this helps to set a purpose for reading. When you have predicted what you will read, go back after you finish reading to see if you were correct.

March 12, 2011
1221 Sea Gull Way
Gulliver, Florida

Dear Rachel,

How are you? It has been ten weeks now since we moved to Florida so my mom could do her ocean research. Our new town is very different from New York. It doesn't snow here, and the temperature is too hot for me.

There's not much going on in this area, and there aren't very many places to go other than the beach. We live in a very small town near the ocean. There's not much to do most of the time, but sometimes I get to go with my mom when she does her research, and that's great. Still, I miss all the activity and all the people in the big city. Remember how we used to go to shows and get the best pizza slices? There's a lot of seafood to eat here, which is pretty gross since I don't like it. It is so much fun where you are, where there is always something to do.

My new school is called Marina Bay School. Last week, we were studying the ocean, and my mom came to give a presentation. That made me feel like I fit in a little bit better with some of the kids in this new town.

At recess, I usually sort of sit on the sidelines and watch the other kids play volleyball or kickball. There's no one like you here. Are you doing all right? Are you still racing with Ellen and Juanita at recess like we used to? That was awesome!

Sincerely,
Lydia

Strategy What do you predict this letter will be about? What purpose will you set for reading?

Skill Which conclusion can you draw about Lydia's view of her new home?
a) She felt more comfortable in New York.
b) She wishes things were quieter where she lives now.
c) She likes her new home better than her old home.

Skill What conclusion can you draw about how Lydia is feeling?

Your Turn!

⏸ **Need a Review?** See the *Envision It! Handbook* for help with drawing conclusions and predicting and setting a purpose for reading.

▶ **Ready to Try It?** Use what you've learned about drawing conclusions as you read *Deep-Sea Danger*.

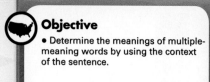

Envision It! | Words to Know

hatch

submersible

tentacles

ego

intrepid

propulsion

silt

Vocabulary Strategy for

Multiple-Meaning Words

Context Clues Some words have more than one meaning. You can use the words and sentences around a multiple-meaning word to figure out which meaning the author is using.

1. Read the words and sentences around the multiple-meaning word.

2. Think about the possible meanings of the word. For example, *refrain* can mean "to keep oneself back" or "a phrase repeated over and over."

3. Decide which meaning makes sense in the sentence. For example, "Everyone said the same *refrain*." Reread the sentence and think of the the meaning you chose.

4. Does this meaning make sense? If not, try another meaning.

Read "Exploration!" on page 115. Use context clues to determine the meanings of any multiple-meaning words you find.

Words to Write Reread "Exploration!" What do you think it would be like to take a tour of an underwater cavern? Write a description of what you imagine, using as many words from the Words to Know list as you can.

Exploration!

I couldn't wait to join my aunt, a famous underwater explorer, for a trip to explore underwater caverns. I knew we would slide into the small submersible and dip down into the caverns and see extraordinary sights!

We'd have to start our trip in a large submarine, but then we could use the submersible's strong propulsion to jet away from the large craft. I knew we'd have to plug in some of the equipment pieces, like flashlights and recorders, to charge them before leaving the submarine. The power sources in the submersible were limited, and it would be important to have all of the equipment ready at a moment's notice.

I'd developed a pretty healthy ego and had bragged to all of my classmates about the trip. I knew they all wished they could go along with me, but I was the only one who would be the intrepid young sailor on this trip. I was absolutely fearless, and I was ready to open the hatch and race into the submarine to head out on the voyage.

I knew that once we landed, we would stir up fine grains of silt, but we had all the equipment to be prepared. We were even ready to deal with any tentacles that an octopus or squid might try to wrap around our submersible. What a story I would have to share when I got back to school!

Your Turn!

⏸ **Need a Review?** For help using context clues to determine the meanings of multiple-meaning words, see *Words!*

▶ **Ready to Try It?** Read *Deep-Sea Danger* on pp. 116–131.

115

Deep-Sea Danger

by
Judy Freed

illustrated by
Nathan Hale

Genre

A **drama** is a story written to be acted for an audience. The story is told by the characters, whose speech is called "dialogue."

Question of the Week
Why do explorers seek out other worlds?

CHARACTERS

Crew of the research vessel Neptune:

MARCUS, Electrician

LU, Navigator

RONNIE, Radio Operator

CHRIS, Cook

SAMANTHA, Pilot-in-Training

STAN, Deck Hand

WILLIE, Deck Hand

Crew of the submersible Explorer:

DALE, Junior Scientist

THE PROFESSOR, Senior Scientist

ISABEL, Pilot

176 / 180

Scene 1

TIME: The not-so-distant future.

SETTING: The deck of the Research Vessel *Neptune*. Somewhere in the Pacific Ocean. *Explorer*, a deep-sea submersible, is stage left. The *Neptune's* radio room is stage right. Its crew lounge, an open area next to the radio room, is center stage.

AT RISE: MARCUS, CHRIS, LU, and SAMANTHA work on *Explorer*. They are preparing the submersible for launch. RONNIE sits at the radio controls. DALE, THE PROFESSOR, and ISABEL watch the crew work.

SAMANTHA: Lights?

MARCUS: Check.

SAMANTHA: Oxygen?

MARCUS: Check.

SAMANTHA: Emergency oxygen supply?

MARCUS: Three days' worth of oxygen are ready to go.

RONNIE *(speaks into the radio)*: Testing. Testing. Lu, do you copy?

LU *(from inside the submersible)*: I hear you loud and clear, Ronnie. The radio is fully functional.

CHRIS: Here's lunch, dinner, and plenty of water.

SAMANTHA: What about the emergency food supply?

CHRIS: There are three days' worth of meals under the seats.

SAMANTHA: Then all systems are go. Isabel, the submersible is ready to launch.

ISABEL *(to the research vessel crew)*: Thank you, Samantha. Great work, crew. Attach the cable, and lower us into the water on my command.

THE PROFESSOR *(to DALE)*: Dale, it's time to go.

ISABEL *(to THE PROFESSOR)*: Are you and your assistant ready, Professor?

THE PROFESSOR: Of course we're ready! We spent three days using robots to map the floor of this particular deep-sea canyon. Now we're going to be the first humans to explore it.

ISABEL: Then let's go for a dive!

(ISABEL and THE PROFESSOR head toward the submersible. DALE stays stage right.)

DALE *(nervously)*: Wait, wait. . . .Tell me again. . . . What happens if there's a really bad storm and we have to stay underwater until the weather clears?

CHRIS: Don't worry. I gave you enough food and water to last three days.

DALE: What if Isabel gets sick and can't bring us back to the surface?

SAMANTHA: I showed you how to use the controls, remember? If Isabel can't pilot the *Explorer,* just call us on the radio. We'll help you get back to the surface.

DALE: And what if there's a problem with the electricity and the oxygen fails and we can't breathe?

MARCUS: Don't worry, Dale. I—

THE PROFESSOR *(doesn't let MARCUS finish his sentence)*: That's right, Dale. Stop worrying! I've explored many deep-sea canyons, and nothing has ever gone wrong.

ISABEL: Would you like to take a picture before you go?

THE PROFESSOR: Of course! A photo of the intrepid crew that's going to make our mission a success. *(to MARCUS)* You. What's your name?

MARCUS: Marcus.

THE PROFESSOR: You're the electrician, aren't you?

MARCUS *(proudly)*: That's me.

THE PROFESSOR: Marcus, stand right here.

(MARCUS stands in front of the submersible.)

THE PROFESSOR: Isabel, you stand here. Dale, over here.

ISABEL: All right.

(ISABEL and DALE stand in front of the submersible.)

THE PROFESSOR *(to MARCUS)*: Here's my camera, Marcus. Careful! It's an expensive piece of equipment.

MARCUS: You want me to take the picture?

THE PROFESSOR: Wait until we're ready. Then push the button on the top.

MARCUS: I know how to take a picture!

THE PROFESSOR: I'll stand here in the middle. Don't take the picture yet.

(THE PROFESSOR stands in front of the submersible between DALE and ISABEL.)

THE PROFESSOR: All right. We're ready. *(to MARCUS)* Now!

(MARCUS snaps the picture.)

THE PROFESSOR: Did you get a good shot? Let me see.

DALE: Thanks, Marcus. It looks great.

ISABEL: Professor, Dale, get on board. It's time to launch our mission.

(DALE, THE PROFESSOR, and ISABEL climb into the submersible.)

LU, CHRIS, SAM *(speak all at once and wave):* Good luck! Happy hunting! Have a great mission!

ISABEL: In two hours we'll be exploring a deep-sea canyon!

TIME: Two hours later.

SETTING: Split scene. DALE, THE PROFESSOR, and ISABEL sit inside *Explorer*. The submersible is now deep in the Pacific Ocean. Aboard *Neptune*, RONNIE sits at the radio controls. EVERYONE ELSE stands in the crew lounge. Throughout this scene, focus shifts between the three areas of the stage. Actors freeze when their area is not active. If lights are available, lighting can highlight active areas of the stage.

AT RISE: ISABEL steers the submersible while DALE and THE PROFESSOR work.

THE PROFESSOR: Look, Dale. There's coral growing on the canyon walls.

DALE: This is amazing!

THE PROFESSOR: I told you, this will be the adventure of your life.

ISABEL: We're about to touch down on the bottom.

THE PROFESSOR: Excellent.

(A gentle THUD. The submersible rocks gently as it settles at the bottom of the canyon.)

THE PROFESSOR: I'll get the camera. Dale, you collect samples of the silt.

DALE: What's that animal? The glowing blue one?

THE PROFESSOR: Just use the robotic arm and put it in the sample case. We may have found a new species.

(In the radio room, RONNIE speaks.)

RONNIE *(to the research vessel's radio):* *Explorer*, do you copy?

ISABEL *(to the submersible's radio):* We hear you loud and clear.

RONNIE: How's the weather down there?

ISABEL: The current is strong, but the fishing is great!

RONNIE: Call us if you need anything.

ISABEL: Will do.

(In Neptune's crew room. LU and SAMANTHA are charting the submersible's course, while MARCUS and CHRIS relax.)

SAMANTHA: You've been complaining ever since *Explorer* left. Let it go!

CHRIS: What's wrong with Marcus?

MARCUS *(imitating THE PROFESSOR)*: "Careful. That's an expensive piece of equipment." Like I don't know how to take a picture.

LU: I think he has a bruised ego.

MARCUS: Those scientists act like the pilot is the only one on the crew that matters. Like the rest of us don't even exist.

LU: That's it, all right.

MARCUS: When was the last time a scientist took a picture of the navigator? Or the cook? Or the radio operator? It's always about the pilot!

CHRIS: What do you expect? The pilot takes them deep into the sea. We stay up here.

MARCUS: Doesn't that bother you?

SAMANTHA: It's just a picture. Get over it!

MARCUS: Someday I wish they'd take *my* picture. Is that so much to ask?

(On the Explorer.)

DALE: What's that big thing?

THE PROFESSOR: Be more specific.

DALE: That creature swimming toward us.

THE PROFESSOR: It looks like a giant squid.

DALE: It's enormous!

THE PROFESSOR: Yes. Giant squid can grow to a length of fifty-nine feet and weigh nearly a ton . . .

DALE: It's wrapping its tentacles around us!

THE PROFESSOR: . . . and notice how the suction cups are lined with sharp, sawlike rings.

DALE: Is it trying to eat us?

THE PROFESSOR: I seriously doubt it. *(pause)* I've never seen a live giant squid before.

(SOUND of a loud BAM. The submersible rocks. The LIGHTS flicker off and on.)

ISABEL *(to radio):* Mayday! Mayday! We are under attack by a giant squid!

RONNIE: *Explorer!* What happened?

ISABEL: The squid slammed us into a canyon wall!

THE PROFESSOR: Get us out of here!

ISABEL: I can't. I've lost propulsion. That squid has its tentacles wrapped around our rear propellers.

(The ENTIRE RESEARCH VESSEL CREW rushes to the radio room.)

SAMANTHA: Can you use the side propeller?

ISABEL: Affirmative.

SAMANTHA *(to radio):* Scrape up against the side of the canyon wall. Maybe that will make the squid let go.

ISABEL: I'll give it a try.

(SOUND of another loud BAM. The submersible rocks. LIGHTS flicker again.)

SAMANTHA:	Is it working?
ISABEL:	Negative. It's still hanging on.
THE PROFESSOR:	We're in its territory. Now it's released a cloud of black ink!
LU	*(to radio):* Dale, use the robotic arm. Try to loosen the squid's grip on your propellers.
DALE:	I can't see the propellers. The ink is in the way!
CHRIS:	What about the eel gun?
LU:	The what?
CHRIS:	The eel gun. Tell them, Marcus.
MARCUS:	I've been working on a plan to turn the robotic arm into a stun gun—for research about electric eels.
ISABEL:	Does it work?
MARCUS:	It fires a powerful electric charge. Dale, do you see the red button under the robotic arm?
DALE:	Yes.
MARCUS:	Touch the squid with the robotic arm. Then push the red button.
DALE:	Okay.
MARCUS:	What happened?
DALE:	The squid felt it.
MARCUS:	Try it again.
DALE:	It's rewrapping its tentacles.
THE PROFESSOR:	It's releasing more ink!
MARCUS:	This time, hold the button down for as long as you can.
DALE:	*This* ought to do it!

126

(SOUND of a loud THUD. Submersible rocks. LIGHTS flicker.)

THE PROFESSOR: It's swimming away! We're free!

(The RESEARCH VESSEL CREW whoops and cheers.)

ISABEL: I still have no propulsion from our rear propellers.

MARCUS: The circuit breaker probably tripped. Check the Number Four circuit breaker.

DALE: I'll check it.

THE PROFESSOR: How do you know where to find the circuit breaker?

DALE: Marcus showed us in safety training. Don't you remember?

(*DALE opens a panel near the controls.*)

MARCUS: Is Number Four off?

DALE: Yes. I'll reset it.

(*DALE switches on the circuit breaker.*)

ISABEL: *Neptune*, I have rear propulsion. All systems are go.

LU: *Explorer*, I've plotted your course back home. Prepare to receive the coordinates.

ISABEL: Thanks, *Neptune*. See you in a few hours.

THE PROFESSOR: Here comes that squid again!

DALE: I'll get the stun gun.

ISABEL: Brace yourself!

(*SOUND of another THUD, the loudest one yet. The submersible rocks. The LIGHTS flicker again.*)

ISABEL: We've lost oxygen. Put on your emergency breathing apparatus!

(*DALE, THE PROFESSOR, and ISABEL suddenly stop moving.*)

RONNIE (*speaks into the radio*): *Explorer*? *Explorer*, can you hear me?

MARCUS: What happened?

RONNIE (*speaks to the research vessel crew*): We've lost communication with *Explorer*.

SAMANTHA: Will they be able to surface?

CHRIS: Will they be able to breathe?

RONNIE: We'll have to wait and see.

Scene 3

TIME: Two hours later.

SETTING: The deck of the *Neptune*. At stage left DALE, THE PROFESSOR, and ISABEL sit frozen.

AT RISE: EVERYONE on the *Neptune* is pacing, or looking stage left.

MARCUS: How long has it been since we heard from *Explorer*?

RONNIE: Almost three hours.

SAMANTHA: I see something. Over there.

CHRIS: It's *Explorer*!

LU: Grab the cable. Let's pull them in.

CHRIS: If I ever get my hands on that squid, I'm going to turn it into calamari!

LU *(to SAMANTHA):* There go Stan and Willie, diving in to hook the cable.

STAN: Grab the cable, Willie!

WILLIE: There! I've got it!

MARCUS: Swim clear! We'll lift *Explorer* onto the deck!

(MARCUS and CHRIS operate the controls that lift the submersible out of the water and onto the ship. STAN and WILLIE swim back to Neptune.*)*

MARCUS: I'm opening the hatch.

CHRIS: Are they all right?

(ISABEL, THE PROFESSOR, and DALE emerge from the Explorer.*)*

ISABEL: Well, that was an adventure!

THE PROFESSOR: It was horrible. *Horrible!* This is the last submersible trip for me!

ISABEL: I've heard that before, Professor.

DALE: Are you kidding? That was amazing! I can't wait to go on another deep-sea mission! I wonder why that squid attacked us. Do you think it was attracted to the lights? Can we dive down tomorrow and find out?

ISABEL *(laughs):*   Tomorrow *Explorer* isn't going anywhere. Tomorrow *Explorer* is having a complete systems check.

MARCUS *(to DALE):* Congratulations on your first mission, Dale. Do you want me to take your picture?

DALE: Thanks, Marcus! Here's the camera. *(takes camera from THE PROFESSOR and gives it to MARCUS)* Professor, Isabel, stand with me in front of *Explorer*.

(ISABEL, THE PROFESSOR, and DALE line up in front of Explorer.)

DALE *(to MARCUS):* Are we all in focus, Marcus?

MARCUS: Yes. Smile, everyone!

DALE: Wait, wait, not yet! Do you see the button on the side of the camera?

MARCUS: Yes.

DALE: That's the timer. We need everyone in this picture! Lu. Chris. Ronnie. Samantha. Marcus. Stan. Willie. Everyone line up! We wouldn't have made it without all of you.

(ALL but MARCUS line up together in front of the submersible.)

MARCUS: Ready?

ALL BUT MARCUS: Ready!

(MARCUS sets down the camera facing the submersible and joins the others.)

MARCUS: Everybody smile!

(ALL smile. LIGHTS flicker off, then on briefly, like the flash on a camera. BLACKOUT.)

The End

Objectives

• Provide evidence from the text to support understanding. • Read independently for a sustained period of time and paraphrase the reading.

Envision It! Retell

Think Critically

1. Describe another story you have read that has a similar plot to that of *Deep-Sea Danger*. Is it also a drama? How is it similar? Text to Text

2. Why do you think the author includes the scene on page 120 where the Professor tells Marcus how to take a picture? Author's Purpose

3. Who was the calmest person in the *Explorer* during the squid attack on pages 124–128? Give examples of behavior that show someone is staying calm. Draw Conclusions

4. The play begins immediately with action. As soon as you read about "oxygen supply," what do you want to find out next? At this point, what do you think the play will be about?
Predict and Set Purpose

5. **Look Back and Write** Look at page 131 to find out who is in the final picture. Explain how and why the picture at the beginning of the play is different. Provide evidence to support your answer.

TEST PRACTICE Extended Response

Meet the Author

Judy Freed decided she wanted to write for the theater in her senior year of high school in the Chicago suburbs, when she coauthored two student shows. At that time she also watched earlier graduates of her high school form a theater company that would become famous: Chicago's Steppenwolf. After she graduated from Harvard University, Ms. Freed became an award-winning playwright. She has seen her plays and musicals performed in London, New York, Chicago, California, Washington, Massachusetts, and throughout the Midwest. Her works for young audiences include the play *The Boy Who Kicked the Sun* and the musicals *Tickle Cakes* and *Tantrum on the Tracks.* Ms. Freed lives with her family in the Chicago suburbs.

Other books about deep-sea adventure: *Ocean* and *The Incredible Record-Setting Deep-Sea Dive of the Bathysphere*

Use the Reading Log in the *Reader's and Writer's Notebook* to record your independent reading.

133

Let's Write It!

Key Features of a Drama

● written to be performed

● tells a story through character dialogue

● includes stage directions

● provides a character list and brief description of setting

READING STREET ONLINE
GRAMMAR JAMMER
www.ReadingStreet.com

Drama

Drama tells a story through the words of characters. A dramatic script includes a title, list of characters, and brief line about the setting. The student model on the next page is an example of drama.

Writing Prompt Write a drama, using dialogue and stage directions, in which characters encounter a problem they must solve.

Writer's Checklist

Remember, you should ...

☑ write a drama in which one or more characters solve a problem.

☑ include a character list.

☑ tell the setting of your drama.

☑ use parentheses to enclose stage directions and tell how actors are to speak their lines.

A Journey's Beginning

CHARACTERS: John Lewis, his wife Sarah, their four children, a riverboat captain

SETTING: (The bank of the Mississippi River. Family members are carrying all of their belongings.)

Lewis (shouting out to a riverboat): Sir! Sir! No one will listen to me! My family needs to be on this boat. I can pay!

Captain: Sorry, but I'm afraid I can't help you. Find yourself another boat.

(Captain steers boat away from shore.)

Lewis (persistent): We have been walking for days!

Captain: That's not my problem!

Lewis (running alongside the boat): But sir! If you let us on your boat, we will not only pay for the passage, but also help you work on the boat! We would be so thankful!

Captain (sighs): It would be hard to refuse anybody when you put it that way. Stand back, I'm coming ashore. Let me grab your bags for you.

(The boat approaches the shore.)

**Genre
Drama** tells a story using character dialogue and stage directions.

**Writing Trait
Organization**
The writer begins a new line when switching between characters.

Indefinite and reflexive pronouns are used correctly.

Conventions

Indefinite and Reflexive Pronouns

Remember Indefinite pronouns may not refer to specific words, and include *someone, somebody, anyone, everybody, something,* and *many*. **Reflexive pronouns** end in *-self* or *-selves*, and include *himself, myself, itself, yourself, ourselves, yourselves,* and *themselves*.

21st Century Skills
INTERNET GUY

Evaluating Online Reference Sources

What is the first thing to do at a new Web site? Find out who wrote the information. Use the "About This Site" button. Can you believe what you find there?

- On Internet Web sites you can find reference sources such as atlases and encyclopedias. They look like printed resources and usually follow a formal organization.

- When you are looking for information for a report, be careful that you are searching the most reliable sources.

- Read "Deep-Sea Explorer"and see the different kinds of information you can find on the Internet's online reference sources.

Deep-Sea Explorer

After reading *Deep-Sea Danger*, you might want to choose the topic of a real life deep-sea scientist for a report. You perform an Internet search. Which of these might prove useful for your report? Note both the source of the information and the description of the information.

File   Edit   View   Favorites   Tools   Help

http://www.url.here

Search Engine

deep-sea exploration

[Search]

This is a .com Web site. The letters *com* are short for *commercial*. A .com site often wants to sell something. It may or may not be reliable. After you read the description, you decide it's not useful.

Sea Exploration SCUBA equipment. Diving classes. Everything needed for an undersea experience. www.website_here.com

Sea Explorers Same crew who discovered the wreck of the *Titanic* finds new discovery. www.website_here.edu

This is a .edu Web site. The letters *edu* are short for *education*. A .edu site is usually a school. It is probably reliable. After you read the description, though, you decide it is not useful.

NOAA Place A great place to learn all about our oceans and the people who explore them! www.website_here.gov

Sea Story The story of a boy who discovers a sea serpent and keeps it as a pet. www.website_here.com

This is a .gov Web site. The letters *gov* are short for *government*. It is probably reliable. As you read the description, you decide it is worth looking at. You click on the link NOAA Place. This Web site is from National Oceanic and Atmospheric Administration. It should definitely be reliable.

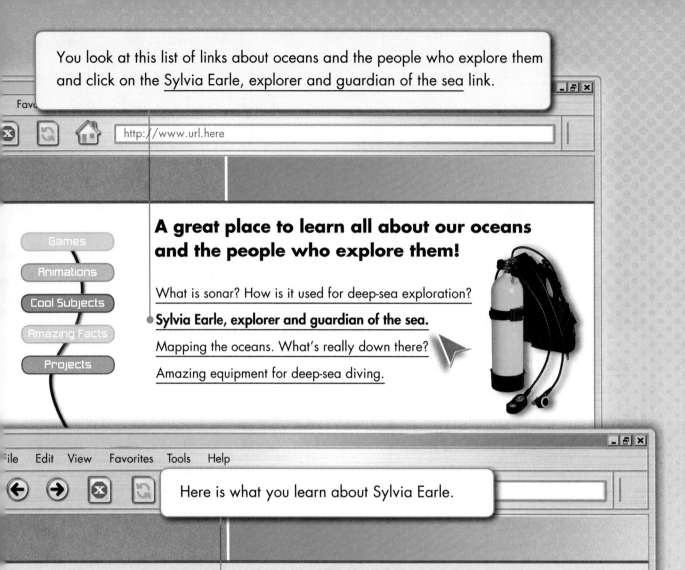

You look at this list of links about oceans and the people who explore them and click on the Sylvia Earle, explorer and guardian of the sea link.

http://www.url.here

Games
Animations
Cool Subjects
Amazing Facts
Projects

A great place to learn all about our oceans and the people who explore them!

What is sonar? How is it used for deep-sea exploration?

Sylvia Earle, explorer and guardian of the sea.

Mapping the oceans. What's really down there?

Amazing equipment for deep-sea diving.

File   Edit   View   Favorites   Tools   Help

Here is what you learn about Sylvia Earle.

Sylvia Earle, Explorer and Guardian of the Sea

Sylvia Earle is an oceanographer and the author of many books. Dr. Earle has done much to develop equipment necessary for underwater exploration. She has been a pioneer in the study of ocean life. Dr. Earle was Chief Scientist at NOAA (National Oceanic and Atmospheric Administration) from 1990–1992. In 1992 she co-founded two companies that design, operate, and consult on manned and robotic submarine sea systems. Today Dr. Earle is the explorer-in-residence at the National Geographic Society.

Diving Records
Dr. Earle, sometimes called "Her Deepness," is an aquanaut who holds a depth record for solo diving. In 1979 she descended to 1,250 feet while strapped to the front of a submarine.

Personal Information
Sylvia Earle was born on August 30, 1935, in Gibbstown, New Jersey. She made her first dive at the age of seventeen. In 1955 she graduated from Florida State University. She received her master's and doctoral degrees from Duke University. She has received many honorary degrees.

Expeditions and Research
Dr. Earle has led more than sixty expeditions throughout the world. She has spent more than 7,000 hours doing underwater research. From 1998 to 2002 she led the Sustainable Seas Expeditions, a five-year program to study the National Marine Sanctuary System. Dr. Earle is an expert on oil spills and led research trips during the Gulf War (1990–1991) and following oil spills of the ships *Exxon Valdez* in 1989 and *Mega Borg* in 1990.

The Tektite Project and Beyond
In 1970, Dr. Earle took part in a government/industry experiment called The Tektite Project, which built an underwater habitat near the U.S. Virgin Islands. For two weeks she led a team of women aquanauts who lived and worked in the underwater city fifty feet under the surface. Her time on that project increased her commitment to the oceans.

She has noted the damaging effects of manmade pollutants and global warming on coral reefs. Asked what she thinks might be the greatest threat to the oceans, she has replied, "Ignorance, lack of understanding, a failure to relate our destiny to the sea."

Asked what she thinks it is that drives explorers to push themselves to their limits and to create the technologies needed to get them to the outer reaches of space or the depths of the oceans, she has replied, "The same thing that drives little kids—curiosity and a sense of wonder about the world around them."

for more practice

Get Online!
www.ReadingStreet.com
Evaluate online reference sources about underwater exploration.

21st Century Skills Online Activity
Log on and follow the step-by-step directions to determine the reliability and usefulness of online reference sources about underwater exploration.

READING STREET ONLINE
ONLINE STUDENT EDITION
www.ReadingStreet.com

Vocabulary

Multiple-Meaning Words

Context Clues Multiple-meaning words may be spelled the same and even pronounced the same but have different meanings. Let context clues be your guide. You may also refer to the *Words!* handbook at the back of this book.

Practice It! Read the sentences below. Think of at least one other meaning that does not make sense for the multiple-meaning word in each sentence.

- I winced when I saw her *jam* her finger against the basketball.

- We had to *row* the boat across the lake.

Fluency

Expression

If you are reading aloud the words a character says, think about the story events. Then think about what the character is feeling and might be thinking. This will help you say the words in a natural, believable way.

Practice It! With a partner, practice reading aloud the spoken lines on pages 118–119 of *Deep-Sea Danger*. How should you read these lines with the expression the characters would use?

140

Listening and Speaking

When you act out a scene from a play, work as a team with your fellow actors.

Dramatization

A dramatization is a version of a story that is performed for an audience. Dramatizations focus on using dialogue to show what happens in the story.

Practice It! Work with a group to act out the scene from *Deep-Sea Danger* when the crew meets the giant squid. Rehearse your scene and then present it to the class. When you're finished, discuss with the class the similarities and differences between reading the scene and acting out the scene.

Tips

Listening . . .

- Listen attentively to each speaker.
- Pay attention to facial expressions to help interpret what the speaker is saying.

Speaking . . .

- Make eye contact with the audience.
- Speak clearly and loudly enough to be heard.
- Stick to the script you have written.

Teamwork . . .

- Participate in discussions that ask for and consider suggestions from others in your group.

141

Objectives

• Listen to and interpret a speaker's message and ask questions. • Identify the main ideas and supporting ideas in the speaker's message.

Oral Vocabulary

Let's Talk About

Inventions

- Share what you know about how an invention happens.

- Describe several significant inventions and tell how they changed people's lives.

- Ask questions about the role the U.S. Patent Office plays in protecting inventions.

READING STREET ONLINE
CONCEPT TALK VIDEO
www.ReadingStreet.com

You've learned
1 9 0
Amazing Words
so far this year!

143

Envision It! | Skill Strategy

Skill

Strategy

Comprehension Skill

Author's Purpose

- Authors may write to inform, persuade, express feelings or ideas, or entertain. Preview the title, headings, and pictures to help predict an author's purpose in writing something.

- When you finish reading, ask yourself, "How did the language or style help meet that purpose?"

- Make a graphic organizer like the one below in order to determine the author's main purpose in writing "The Age of Inventions."

Before Reading
Preview to decide purpose.

↓

During Reading
Look for clues about purpose.

↓

After Reading
Ask if purpose was met and how.

Comprehension Strategy

Monitor and Clarify

Good readers make sure they understand what they are reading. If you are not sure you understand the text, stop to clarify what you have just read. If you discover, for example, that the author is giving you brand-new information using difficult words, stop and think about the meaning of each word and then reread the section that stopped you.

The Age of Inventions

The period from the mid-1800s to the early 1900s was one of great significance in human history. Many of the machines invented during this time changed the world.

First, new ways to power machines were developed. Inventors learned to generate and use electricity, leading to the widespread use of electric lights and trains. The first gasoline-fueled engine was perfected in 1859, and these engines were soon used in many factories.

Second, transportation changed dramatically. The first motorcycles and motorcars were introduced in 1855. The first large iron ships were constructed during this time as well and soon replaced ships powered by sails. The Wright brothers piloted the first plane flight in 1903.

Third, people were able to communicate in more sophisticated ways. For example, the telephone, which was made in 1876, and the wireless telegraph, invented in 1895, let people converse across long distances. The radio was invented in 1901.

The world changed in very many ways from the mid-1800s to the early 1900s. Was it a better place because of all these inventions? Many people would say yes. However, some might disagree. Transportation and communication were speedier, but noise, pollution, and a faster pace of life resulted.

Skill What do you predict is the main purpose of this article?
a) to inform you which machines were invented during this time
b) to entertain you by joking about inventions of the 1800s
c) to persuade you that this time was very popular

Strategy Are you understanding the author's purpose and the information in the article? Do you need to stop and think?

Skill What does the purpose of this final paragraph seem to be—to inform, to entertain, or to express ideas?

Your Turn!

⏸ **Need a Review?** See the *Envision It! Handbook* for help with author's purpose and monitoring and clarifying.

▷ **Ready to Try It?** Use what you've learned about author's purpose as you read *Inventing the Future*.

Inventing the Future

145

percentage

reproduce

transmitted

converts

devise

efficiency

generated

proclaimed

Vocabulary Strategy for

Prefixes *re-*, *pro-*, and *trans-*

Word Structure A prefix is a word part that is added to the beginning of a base, or root, word. The prefix changes the base word's meaning. When you come across an unfamiliar word with a prefix, knowing the meaning of the prefix can help you to figure out the word. The prefix *re-* means "again"; *pro-* means "forth" or "forward"; and *trans-* means "across," "beyond," or "through."

1. Look at an unfamiliar word to see if it has a base word you know.

2. Check to see if the prefix *re-*, *pro-*, or *trans-* has been added to the base word.

3. Think about what meaning the prefix adds to the meaning of the base word.

4. Try the meaning and the base word together.

5. See if the meaning you come up with makes sense in the sentence. If it doesn't, look up the word in a glossary or a dictionary.

Read "Hats Off to Inventors." Look for words that have prefixes. Use the prefixes to help you figure out the meanings of the words.

Words to Write Reread "Hats Off to Inventors." Choose an invention you think is important. Write about how it has changed people's lives. Use as many words from the Words to Know list as you can.

Hats Off to Inventors

We owe the comfort and convenience of our lives to inventors. These creative geniuses devise better ways to do or make something. Sometimes this means coming up with a whole new invention, such as the telephone. Thanks to this machine, sound is transmitted over great distances. At other times, inventors have just improved the efficiency of a machine that already exists. The radial tire, for example, meant that cars would get better gas mileage. Even simple inventions can make a big difference. For example, the sticky-note converts paper into a message that can be placed right where you want it. The inventor is a practical dreamer. He or she wants to make a product that is easy to reproduce and useful so that the public will buy it.

Inventors have been around for thousands of years, but in the last 150 years they have generated by far the greatest percentage of new gadgets ever invented. In many ways, their work has made life better for us all. Don't you think a special Inventors Day should be proclaimed?

Your Turn!

⏸ **Need a Review?** For help using prefixes, see *Words!*

▷ **Ready to Try It?** Read *Inventing the Future* on pp. 148–165.

Inventing the Future

Future

A Photobiography of Thomas Alva Edison

by Marfé Ferguson Delano

Genre

A **biography** is the story of a real person's life written by another person. Before you read, think about what you may already know about Thomas Edison.

Question of the Week
How do inventions happen?

149

In 1868, Thomas Edison took a job in the Western Union telegraph office in Boston. He found the city an exciting place. Not only did it have a large telegraphic community, it was filled with inventors. One of them was Alexander Graham Bell, who in 1876 would invent the telephone. Edison worked nights as a press operator and spent his days exploring the shops where telegraphs and other electrical devices were designed and made. Inspired by all the activity he found, Edison soon quit his job to focus full time on bringing out inventions. He met with people who had money to invest and persuaded them to provide the funds he needed to develop his ideas and have his inventions made. He specialized in telegraphic devices, but he also worked on other inventions.

Pictured here during his "tramp telegrapher" days, Edison preferred to work night jobs, which he said gave him "more leisure to experiment."

When he was 22 years old, Edison received his first patent. It was for an electric vote recorder. A patent is an official document issued by the government that gives a person or company the sole right to make or sell an invention. Edison hoped the device would be used by state legislatures, but lawmakers were not interested in buying it. The experience taught him a valuable lesson: Never again would he invent something that people didn't want to buy.

In 1869, Edison moved to New York City. Many telegraph companies, including Western Union, had their headquarters in the city, which brimmed with business opportunities for an ambitious young inventor. Edison worked for a while for the Laws Gold Indicator Company, where he repaired and improved the company's stock printers. Also called stock tickers because of the noise they made, stock printers were a kind of telegraph that sent minute-by-minute reports of the changing price of gold to stockbrokers' offices.

"Anything that won't sell, I don't want to invent. Its sale is proof of utility, and utility is success."

That fall, Edison started a business called Pope, Edison and Company with a fellow inventor named Franklin Pope. They advertised themselves as electrical engineers who could "devise electrical instruments and solve problems to order." The company offered a variety of services having to do with telegraph technology and was also committed to bringing out new devices—Edison's specialty. He patented a number of telegraphic improvements that were eagerly bought by the telegraph industry. Finally he was inventing what people wanted and were willing to pay for.

By the age of 23, Edison had earned a reputation as one of the best electrical inventors in the country, which helped him attract more financial backers. In 1870, his partnership with Pope broke up, and Edison opened his very own manufacturing company and laboratory in Newark, New Jersey.

Edison hired more than 50 employees to make and sell his stock printers and other equipment and to assist with his many experiments. Among the skilled machinists and clockmakers he hired were Charles Batchelor and John Kruesi. A British-born machinist and draftsman, Batchelor soon became Edison's right-hand man as well as his friend. They worked closely together for nearly 25 years. Kruesi, born in Switzerland and trained as a clockmaker, worked with Edison for 20-some years.

Manufactured at his Newark factory and embellished with his name, Edison's Universal Printer, a stock ticker, was among his first commercially successful inventions.

In the fall of 1871, 24-year-old Edison started his own news service, the News Reporting Telegraph Company. Among the company's employees was a pretty 16-year-old clerk named Mary Stilwell, a Newark girl whose father worked in a sawmill. Edison set his sights on Mary, and after a brief courtship, they married on Christmas Day, 1871. When the couple's first child was born, a daughter named Marion, Edison

Mary Stilwell (top) married Edison on Christmas Day, 1871. The couple had three children: Marion (middle), Thomas Alva, Jr., (bottom right), and William (bottom left).

nicknamed her "Dot," after the telegraph signal. Their second child, Thomas Alva, Jr., was dubbed "Dash," of course. The Edisons' third child was named—and called—William.

Soon after their marriage, Mary discovered that she played second fiddle to her husband's true love—inventing. He often spent several days straight at the lab, working through the nights and catching naps on a workbench or desktop when exhaustion overwhelmed him. Whenever Edison was involved with a project, he became totally wrapped up in it. And since he almost always had dozens of inventions going at once, he had little time for anything else.

In Newark, Edison first developed the method of team inventing that would characterize the rest of his career. Whenever a new idea for an invention inspired him, he sketched it out in a notebook and then shared the drawing with Batchelor and Kruesi or other trusted assistants. Their job was to take the sketch and see that it was made into a working model. Lab workers then experimented with the model to see how the invention worked—or did not work, which was often the case. Edison was not discouraged when things went wrong. He and his workers would just keep trying until they found out what did work.

Edison's workers tended to be very loyal to "the old man," as they called their young boss. They admired and respected him for the way he worked alongside them, plunging into the dirtiest jobs with enthusiasm and putting in longer hours than anyone else. Moreover, Edison could be generous. He often gave assistants who worked closely with him on an invention a percentage of the profits it made.

"Negative results are just what I want. They're just as valuable to me as positive results. I can never find the thing that does a job the best until I find the ones that don't do."

Although Edison's Newark laboratory focused mainly on devices that improved the speed and efficiency of the telegraph, other electrical inventions were also under development. One of these was the electric pen, which could create multiple copies of a handwritten document. Business owners, from lawyers to mapmakers, immediately saw the value of the device, and it sold well. Although Edison manufactured and sold many of his inventions, he also sold the patents for many others. This gave the buyer the exclusive right to make and sell a device. Despite the income this generated, Edison was usually short of cash. That's because he tended to spend most of what he earned from one invention on the next.

In 1876, Edison sold his Newark business. He moved his family and about 20 of his best workers—including Batchelor and Kruesi—

The electric pen was among the inventions Edison developed and manufactured at his Newark facility. An advertisement for the device claimed that it could produce "5,000 copies from a single writing."

Edison (seated at center wearing a cap and scarf) and his muckers take a break in his Menlo Park "invention factory." Among the projects he worked on there was an improved telephone transmitter. To find the material that would work best in it, Edison and crew experimented with more than 2,000 different substances, including rubber, ivory, tobacco leaf, and fish bladder.

to a small farming village in New Jersey called Menlo Park, located about 20 miles from New York City. There he had a two-story laboratory built to his design. Unlike most other labs of the time, which combined inventing with manufacturing, Edison's new laboratory was devoted exclusively to researching and developing his ideas. It contained well-equipped chemistry and electrical labs and a machine shop for making models of his inventions. Edison often referred to the place as his "invention factory." He bragged that it would turn out "a minor invention every ten days and a big thing every six months or so."

Edison and his "muckers," as he fondly called his crew of fellow experimenters, lived up to the boast. Known as the "Chief Mucker," Edison patented 75 different inventions in the first two years at Menlo Park. Among them was an improved version of Alexander Graham Bell's telephone.

"Genius is 1 percent inspiration and 99 percent perspiration."

The biggest problem with Bell's telephone was that the sound it transmitted, or sent, was weak. A caller had to shout into it in order to be heard on the other end of the line. Edison felt sure he could not only find a way to make the telephone sound louder and clearer, he also could make it send messages over longer distances. Eager to gain the advantage in the budding telephone industry, Western Union hired him to do just that.

Edison knew that improving the transmitter—the device that converts the sound of a speaker's voice into electrical signals—was the key to better quality sound. The challenge was to find the material that would work best in it.

In 1877, less than a year after Bell's invention of the telephone, Edison discovered that tiny pieces of carbon encased in a small container, or button, gave the best results. Called the carbon button transmitter, the invention not only produced excellent sound, but greatly increased the range of the telephone. A version of it is still used in most telephones today.

Paying customers listen through earphones to a recording in a "phonograph parlor" in Salina, Kansas, in the 1890s. Edison manufactured phonographs with a special coin-in-slot device for use in saloons and other places of entertainment.

"I had the faculty of sleeping in a chair anytime for a few minutes at a time."

A taker of catnaps since his days as a young telegrapher, Edison wasn't picky about where he nodded off. Here he snoozes atop a lab table in his West Orange laboratory in 1911.

While he was working on the telephone, another sound-related idea occurred to Edison. If the human voice could travel over wires, he reasoned, then there should be a way to record the sound so that it could be listened to later. In November 1877, Edison gave a sketch of an invention he called the phonograph to John Kruesi and asked him to build it. A few days later, Kruesi had a model ready for testing. A simple machine, it consisted of a hand-cranked cylinder covered in tinfoil, a mouthpiece with a metal disk called a diaphragm, and a needle.

With his muckers gathered around him, Edison turned the handle of the machine while he shouted a nursery rhyme into the mouthpiece. As the sound waves of his voice vibrated the diaphragm, the attached needle scratched grooves in the foil. When he finished reciting, he rewound the cylinder, put the needle into the tracks it had made, and cranked the handle again. To everyone's surprise, the machine worked the very first time! Out of the phonograph came Edison's voice, faint but clear: "Mary had a little lamb, its fleece was white as snow, and everywhere that Mary went, the lamb was sure to go." The excited experimenters stayed up all night recording themselves with the invention, which was the ancestor of modern CD players.

The next morning Edison took his brand-new "baby" to New York City and dazzled the editors of *Scientific American* magazine with a demonstration. Word of the amazing invention spread rapidly, and Edison became a celebrity overnight. The phonograph's ability to reproduce human speech seemed like a miracle. Newspaper headlines proclaimed him the "Inventor of the Age" and the "Wizard of Menlo Park."

Edison, who enjoyed the attention the phonograph attracted, envisioned a variety of commercial uses for the device, including toys and dictation machines. He soon set it aside, however, to concentrate on the greatest challenge of his career—the development of an electric lighting system that could be used in homes and businesses.

Electric lighting was not a new idea. Brightly burning lamps called arc lights (which glowed when a current of electricity jumped between two carbon rods) had already replaced gas street lamps in some large cities by the 1870s. But they were not suitable for home use. Not only

> *"This [the phonograph] is my baby and I expect it to grow up to be a big feller and support me in my old age."*

In 1878, Edison demonstrated his phonograph at the National Academy of Sciences in Washington, D.C. While there, he posed with his invention for this photograph taken by famed Civil War photographer Mathew Brady.

Over the years, Edison produced a variety of phonographs for home use. The records he made to play on them were delivered to homes and could also be bought in stores.

was their glare too intense for indoors, they were also smelly. So people still used candles, oil lamps, or gas lamps to light their homes after dark.

Aware that other inventors were racing toward the same goal as he, Edison vowed to get there first. To gain the financial support he needed, he took a gamble. In September 1878, he announced to reporters that he was very close to developing a practical incandescent lamp, or light bulb. Not only that, he said he expected to have a safe, affordable electric lighting system ready to go in just six weeks. He was exaggerating his progress greatly, but so strong was his reputation at the time that few questioned his claim. Confident of Edison's genius, several rich investors established the Edison Electric Light Company to cover his expenses. Edison's gamble paid off. It was time for the real work to begin.

The groundwork for the incandescent light bulb had been laid many years earlier by an English chemist named Sir Humphry Davy. In 1802, Davy discovered that by passing an electric current through strips of metal, he could make them hot enough to glow brightly, or incandesce, for a few seconds before they burned up.

The Menlo Park lab hummed with round-the-clock activity as Edison and his muckers—including several newly hired electrical experts—tackled the problem of the light bulb. Edison set some of his associates the task of finding a way to get all the air out of the glass bulb, so that the material giving off the light, called the filament, would not burn up too quickly. Other workers tested more than 1,600 materials—including horsehair, coconut fibers, fish line, spider webs, and even the hair from John Kruesi's beard—to find the best filament.

Finally his persistence was rewarded. In the fall of 1879, Edison and his muckers tested a piece of cotton sewing thread. First they carbonized it by baking it until it charred and turned into carbon. Then they inserted the carbonized thread into the glass bulb, forced out the air with a special vacuum pump, and sealed the glass. When connected to an

THE DAILY GRAPHIC

The front page of *The Daily Graphic* from July 9, 1879, (top) pictures Edison in sorcerer's garb, a reference to his nickname, the "Wizard of Menlo Park." The cartoon below it illustrates the fear electrical wiring inspired in some people in the 1880s.

This portrait of Edison associate Charles Batchelor is the first photograph ever taken by electric light. Edison sketched hundreds of different designs and tested more than 1,600 different materials in his quest to invent a practical, long-burning light bulb.

161

The inventor mixes chemicals in his West Orange laboratory.

electric current, the bulb glowed steadily for more than 13 hours! Within a few weeks, the lab had produced an improved bulb that burned many hours longer.

In late December 1879, Edison invited the public to Menlo Park to see his marvelous new invention. As visitors got off the train in the evening, they were astounded by the brightly shining electric street lamps lighting their way. Even more impressive was the laboratory, which one newspaper article described as "brilliantly illuminated with twenty-five lamps."

This lab sketch from 1879 expresses the jubilation felt by Edison and his Menlo Park muckers at finally producing a long-burning light bulb.

Over the next two years, Edison and his crew worked feverishly to invent the many other devices besides the light bulb that were needed to get a full lighting system up and running. At the top of the list was an efficient generator, or dynamo, to produce the electricity. They also developed wires and cables to deliver the electricity from the generators, which would be housed in central power stations, to streets and buildings. Sockets, switches, safety fuses, and lamp fixtures also had to be designed. Ever practical, Edison didn't forget to devise a meter to measure the amount of electricity that customers used, so they could be charged accordingly. His lighting would be cheap, yes, but not free!

By 1882, Edison had set up the world's first commercially successful electric power station, on Pearl Street in New York City. He and his family had moved to the city sometime earlier, so that he could personally supervise the installation of his lighting system. On September 4 of that year, he was finally ready to deliver what he had promised four years earlier. Standing in the office of millionaire businessman J. P. Morgan— one of his investors—Edison flicked a switch and current from the Pearl Street station lit the office lamps.

By nightfall, some two dozen buildings in the city's financial district glowed with Edison's electric lights. As crowds gathered in the streets to

Edison's earliest movies were filmed in West Orange. They were viewed through a peephole machine called a kinetoscope (above).

marvel at the latest magic from the Wizard of Menlo Park, his fame soared even higher.

Edison devoted the next few years to improving his electrical system and spreading it around the country and the world. He set up numerous companies to handle the manufacturing and installation of his products and made millions of dollars.

In 1887, Edison built the laboratory of his dreams. Located about a mile from Glenmont, it was the largest, best-equipped research facility in the world. Ten times bigger than Menlo Park, the main lab was three stories high and 250 feet long. Housed in separate buildings were a physics lab, a chemistry lab, and a metallurgical lab. In his new laboratory, Edison continued to improve his lighting system.

Edison's West Orange lab also contributed to the birth of the motion picture industry. Around 1889, Edison and a team of muckers led by William K. L. Dickson started work on "an instrument which does for the Eye what the phonograph does for the Ear."

In a few years, they had invented a movie camera, called a kinetograph, and a peep-hole machine, called a kinetoscope, for watching the movies. To make films for the kinetoscopes, Edison opened the world's first motion picture studio in West Orange in 1893. Only 20 to 30 seconds long, these early movies featured a variety of subjects, from acrobats to boxers to ballet dancers.

Edison also returned to his "baby," the phonograph, in West Orange. While Edison had been working on electric lights, inventors Chichester Bell (a cousin of Alexander Graham Bell) and Charles Tainter had created

TIME LINE OF EDISON'S INVENTIONS

		1877—Tinfoil phonograph	
	1875—Electric pen	1877—Carbon-button	
1869—Electric vote recorder	1875—Quadruplex telegraph	telephone transmitter	1879—First practical light bulb

As part of the 1929 Jubilee, Edison (seated) reenacts the lighting of his famous bulb 50 years earlier. Looking on are Henry Ford (standing, left) and former Edison employee Francis Jehl.

their own, improved version of the machine, which used wax cylinders rather than tinfoil for recording. Spurred by the competition, Edison developed an even better wax-cylinder phonograph. Although he originally envisioned the device as a business machine for taking dictation, people were eager to purchase it for home entertainment. Edison was happy to satisfy them. Not only did he produce a variety of phonographs for home use over the next 40 years, he also made prerecorded cylinders, or records, of popular tunes to play on them. In the process, he helped to create what we now call the recording industry.

Edison phonograph from 1911

| 1888—'Perfected' phonograph | 1893—System for making and showing motion pictures | 1909—Storage battery |

Objectives
• Provide evidence from the text to demonstrate understanding.
• Read independently for a sustained period of time and paraphrase the reading.

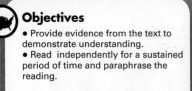

Envision It! Retell

Think Critically

1. Choose an invention in your home that you think is important. Write about how it has changed people's lives. **Text to World**

2. The biographer organizes this article by time. She lists a date followed by Edison's accomplishments during that time and then moves on to another date and another set of accomplishments. Why do you think she follows this chronological pattern? **Think Like an Author**

3. The author's purpose for writing *Inventing the Future* was to inform about Thomas Alva Edison's inventions. What might be another purpose the author had for writing this? Why do you think that? **Author's Purpose**

4. Some of Edison's inventions were improvements of other people's inventions. Create a T-chart. On the line, write "Telephone" at the top left and "Light Bulb" at the top right. Under each heading, record the ways in which Thomas Edison improved upon each of these inventions. **Monitor and Clarify**

5. **Look Back and Write** Look back through *Inventing the Future* for key qualities that Thomas Alva Edison possessed both as an inventor and as a co-worker. Make a list of these qualities and then write a paragraph about Mr. Edison as a person you would like to meet.

   TEST PRACTICE Extended Response

Marfé Ferguson Delano

Marfé Ferguson Delano is an award-winning author. Her book *Inventing the Future: A Photobiography of Thomas Alva Edison* was named a 2003 Notable Book for Children by the American Library Association. She teamed with Nancy Aulenback, an elementary schoolteacher, and Hazel Barton, a microbiologist and award-winning mapper of caves, to write *Exploring Caves: Journeys into the Earth.* That book was recognized by the National Science Teachers Association in 2002. Ms. Delano has written many books for the National Geographic Society about nature subjects, including three books in the Animal Safari series: *Kangaroos, Tree Frogs,* and *Sea Otters.* She is a graduate of Duke University and lives in Virginia with her husband and three children.

Other books by Marfé Ferguson Delano: *Exploring Caves* and *Wildflowers*

Use the Reading Log in the *Reader's and Writer's Notebook* to record your independent reading.

Let's Write It!

Key Features of a Summary

● tells what a selection is about

● includes only the most important ideas and details

● leaves out unnecessary details

READING STREET ONLINE
GRAMMAR JAMMER
www.ReadingStreet.com

AN UNRESTRAINED DEMON.

168

Expository

Summary

A **summary** is a retelling of the main points of a story. The student model on the next page is an example of a summary.

Writing Prompt Think about an interesting article or story that you have read recently. Now write a summary explaining what the article or story is about.

Writer's Checklist

Remember, you should . . .

 look for key words to help determine main ideas.

☑ begin with a clear topic sentence.

☑ support main ideas with important details.

☑ arrange your sentences in logical order.

Summary of <u>The Chimpanzees I Love</u>

    The first section of <u>The Chimpanzees I Love</u> discusses the mind of the chimpanzee. Scientists are researching how chimps communicate, learn, and remember. Chimpanzees have been observed using tools, and some have even been taught to speak in sign language.

    The second section talks about the negative consequences of chimps kept in captivity. Many chimps have been taken from their homes for research or to perform in circuses. They live in prison-like cages. Many zoos are making lives better for captive chimps, however, by re-creating the chimps' wild habitat in the cages.

    The story also gives information on challenges that face chimpanzees today. As the trees in African forests are cut down, chimps are losing their habitats. People *who* are working to solve these problems believe they must move fast. Jane Goodall, *whom* many around the world admire for her work, wrote about people *who* are trying to help chimpanzees both in the wild and in captivity.

Writing Trait Focus/Ideas
The beginning focuses on the topic and purpose of the summary.

Genre
A **summary** tells only the most important ideas from a text.

The pronouns *who* and *whom* are used correctly.

Conventions

Who and Whom

Remember Use the pronoun **who** as the subject of a sentence or clause. Use the pronoun **whom** as the object of a verb or preposition. These pronouns can be used to ask a question: *Who* called me? *Whom* did you tell?

Objectives

● Identify the language and devices used in biographies, including how authors present major events in a person's life. ● Make connections between and among texts.

Science in Reading

Genre
Biography

● A biography is the story of a real person's life, written by another person.

● Biographies are usually organized according to time, or the sequence in which events happened in the person's life.

● Read "Garrett Augustus Morgan" and see how it is an example of a biography about an important American inventor.

GARRETT AUGUSTUS MORGAN

Garrett Augustus Morgan was an African American businessman and inventor whose curiosity and innovation led to the development of many useful and helpful products. A practical man of humble beginnings, Morgan devoted his life to creating things that made the lives of other people safer and more convenient.

Among his inventions was an early traffic signal that greatly improved safety on America's streets and roadways. Indeed, Morgan's technology was the basis for modern traffic signal systems and was an early example of what we know today as Intelligent Transportation Systems.

THE INVENTOR'S EARLY LIFE

The son of former slaves, Garrett A. Morgan was born in Paris, Kentucky, on March 4, 1877. His early childhood was spent attending school and working on the family farm with his brothers and sisters. While still a teenager, he left Kentucky and moved north to Cincinnati, Ohio, in search of opportunity.

Although Morgan's formal education never took him beyond elementary school, he hired a tutor while living in Cincinnati and continued his studies in English grammar.

In 1895, Morgan moved to Cleveland, Ohio, where he went to work as a sewing machine repairman for a clothing manufacturer. News of his proficiency for fixing things and experimenting traveled fast and led to numerous job offers from various manufacturing firms in the Cleveland area.

In 1907, Morgan opened his own sewing equipment and repair shop. It was the first of several businesses he would establish. In 1909, he expanded the enterprise to include a tailoring shop that employed 32 employees. The new company turned out coats, suits, and dresses, all sewn with equipment that Morgan himself had made.

In 1920, Morgan moved into the newspaper business when he established the *Cleveland Call*. As the years went on, he became a prosperous and widely respected businessman, and he was able to purchase a home and an automobile. Indeed it was Morgan's experience while driving along the streets of Cleveland that led to the invention of the nation's first patented traffic signal.

A SEWING MACHINE FROM THE EARLY 1900S

Let's Think About...

What are some of the features that help you recognize this article as a biography?
Biography

Let's Think About...

How might you keep track of Garrett Morgan's age as he moves through his life?
Biography

THE GARRETT MORGAN TRAFFIC SIGNAL

Let's **Think** About...

What facts and details do you find most interesting about Garrett Morgan's life?
Biography

The first American-made automobiles were introduced to U.S. consumers shortly before the turn of the century. The Ford Motor Company was founded in 1903, and with it American consumers began to discover the adventures of the open road.

In the early years of the 20th century, it was not uncommon for bicycles, animal-powered wagons, and new gasoline-powered motor vehicles to share the same streets and roadways with pedestrians. Accidents were frequent. After witnessing a collision between an automobile and a horse-drawn carriage, Morgan was convinced that something should be done to improve traffic safety.

BEFORE THE INVENTION OF THE TRAFFIC SIGNAL, ROAD INTERSECTIONS WERE OFTEN CHAOTIC AND DANGEROUS.

While other inventors are reported to have experimented with and even marketed traffic signals, Garrett A. Morgan was the first to apply for and acquire a U.S. patent for such a device. The patent was granted on November 20, 1923. Morgan later had the technology patented in Great Britain and Canada as well.

The Morgan traffic signal was a T-shaped pole unit that featured three positions: Stop, Go, and an all-directional Stop position. This "third position" halted traffic in all directions to allow pedestrians to cross streets more safely.

Morgan's traffic management device was used throughout North America until it was replaced by the red-, yellow-, and green-light traffic signals currently used around the world. The inventor sold the rights to his traffic signals to the General Electric Corporation for $40,000. Shortly before his death, in 1963, Morgan was awarded a citation for his traffic signal by the United States government.

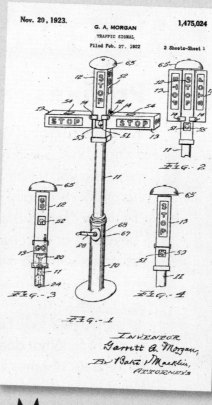

Nov. 20, 1923.   G. A. MORGAN   1,475,024
                        TRAFFIC SIGNAL
                      Filed Feb. 27, 1922   2 Sheets-Sheet 1

MORGAN'S SKETCH OF HIS INVENTION AS SUBMITTED TO THE U.S. PATENT OFFICE

Let's Think About...

Why might the author think that Garrett Augustus Morgan is a good choice for a biography?
Biography

OTHER MORGAN INVENTIONS

Garrett Morgan was constantly experimenting to develop new concepts. Though the traffic signal came at the height of his career and became one of his most renowned inventions, it was just one of several innovations he developed, manufactured, and sold over the years.

Morgan invented a zig-zag stitching attachment for manually operated sewing machines. He also founded a company that made personal grooming products such as hair-dying ointments and the curved-tooth pressing comb.

Let's Think About...

Reading Across Texts How were the two inventors, Thomas Edison and Garrett Morgan, alike and different?

Writing Across Texts Write at least two similarities and two differences between these two inventors.

Let's Learn It!

READING STREET ONLINE
ONLINE STUDENT EDITION
www.ReadingStreet.com

Vocabulary

Prefixes *re-, pro-, trans-*

Word Structure When you find a word you do not know, see if it begins with a prefix that may help you figure out the word. For example, the prefix *re-* usually means "again"; *pro-* means "forth" or "forward"; and *trans-* means "across," "beyond," or "through." Combine the meaning of the prefix with the meaning of the base word.

Practice It! Find the word *transmitted* on page 155. What does the prefix *trans-* mean? Make a list of other words with the prefix *trans-*. What is the meaning of each base word? How does the prefix change the meaning? You may also consult the glossary or a dictionary.

Fluency

Appropriate Phrasing

When you use appropriate phrasing, you group words together as you read, using the sentence's punctuation as a guide. Pause briefly at a comma; pause for a longer time at a dash, colon, or semicolon; and come to a full stop at a period, question mark, or exclamation point. Use punctuation signs as cues to your reading.

Practice It! With a partner, practice reading a page from *Inventing the Future*. Before you begin, scan to see which words make sense to group together. Use punctuation cues to guide you. If you see an exclamation point, express surprise.

Listening and Speaking

Get Ready For High School

When you give an informational speech, do your research and speak with confidence.

Informational Speech

In a speech, a speaker gives a formal talk to an audience for a specific purpose. The purpose of an informational speech is to provide listeners with facts about a topic.

Practice It! Choose one of Thomas Edison's inventions and research it. Explain what it is, what it does, and why it was significant. Next write three or four paragraphs that tell about the invention, using your own words. Practice with a partner to be sure you're staying on topic. Then present your speech to the class.

Tips

Listening . . .

- Listen to the speaker.
- Determine the speaker's main idea.
- Ask relevant questions.

Speaking . . .

- Use notes to stay focused on the invention you're telling about.
- Explain your topic clearly.
- Speak loudly enough to be heard.
- Make eye contact.

Teamwork . . .

- Hold up your hand if you can't hear the speaker.
- Listen to your partner for feedback.

175

Poetry

- **Humorous poems** are meant not only to please but also to make the reader smile or even laugh.

- Humorous poems can take any form. They can rhyme or not, follow a **meter** or not, or even use punctuation or not.

- Humorous poems often surprise the reader.

- How does the author of "Science Fair Project" use rhyme to make the poem funny? What kind of imagery does she use?

- Compare the imagery in "Science Fair Project" with that in "Seeds" to see how important using sensory details can be to enjoying poems.

Science Fair Project

by Carol Diggory Shields

PURPOSE:
The purpose of my project this year
Is to make my brother disappear.

HYPOTHESIS:
The world would be a better place
If my brother vanished without a trace.

MATERIALS:
3 erasers
White-out
Disappearing ink
1 younger brother
1 kitchen sink

PROCEDURE:
Chop up the erasers.
Add the white-out and the ink.
Rub it on the brother
While he's standing in the sink.

RESULTS:
The kid was disappearing!
I had almost proved my theorem!
When all at once my mom came home
And made me re-appear him.

CONCLUSION:
Experiment a failure.
My brother is still here.
But I'm already planning
For the science fair *next* year.

Seeds

by Ann Turner

When the dust gets in my mouth
I remember the taste of pork
roasted over hickory wood
the night before we left
and how Gran filled a sack
with peach pits,
like dried brown hearts to carry west.
Someday I'll dig some black sweet soil,
set each seed to catch the light,
and one day I'll watch those peaches ripen.
Each bite
will be a taste of our old farm.

Let's **Think** About...

What key elements make "Science Fair Project" a humorous poem? List them.

Let's **Think** About...

Both "Science Fair Project" and "Seeds" use vivid details for their subjects. Which do you like better? Why?

The Explorers

by Carole Boston Weatherford

Esteban set out to search for gold.
Henson braved ice to find the Pole.
Beckwourth trekked beyond the bounds,
and du Sable settled Chicago town.
They basked in sunsets few had seen
and hiked where hidden springs ran clean.
They forded rivers, bathed in creeks,
camped on cliffs and climbed high peaks.
Bound for glory, compass in hand,
they boldly conquered newfound lands.
Some sailed seas and some rode west,
but one went farther than the rest.
Mae Jemison gazed at this earthly sphere,
rocketed through the space frontier.

Bronze Cowboys

by Carole Boston Weatherford

When bison roamed the wild, wild West
dark riders rode the Pony Express
over the mountains, across the plains,
past coyotes, bobcats and wagon trains.
Bronze cowboys rode in cattle drives
where deserts met the turquoise skies.
They busted broncos and bulldogged steer,
made peace with the Indians and showed no fear.
A mail carrier named Stagecoach Mary
fought off wolves on the lonesome prairie.
Nat Love was the surest shot in the land.
Bill Pickett was known as a mean cowhand.
Around the campfire, they strummed guitars,
imagined they could lasso stars.

What are resources and why are they important to us?

RESOURCES

Objectives
● Listen to and interpret a speaker's message and ask questions. ● Identify the main ideas and supporting ideas in the speaker's message.

Oral Vocabulary

Let's Talk About

Family Relationships

● Express opinions about the importance of family histories.

● Share what you know about how to document a family history.

● Describe several ways that older family members are important to younger ones.

READING STREET ONLINE
BIG QUESTION VIDEO
www.ReadingStreet.com

Skill

Strategy

Comprehension Skill

Literary Elements: Plot and Theme

- Recognizing literary elements—plot, characters, setting, theme—will help you better understand the stories and books that you read.

- The plot includes (1) a *problem,* or *goal;* (2) *rising action,* or events when a character tries to solve the problem or meet the goal; (3) a *climax,* when the character meets the problem or goal head-on; and (4) a *resolution,* or outcome.

- The theme is the main idea of a story.

- Make a graphic organizer like the one below to help you chart the plot in "Jarrett's Journal."

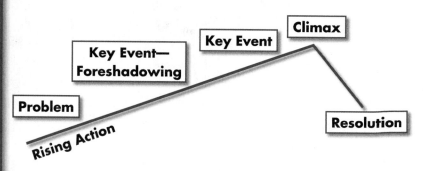

Comprehension Strategy

Summarize

Good readers can better understand a story by summarizing, or briefly stating in their own words, the story's plot and theme. When you summarize a story, concentrate on the main events rather than the details.

JARRETT'S JOURNAL

April 16—It's a very relaxing evening—the very opposite of today! Today I was going to host a dinner at 6 o'clock in my new apartment for my grandparents, parents, and 12-year-old brother, Billy. <u>Was going to</u> is the operative phrase.

This morning I rolled over in bed and glanced at the clock. It was noon! I was so exhausted from moving that I'd neglected to set my alarm. I darted out of bed and started sweeping and scrubbing and piling boxes and stuff that was lying around into closets and my dresser drawers.

Then I dashed out to the supermarket. When I got back, I rinsed the chicken I'd just bought, plopped it into a pan, poured a gourmet sauce over it, and stuck it in the oven.

Next I got the potatoes and salad ready and set the table. Finally I readied myself, showering and putting on a clean pair of jeans. Six o'clock—the security buzzer rang.

With my family peering over my shoulder, I opened the oven and voila! a pink, flabby, RAW chicken. I'd forgotten to turn on the oven!

"Nice going," my brother said with a smirk. "Now what are we going to eat?"

It's a good thing there's an outstanding pizza parlor just down the block.

Skill What is the problem in this story?

Skill What is the climax? What is the resolution?

Strategy Use the main events of the story to summarize.

Your Turn!

⏸ **Need a Review?** See the *Envision It! Handbook* for help with literary elements—plot and theme—and summarizing.

Let's **Think** About...

▶ **Ready to Try It?** Use what you've learned about plot and theme as you read *The View from Saturday*.

decline

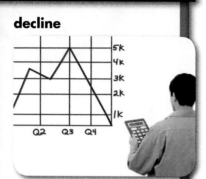

former

unaccompanied

accustomed

presence

Vocabulary Strategy for

🎯 Antonyms

Context Clues Antonyms are words that mean the opposite of one another. You can use analogies, or comparisons that show relationships, to help you understand antonyms. For example, *tall* is to *short* as *few* is to *many*. Sometimes a writer uses an antonym near an unfamiliar word to help readers understand the unfamiliar word.

Choose one of the Words to Know and follow these steps.

1. Reread the words and sentences around the unfamiliar word. Are two things being contrasted? Look for words and phrases that point to opposites such as *unlike, not, however, but,* and *on the other hand.*

2. If there is an antonym, think about a word that means the opposite and substitute it for the unfamiliar word.

3. Does this meaning make sense in the sentence?

4. If not, look up the unfamiliar word in the dictionary.

Read "An Invitation to a Wedding." Look for antonyms that help you understand the meanings of any unfamiliar words.

Words to Write Reread "An Invitation to a Wedding." Then write a description of a wedding you have attended or watched on TV. Use as many words from the Words to Know list as you can.

An Invitation to a Wedding

The invitation began "Mr. and Mrs. Harold Smith request the honor of your presence. . . ." I thought to myself, *Oh, no! Not another wedding!* And I began thinking of ways to excuse myself from this celebration.

I didn't always feel this way. I enjoyed the joyous occasion and the party that followed as much as the next person. But as I grew older, my enthusiasm for weddings went into a decline. The more friends and cousins married, the more people asked me, "Isn't it time that you get married?" If I attended a wedding unaccompanied, people shot me sympathetic glances.

(*Poor thing,* they thought. *All alone again.*) If I escorted a friend to the wedding, we were at once claimed by the hordes of matchmakers who seem to live for weddings. (*Have you set a date yet?*)

One day I'll meet the right person. Then I'll be ready to take my turn in front of the well-wishers. My former distaste for weddings will dissolve as I relish my own future wedding. By then, my family will have become so accustomed to my single state that it will be hard for them to get used to the idea that I'm getting married!

Your Turn!

⏸ **Need a Review?** For help using context clues with antonyms, see *Words!*

Let's **Think** About...

▶ **Ready to Try It?** Read *The View from Saturday* on pp. 188–205.

The View from Saturday

by E. L. Konigsburg
illustrated by Janan Cain

Question of the Week
**How can different
generations be resources?**

My mother insisted that I write a B & B letter to my grandparents. I told her that I could not write a B & B letter, and she asked me why, and I told her that I did not know what a B & B letter was. She explained—not too patiently—that a B & B letter is a *bread and butter letter* you write to people to thank them for having you as their houseguest. I told her that I was taught never to use the word you are defining in its definition and that she ought to think of a substitute word for *letter* if she is defining it. Mother then made a remark about how Western Civilization was in a decline because people of my generation knew how to nitpick but not how to write a B & B letter.

I told her that, with all due respect, I did not think I owed Grandma and Grandpa a B & B. And then I stated my case. **FACT:** I was not just a houseguest, I was family; and **FACT:** I had not been their houseguest by choice because **FACT:** She had sent me to them because she had won a cruise for selling more houses in Epiphany than anyone else in the world, and if she had shared her cruise with Joey and me instead of with her husband, my father, I would not have been sent to Florida in the first place and **FACT:** She, not me, owed them thanks; and further **FACT:** I had been such a wonderful help while I was there that Grandma and Grandpa would probably want to write me a B & B.

My brother Joey had been sent to my other set of grandparents, who live in a normal suburb in Connecticut. "Is Joey writing a B & B to Grandma and Grandpa Eberle?"

"Even as we speak," Mother replied.

"Well, maybe he has something to be thankful for," I said.

Let's **Think** About...

What kind of information does the author seem to tell in the "FACT:" points? **Story Structure**

190

Mother drew in her breath as if she were about to say something else about what children of my generation were doing to Western Civilization, but instead, she said, "Write," and closed my bedroom door behind her. I opened the door and called out to her, "Can I use my computer?"

She said, "I know you can use the computer, Noah, but you *may* not." I was about to make a remark about who was nitpicking now, but Mother gave me such a negative look that I knew any thoughts I had had better be about bread and butter and not nitpicking.

I gazed at my closed bedroom door and then out the window. Door. Window. Door. Window. There was no escape.

I took a box of notepaper out of my desk drawer. The notes were bigger than postage stamps, but not by much. I took out a ballpoint pen and started pressing it against a piece of scrap paper, making dents in the paper but not making a mark. Ballpoint pens sometimes take a while to get started. When I was down in Florida, Tillie Nachman had said, "The ballpoint pen has been the biggest single factor in the decline of Western Civilization. It makes the written word cheap, fast, and totally without character." My mother and Tillie should get together. Between them, they have come up with the two major reasons why Western Civilization is about to collapse.

Not because I was trying to save Western Civilization but because I wanted to actually get my B & B letter written, I put the ballpoint pen back into the drawer and took out my calligraphy pen, the one that uses wet ink. I didn't fill it. I would fill it when I was ready to write. I also took out a sharpened pencil and a pad of Post-it notes to jot down any ideas that might come to mind.

I wrote *red wagon.* The red wagon had definitely been a gift—even though, under the circumstances, I didn't bring it back to Epiphany with me. I thought a while longer and wrote *tuxedo T-shirt.* It, too, had been a gift, but I didn't have

Let's **Think** About...

What has Noah told so far about his visit to his grandparents in Florida?

Summarize

191

that either. I wrote *calligraphy pen and bottle of ink.* A wet ink pen and a bottle of ink had been given to me, but the ones I took out of my desk drawer were ones I had bought myself. The calligraphy pen made me remember about the Post-it notes I had bought to correct the problem that had developed with the ink. Even though I had bought the Post-it notes myself, I added *Post-it notes* to my list. I peeled off the Post-it note containing my list and stuck it on the wall in front of my desk, and then, as my mother had commanded, I thought again.

red wagon
tuxedo T-shirt
calligraphy pen
and bottle of ink
Post-it notes

Century Village, where my Gershom grandparents live, is not like any place I had ever been to. It is in Florida, but it is not exactly Disney World or Sea World or other regular destinations. It is like a theme park for old people. Almost everyone who lives there is retired from useful life. Grandma Sadie and Grandpa Nate fit in nicely.

It all started when Margaret Draper and Izzy Diamondstein decided to get married, and the citizens of Century Village called a meeting in the clubhouse to organize the wedding.

In their former lives, Grandma Sadie and Grandpa Nate had owned a small bakery right here in Epiphany, New York, so Grandma volunteered to do the wedding cake, and Grandpa Nate, whose chief hobby had always been violin playing, promised to arrange for the music.

Mr. Cantor, a retired postman from Pennsylvania, who was devoted to growing orchids, said that he would have enough blossoms for the corsages. And Mrs. Kerchmer said that she would lend her African violets for the centerpieces.

Tillie Nachman volunteered to do the invitations, and Rabbi Friedman, who was a rabbi in his former life, said he would perform the ceremony even though Margaret Draper was not Jewish and Izzy Diamondstein was. This was a late second marriage, and there wouldn't be any concern about what religion they should choose for their children since all their children were already grown up and chosen. Grandpa Nate later explained to me that unlike the average citizen of Century Village, rabbis don't have former lives. They are what they were; once a rabbi, always a rabbi.

Many citizens of Century Village were widows who had once been great family cooks, so they formed a committee to plan the wedding dinner. Everyone agreed to share the cost, and they made up a menu and a master shopping list.

After that first meeting, Grandpa Nate and I took Tillie Nachman, a former New York City person who had never learned to drive, to the stationery store so that she could buy the invitations. While she shopped for the invitations, Grandpa and I went to Wal-Mart to pick up Grandma's prescription, and that is when we saw the red wagon special. Grandpa bought it for me, and it's a good thing he did. It came in handy until Allen came along.

I checked my list. *Post-it notes.* I had bought them when we ran out of invitations. Of course, we didn't run out of invitations until Tillie's cat got its paws into the ink.

Tillie was filling in the *who-what-when-and-where* on the invitations when I noticed that she had the prettiest handwriting I had ever seen. "Calligraphy," she said. "It means beautiful writing," and she asked me if I would like to learn how to write like her. I said yes. She said she would give me lessons if I would help her address the envelopes. So Grandpa drove us to an art supply store where she bought me a calligraphy pen and a bottle of ink. It was while Tillie was trying out various pen points (called *nibs*) that she made

Let's Think About...

From what you have read so far, what do you think will happen next? **Predict and Set Purpose**

193

the remark about the ballpoint pen being the biggest single factor in the decline of Western Civilization.

After choosing a nib Tillie said, "I hope in the future, Noah, that you will use a ballpoint pen only when you have to press hard to make multiple carbons."

I couldn't promise that. There were times in school when a person had to do things fast, cheap, and without character.

Tillie said, "There are pens that come with ink in a cartridge, Noah, but I will have nothing to do with them." So when we were back at her condo, Tillie taught me how to fill a pen, or, as she said, "How to *properly* fill a pen."

One: Turn the filling plunger counterclockwise as far as it will go. Two: Dip the nib completely into the ink. Three: Turn the filling plunger clockwise until it stops. Four: Hold the nib above the ink bottle and turn the plunger counterclockwise again until three drops of ink fall back into the bottle. Five: Turn the plunger clockwise to stop the drops. Six: Wipe the excess ink completely from pen and nib.

When I told Tillie that six steps seemed a lot to have to do before you begin, she said, "You must think of those six steps not as preparation for the beginning but as the beginning itself."

I practiced my calligraphy. I practiced all twenty-six letters of the alphabet, including *X,* which was not part of any of the who-what-when-and-wheres or any of the addresses but is a very good letter to practice because **FACT:** It is not easy.

When Tillie decided that I was good enough to help with the invitations, I sat on the floor of her living room and used her coffee table as my desk. She sat at the kitchen table. **FACT:** Many of the domiciles in Century Village do not have family rooms with desks.

There was a lot of writing to do because at the bottom of each and every one of those invitations, we wrote: Your presence

Your presence but no presents.

Let's **Think** About...

What steps did Noah follow to begin to learn calligraphy for the invitations?

🔄 **Summarize**

194

but no presents. Tillie said that practically all the invitations that went out from Century Village said that. "Besides," she said, "I think that making the wedding is enough of a present."

I was doing a wonderful job until Thomas Stearns, called T.S., Tillie's cat, pounced into my lap, and I jumped up and spilled the ink, and the cat walked through the spilled ink and onto a couple of the invitations I was addressing. A few—five altogether—now had cat's paws.

Tillie was pretty upset because she had not bought extras because she said, "I don't make mistakes." In her former life Tillie had been a bookkeeper. I heard her say, "I can add up a column of figures with the best of them." I didn't know if she meant the best of the computers or the best of the bookkeepers, and I didn't ask because I was afraid I already knew.

I told Tillie not to worry. I told her that I would think of something. And I did. That's when I bought the Post-it notes. I put a Post-it into each of the invitations that had a cat's paw mark. On the Post-it I wrote (in faultless calligraphy): Bring this specially marked invitation to the wedding and receive a surprise gift. When Tillie asked me what the surprise would be, I told her not to worry, that I would think of something. And I did. But **FACT:** It wasn't easy.

On the day the groceries were to be purchased, the citizens of Century Village formed their version of the Home Shopping Network. They met in the clubhouse again. Everyone sat in rows, holding coupons they'd

Let's Think About...

How does the author portray Noah's attitude toward his job for the wedding?
Inferring

195

clipped since printing began. They asked me to be master of ceremonies.

I sat at a table in front of the clubhouse room and called out items from the master grocery list. It was a lot like a game of Go Fish. I said, "I need one Crisco, four margarines, *pareve*, and let's have all your paper towels." Everyone searched through their fistfuls of coupons and gave me the ones that were needed. Tillie circled the items we had coupons for.

Then we checked the newspaper for supermarket specials and made out lists for each of the stores, depending on which one had the best buy in a particular item. I wrote the Gershom list in calligraphy. It didn't slow things down too much, and the citizens of Century Village are accustomed to waiting.

Later that day, everyone returned to the clubhouse with the groceries and the store receipts. Tillie added, divided, and straightened out who owed and who was owed, and no one bothered to check because everyone knew that Tillie Nachman did not make mistakes. Then we had to check the grocery list against the menu and who was cooking what. I helped distribute the groceries to the proper households, using the new red wagon.

FACT: I did a wonderful job.

On the day of the wedding I was in great demand to take things over to the clubhouse in my wagon. The African violets alone took three trips, and the briskets took two. Next, Mr.

Let's **Think** About...

What did Noah and the citizens of Century Village do to line up the groceries?

Summarize

Cantor and I delivered the orchid corsages to the bride and her maid of honor. In the real world, I had never met anyone who spent as much time with flowers as Mr. Cantor. Mrs. Draper's maid of honor was to be her daughter, Mrs. Potter. Mrs. Draper used to live in my hometown, which is Epiphany, New York, and her daughter, Mrs. Potter, still does. Mrs. Potter bought a new dress and flew down for the wedding, but we didn't fly down together. I had come weeks before—my first trip as an unaccompanied minor.

Mr. Cantor and I took flowers over to the groom and his best man to put in their buttonholes. Allen, who was Izzy Diamondstein's son, was to be best man. They both live in Florida and have the same last name.

Allen Diamondstein still lived in the real world because even though he was Izzy's child and even though he was full-grown, he was too young to live in Century Village. **FACT:** Allen Diamondstein was the most nervous human being I have ever seen in my entire life. **FACT:** His wife had left him. She had moved to Epiphany and taken a job with my father, who is the best dentist in town (**FACT**).

Allen Diamondstein kept saying, "Isn't it ironic? My father is getting married just as I am getting divorced." This was not the greatest conversation starter in the world. No one knew what to say after he said it. Some cleared their throats and said nothing. Others cleared their throats and changed the subject.

I must have heard him say it a dozen times, and I never knew what to say either. At first I wondered if that was because I didn't know the meaning of *ironic*. So I looked it up.

The meaning that best fits (and does not use the same word in its definition) is "the contrast between what you expect to happen and what really happens." But after I looked it up, I couldn't figure out what was ironic about Allen Diamondstein's getting divorced and Izzy Diamondstein's getting married. The way Allen Diamondstein acted, I can tell you that divorce would be the only possible thing you could expect from marriage to him. And the way Izzy acted around Margaret, marriage would not only be expected, it would be necessary.

Let's **Think** About...

By having Noah tell the story this way, how does the author reveal her characters?
Story Structure

197

Sha! a shanda far die kinder. They were embarrassing to watch, but not so embarrassing that I didn't.

Wedding cakes are not baked as much as they are built. In the real world, people don't build wedding cakes. They order in. If you are going to build it yourself, it is not done in a day. It takes three. On the first day, Grandma Sadie baked the layers. On the second, she constructed the cake, using cardboard bases and straws for supports, and made the basic icing to cover the layers. On the third day, she made the designer icing for the rosebuds and put the little bride and groom on top. **FACT:** The cake was beautiful.

Fortunately, Grandpa Nate took its picture right after she finished it, so Grandma Sadie can remember how it looked for a little while.

Allen Diamondstein would tell you that the red wagon was the problem, but I would say that it's ironic that he should say so. It definitely wasn't. He was. How else were we supposed to deliver the cake to the clubhouse? It was too tall to fit in the trunk of the car, and since on an average day the outside temperature in Century Village is body temperature, there would be a major meltdown before the cake got to the clubhouse where the wedding was to take place. That's when I got the idea to load up the wagon with ice, put a sheet of plastic over the ice, put the cake on top of that, and slowly wheel it over there, with me pulling and Grandpa checking the rear.

Grandpa Nate went to the Jiffy store and bought three bags of ice, and we loaded them into the wagon. Too much. Since we didn't want the bed of the wagon filled right

Let's **Think** About...

What do you think will happen to Grandma Sadie's wedding cake?
Predict and Set Purpose

up to the edge, we emptied some, dumping it out on the cement of the patio. That's where we were going to load the wagon so we wouldn't have to wheel the wagon down any steps to get it to the meeting room.

Just after we loaded the cake onto the wagon, Allen Diamondstein came over to Grandma's. He said his father wanted him to pick up a prayer book, but I think his father sent him because he was making the groom nervous.

No one answered when he rang the front doorbell because we were all in the back loading the cake into the red wagon, so he walked around back to the patio.

Unfortunately, he didn't see the wagon handle, so he tripped on it, slid on the wet concrete, fell in the puddle of melted ice, and, unfortunately, toppled the wedding cake.

The little top layer was totally smashed; it fell in the same puddle as Allen, and the little bride and groom were seriously maimed.

So was Allen's ankle. Which fact I detected when he grabbed his foot and started to moan while still sitting in the puddle on the patio. Grandpa Nate called 911. Grandma Sadie returned to the kitchen to whip up a repair batch of icing. Grandpa Nate took the remains of the cake to the clubhouse, and I sat with Allen until the ambulance came. He was not good company.

The groom called to see what was taking Allen so long. I answered the phone, and I thought I would have to call 911 for him, too. "Don't panic," I said. "I'll be your best man."

Let's **Think** About...

What is the climax, or high point, of this story-within-a-story? How do you know?
Story Structure

199

I did not tell Izzy what had happened to the couple on top of the wedding cake because people get very superstitious at weddings, and no one wants a wounded bride and groom sitting on top of the cake with which they are to start a happy marriage. I had seen that sort of thing often enough in the movies: A close-up of the shattered little bride and groom floating in a puddle of melted ice signifying the fate of the real bride and groom. So although I had to tell Izzy Diamondstein what had happened to Allen, I didn't say a word about the top of the wedding cake. I didn't think I could convince him that having the little bride and groom fall into a puddle was ironic.

He seemed to calm down when I volunteered to be best man, which was about the same time that we found out from the ambulance driver that Allen would be back at Century Village in time for the wedding even if he probably wouldn't be able to walk down the aisle.

As soon as the ambulance took Allen away, I ran over to Mr. Cantor's place and asked him to please, please find another orchid for the top of the cake although it would be better if he could find two since the second layer was now the top layer and was bigger. Mr. Cantor found two beautiful sprays of orchids, which Grandma Sadie artistically arranged around the new top layer.

Since I had promised to be best man, not having a tux was a problem. I couldn't fit in Allen's, not that I would have wanted to if I could. That's when Grandpa Nate called Bella Dubinsky.

In her former life, Bella had been an artist. She painted the pictures that went into the pattern books for people who sew their own clothes. In the real world I had never met anyone who sewed her own clothes, but in Century Village, I had met three. Bella had a supply of fabric paints, and within two hours, we had painted a T-shirt that looked like a tuxedo and a red bow tie. I say *we* because I helped color in the lines she drew. It's not easy filling in the lines on T-shirt material; it scrunches up under the weight of the brush, leaving skip marks. You have to go over it again and again. Fortunately, the paints dry fast, and by four o'clock, it was ready to wear.

Repaired, the wedding cake looked beautiful. If Allen had not told, no one would have guessed that those orchids didn't belong on top. But Allen told. He told everyone. He also apologized for my being best man. I didn't think that I was someone he had to apologize for. I had helped a lot, and I looked totally presentable in my tuxedo T-shirt, which was a real work of art.

FACT: Being best man is not hard. You walk down the aisle with the maid of honor. Who, in this case, was a matron of honor because she is married. I admit that having the son of the groom, Allen, as the best man would have been a better match, size-wise, for the daughter of the bride even though one is married and the other divorced, but the essential fact is that I did a very good job. I stood beside the groom. Mrs. Potter stood beside the bride, and the four of us stood in front of the rabbi, and all five of us stood under a bridal canopy, which I know is called a *chupah* and which I think is spelled the way I spelled it. I didn't yawn, sneeze, or scratch any visible thing. I held the wedding ring until the rabbi nodded, and I handed it over.

Let's **Think** About...

What seems to be Noah's attitude toward Allen, the son of Izzy, the groom?
Inferring

201

Let's **Think** About...

What events have happened at the wedding to this point?

🔵 **Summarize**

I did an excellent job of being best man even though when I was under the chupah, I was under a lot of pressure trying to think of surprises for the cat's-paw invitations. The idea came to me at the very moment Izzy smashed the glass and everyone yelled *mazel tov.* Even before Izzy stopped kissing the bride, I knew what I could do. (**FACT:** It was a very long and thorough kiss.)

It wouldn't be easy. It would mean giving up things I loved, but I had to do it.

When everyone except Allen was dancing the *hora,* I slipped out of the clubhouse and ran back to Grandma Sadie's. I took off my tuxedo T-shirt, folded it nicely, and put it in my red wagon. I found the package of Post-it notes, my

calligraphy pen, and bottle of ink and after making sure that the ink was tightly closed, I put those in the wagon, too. When I returned to the wedding party, the dance was over, and everyone was sitting around looking exhausted. My moment had arrived.

I tapped a glass with a spoon as I had seen grown-ups do, and I said, "Ladies and gentlemen, will those lucky few who have the specially marked invitations, please come forward. It is time to choose your surprise gift." I saw them pick up their cat's-paw invitations and walk over to the band where I was standing beside my red wagon. "First," I said, "we have one hand-painted T-shirt, which is an original work of art done by Mrs. Bella Dubinsky. In addition, we have a calligraphy pen, almost new, and a bottle of ink, almost full. These are the perfect instruments for beautiful handwriting. We have one packet of Post-it notes, complete except for five." I swallowed hard and added, "And we have one red wagon."

Tillie Nachman, who could count precisely, said, "But that's only four gifts, and there were five cat's-paw invitations."

"Oh yes," I said, "the fifth gift is the best gift of all."

Everyone asked at once, *Whatisit? Whatisit? Whatisit?*

I sucked in my breath until my lungs felt like twin dirigibles inside my ribs. "The best gift of all is . . . the very best . . . the very best gift of all is . . . to give up your gift."

A thick silence fell over the room. Then Tillie Nachman started clapping. Soon the others joined in, and I noticed Grandma Sadie and Grandpa Nate looking proud.

At first everyone who held a cat's-paw invitation wanted to be the one to give up his gift, but I did not want that. If they didn't take my presents, I would feel as if they didn't matter. Mr. Cantor stepped forward and took the Post-it notes. He

Whatisit? Whatisit? Whatisit? Whatisit?

Let's **Think** About...

How does the author show that Noah is very quick-witted and fast on his feet?
Story Structure

203

said he could use them for labeling his plants. He said that he was donating an orchid plant as the fifth gift. Then Tillie promised calligraphy lessons to the person who took the pen and ink, and Bella promised fabric painting lessons to the person who took the tuxedo T-shirt. In that way each of my gifts kept on giving.

Four cat's-paw gifts were now taken.

Only the red wagon remained. Guess who had the fifth cat's-paw invitation?

Allen, the son of.

Allen said he didn't want the little red wagon. He said that he had no use for a wagon in the real world where he was an accountant.

When Izzy, the groom, rose from the table to make a toast, he lifted his glass of wine and said, "Margy and I want to thank all our friends in Century Village. We don't know if we can ever thank you enough for giving our life together this wonderful start. As you know, Margy and I have pooled our resources and bought a little condo on the ocean. Not exactly *on* the ocean. It is, after all, a high-rise. We will miss the community life here, but we don't want to miss our friends. We'll visit. We want you to visit us. Our welcome mat is out. Always. We leave many memories behind. And we are also leaving this little red wagon. Every time you use it, please think of this happy occasion."

Izzy started to sit down, but halfway he got up again and added, "Consider it a gift to everyone from the best man." He never said which best man he meant, but I'm pretty sure he meant me.

marriage
of
Margaret Draper
and
Izzy Diamondstein

presence but no presents

Let's **Think** About...

How does the author use Izzy's thank-you speech as a way to end the story-within-a-story?
Story Structure

204

Now back in the real world, I sat at my desk and crossed every single item off the list. I didn't have the wagon, the Post-it notes, the T-shirt that Bella Dubinsky had designed, or the pen and ink that Tillie Nachman had bought me. I did have a new pad of Post-it notes and a new calligraphy pen—both of which I had bought with my own money when I got back to Epiphany.

I never had to write a B & B letter when we stayed at Disney World or Sea World. Of course, Century Village is not exactly Disney World or Sea World either. Century Village is not like any other place in Western Civilization. It is not like any other place in the entire world.

I picked up my pen and filled it *properly,* the six-step process that Tillie had taught me. She had said, "You must think of those six steps not as preparation for the beginning but as the beginning itself." I knew then that I had started my B & B. I let my pen drink up a whole plunger full of ink and then, holding the pen over the bottle, I squeezed three drops back into the bottle.

And I thought—a B & B letter is giving just a few drops back to the bottle. I put away the tiny notepad and took out a full sheet of calligraphy paper and began,

Dear Grandma Sadie and Grandpa Nate,
Thank you for a vacation that was out of this world...

Let's **Think** About...

How might a reader retell this story to focus on what Noah learned during his visit to Florida?

Summarize

205

Objectives
• Provide evidence from the text to demonstrate understanding.
• Read independently for a sustained period of time and paraphrase the reading.

Envision It! | Retell

Think Critically

1. Have you ever been to a wedding? Compare your experience to the narrator's experience. If you haven't been to a wedding, compare what you think a wedding might be like to the experience the narrator has. **Text to Self**

2. Although *The View from Saturday* is humorous fiction, the author often introduces information that is important to the story with the word "FACT" in bold letters. Why do you think she does this? **Think Like an Author**

3. Near the beginning of the story, Noah writes "red wagon" on a Post-it® note. What is the wagon used for, and why is it an important part of the story's plot? **Literary Elements**

4. What do you think Noah included in his B & B letter? How do you think his grandparents will react to his letter? Summarize what you think he will write. **Summarize**

5. **Look Back and Write** What was written at the bottom of every wedding invitation (bottom of page 194)? Explain what it means. Provide evidence to support your answer.

TEST PRACTICE Extended Response

206

Meet the Author

E. L. Konigsburg

Elaine Lobl was born in New York City, the second of three daughters, but she grew up in small towns in Pennsylvania. She was the first in her family to go to college, where she majored in chemistry and met her future husband, whose name is Konigsburg. After teaching science at a school for girls and becoming mother to three children, she began to write humor-tinged books that remind her of her own experiences and those of her children and of her students. E. L. Konigsburg says, "Readers let me know they like books that have more to them than meets the eye. Had they not let me know that, I never would have written *The View from Saturday*." That book won the Newbery Medal in 1997. It was the second time one of Ms. Konigsburg's books received the top honor. Her advice to would-be writers is simple: "Finish. Don't talk about doing it. Do it. Finish." Ms. Konigsburg and her husband live on a beach in northern Florida.

Other books by E. L. Konigsburg: *From the Mixed-up Files of Mrs. Basil E. Frankweiler* and *Altogether, One at a Time*

Use the Reading Log in the *Reader's and Writer's Notebook* to record your independent reading.

• Understand the purpose of a review.
• Write a review that includes supported opinions.
• Use correct conventions for titles.
• Use and understand contractions and negatives.

Expository

Let's Write It!

Key Features of a Review

● reviews a work, such as a book or movie

● supports opinions with specific details

● has a clear beginning, middle, and end

● states title and author of work in first paragraph

READING STREET ONLINE
GRAMMAR JAMMER
www.ReadingStreet.com

Review

A **review** examines something, such as a short story, novel, work of art, or movie, and offers a final evaluation of it. The student model on the next page is an example of a literary review.

Writing Prompt Think about a book or story you have read recently. Write a literary review describing the book or story, and offer your opinion of it. Make sure you consider the overall effectiveness of characters, plot, or dialogue.

Writer's Checklist

Remember, you should ...

✓ clearly state your opinion and support it throughout the review.

✓ include details to strengthen your argument.

✓ close by summarizing the review in an interesting way.

Review of <u>A Wrinkle in Time</u> by Madeline L'Engle

> Want to be drawn into a web of time travel and interesting characters? Then you should read <u>A Wrinkle in Time</u>. This time-travel tale, by Madeline L'Engle, tells the story of a sister and brother who must dash through time and space to rescue their father.

The plot is strong and believable in this book, and so are the characters. For example, the character of Charles Wallace is described in Chapter 1 as a five-year-old who teaches himself new words and talks like an adult. Also, the author's language will carry you to the center of the story events; you **won't** want to put down the book until you discover the fate of the children and their father.

While some authors leave all of the problem solving to adults, that **isn't** the case in this book. L'Engle puts the power squarely in the hands of the children. This makes the book very interesting for younger readers.

You **can't** find a better book to take you to new times and places than <u>A Wrinkle in Time</u>.

Writing Trait Conventions The title is correctly punctuated.

Genre A **literary review** evaluates a literary text.

Contractions and negatives are used correctly.

Conventions

Contractions and Negatives

Remember A **contraction** is a shortened form of two words that uses an apostrophe to show where letters have been left out. (*We + have = we've; should + not = shouldn't.*) **Negatives** are words that mean "no" or "not": *no, never, not, none, nothing.* Contractions with *n't* are negatives too.

Genre
How-to Text

- How-to texts explain how to do or make something or even how to solve a problem.

- A how-to article is an example of procedural text.

- Most how-to texts contain a sequence of activities needed to follow a certain procedure.

- Some how-to texts use numbered steps, charts, or even diagrams that tell the order of what to do.

- Read "Be a Family Historian"and see if you can follow the informal directions for becoming your family's historian.

Be a Family
HISTORIAN

By Ann Gadzikowski

Think of yourself as a historian. Everything that happens is part of the history of the world—and that includes your own family history. You can be a historian by researching and writing about your family history. What resources are available to you?

First, look for artifacts. Artifacts are objects that hold information about another time. Old photo albums or scrapbooks that show images of what life was like for family members in the past are examples of good artifacts. Gather together diaries, postcards, letters, and old newspaper articles that describe your family history in words. Sometimes old clothing, watches, blankets, shoes, and even furniture hold memories, if they have been passed down over the years from one generation of your family to the next.

To unlock the memories in your artifacts, use another classic historian's resource: the interview. Parents, grandparents, aunts, uncles, and cousins all have memories of the past. Look over the artifacts you have found and make up a list of questions based on them.

For instance, Where did this quilt come from? Do you know who made it? Or, When was this picture taken? What is that building in the background?

Answers to these kinds of questions will start to give you an idea of what life was like in times past. Be sure to write down the answers accurately. Better yet, if you have a recorder or video camera, record family members in live interviews.

After gathering your information, put it together into a book or series of articles. Or create a family tree, a chart of the people in your family that goes back for generations. It's a kind of map that shows you where you came from. Some family trees have photographs and birthdates as well as names. Web sites on the Internet show how to make a family tree.

When you finish, get together with family members and read and show them your results. Consider a family reunion to present your family history. Let everyone see the memories you have gathered as a family historian!

Let's **Think** About...

What information can old family photo albums, scrapbooks, and other artifacts supply to a family historian?
How-to Text

Let's **Think** About...

Reading Across Texts Describe the basic differences between the first-person story told by Noah in *The View from Saturday* and the how-to text in "Be a Family Historian."

Writing Across Texts Write a paragraph about the importance of family history from Noah's viewpoint.

211

Objectives
● Read aloud with fluency and expression. ● Determine the meanings of unfamiliar words by using the context of the sentence.
● Listen to and interpret a speaker's messages and ask questions.

READING STREET ONLINE
ONLINE STUDENT EDITION
www.ReadingStreet.com

Vocabulary

Antonyms

Context Clues Remember that you can use surrounding words and phrases—context clues—to help you figure out the meaning of an unfamiliar word. Antonyms, or words that are opposite in meaning, are one form of context clue that may help you determine the meanings of words.

Practice It! Read the sentences below. Read each italicized word and then think of an antonym for it. Check your guess in a dictionary.

• In the yard, the lizard was hidden near the rocks, but the red parrot was *conspicuous*.

• Our dog was sad because it was raining, but I was *elated* that I didn't have to walk him.

Fluency

Expression

Reading with expression can bring the characters in a story to life. Expression also adds meaning to the descriptions in a story and lets you express emotions such as excitement or suspense. Adjust the tone of your voice to match what's happening in the story.

Practice It! With a partner, read several paragraphs beginning with "It all started when. . . ." on page 192 of *The View from Saturday*. How can you use your voice to keep the humor in the sentences and descriptions? Before you start to read, skim over the text to figure out what's funny.

Listening and Speaking

When you conduct an interview, ask specific questions of the person you are interviewing.

Interview

In an interview, one person asks another person questions. The purpose of an interview is to find out what the person being interviewed knows about a particular subject or what he or she has done.

Practice It! With a partner, make a list of questions you will each ask one another about an older member of your families. With the class as your audience, ask questions that give a good idea of the older person's personality, his or her main life events, and the influence he or she has had on your partner. Stick to your questions and be brief.

Tips

Listening . . .

- Listen carefully to the interviewer's questions.
- Listen to the interviewee's answers.

Speaking . . .

- Take a moment before you answer the interviewer's question.
- Speak clearly whether you're asking or answering a question.

Teamwork . . .

- Follow your agreed-to questions.
- Look at your interview partner during the interview.

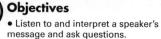

Let's Talk About

Civil Rights

● Describe what you know about civil rights in the United States.

● Ask questions about how people can work together to bring about change.

● Express opinions about why citizens need to exercise their right to vote.

**READING STREET ONLINE
CONCEPT TALK VIDEO**
www.ReadingStreet.com

214

Envision It! | Skill Strategy

Skill

Strategy

Comprehension Skill

Fact and Opinion

- Careful readers watch for statements of opinion as they read. While facts can be proved true or false, opinions cannot be proved. They can, however, be shown to be valid or faulty.

- Valid statements of opinion can be supported by facts, experts, or logic. Faulty statements of opinion cannot be supported.

- Use a graphic organizer like the one below to evaluate the opinions stated in "The Best Job in the World" on page 217.

Opinion	Source	Valid or Faulty

Comprehension Strategy

Text Structure

Text structure is the way a piece of writing is organized. External organization includes titles and headings, special typefaces, and various illustrations and graphics. Internal organization is the way that the writer structures thoughts and ideas. Internal methods of organization include using compare and contrast, cause and effect, sequence, and description.

The Best Job
IN THE WORLD

Movers transport people's belongings from one location to another. Movers have the best job in the world because they are healthy, they get to help people every day, and they get to see many interesting places.

Strategy How can you tell that this writer is using description to organize the text?

Movers use their muscles when they work. I think exercising your muscles makes you strong. Movers are the strongest workers in the world because they use their muscles more than anything.

Skill Which of the following tells you that this statement of opinion is faulty?
a) It is based only on someone's opinion.
b) It was stated by an expert.
c) It is based on incorrect facts.

Movers have the best job because each day they get to help other people, and that makes movers happy. I think movers are happy because Dr. David Kell recently did a study showing that helpful people tend to be happier. Everyone enjoys helping others. Think of how nice it would be to do so all day, every day.

Finally, movers always get to see new and interesting places. Office workers who sit at their desks each day can't say that. Movers get to see mansions, unique apartments, and other types of living places. That is always fun to do.

Skill Is the author's statement of opinion well supported or poorly supported?

In conclusion, movers have the best job in the world because they exercise, help others, and get to see new places every day. Now, don't you want to be a mover?

Your Turn!

Need a Review? See the *Envision It! Handbook* for help with fact and opinion and text structure.

Ready to Try It? Use what you've learned about fact and opinion as you read *Harvesting Hope*.

authority

lush

wilt

access

obstacle

toll

torment

Vocabulary Strategy for
🔄 Homonyms

Context Clues When you come across a word you think you know but that doesn't make sense in the sentence, you may have come across a homonym. Homonyms are two or more words that are spelled the same and pronounced the same but have different meanings. For example, *lean* could mean either "thin" or "to rest against something for support." Always try to use the context—the words and sentences around the puzzling word—for clues to figure out the correct meaning of a homonym.

Follow these steps to use context to determine the meaning of homonyms.

1. Reread the sentence in which the homonym appears.

2. Look for context clues to the homonym's meaning.

3. If you need more help, read the sentences around the sentence with the homonym. Look for clues or for additional information that suggests the homonym's meaning.

4. Try the new meaning in the sentence. Does it make sense? If not, check the glossary.

Read "Migrant Work Is No Picnic." Use context clues to figure out the meaning of any homonyms you find.

Words to Write Reread "Migrant Work Is No Picnic." Imagine that you are working as a migrant worker. Write a journal entry to tell what you feel and see. Use as many words from the Words to Know list as you can.

Migrant Work Is No Picnic

We tend to think of farm work as being healthful. You get fresh air and sunshine and use your muscles. You can lean against your hoe and look at the lush green crops growing in straight rows. It sounds like a satisfactory life, doesn't it?

On the contrary, for migrant workers field work means long hours, poor pay, and torment for the body and mind. With bare hands and bent backs, these workers labor from dawn to dusk in the hot sun. Even a plant will wilt under the sun's punishing rays without enough water. Sometimes the workers are not provided with water. They may not even have access to bathrooms. And, as for fresh air, workers instead often breathe the fumes of powerful insecticides.

All this hard labor takes a toll on workers' health. Yet they often fail to get proper health care. When your pay is scarcely enough to buy food for your family, a doctor's bills become an obstacle that can't be overcome. Getting people the authority to fight for the rights of migrant workers has been an important issue for decades.

Your Turn!

⏸ **Need a Review?** For help using context clues to understand homonyms, see *Words!*

▷ **Ready to Try It?** Read *Harvesting Hope* on pp. 220–231.

Genre

A **biography** is the story of a real person's life that has been written by another person. As you read, notice the clues that tell you this is a story about a real person.

Harvesting Hope

THE STORY OF CESAR CHAVEZ

by Kathleen Krull

illustrated by Yuyi Morales

Question of the Week

How can we combine our resources to make change?

Until Cesar Chavez was ten, every summer night was like a fiesta. Relatives swarmed onto the ranch for barbecues with watermelon, lemonade, and fresh corn. Cesar and his brothers, sisters, and cousins settled down to sleep outside, under netting to keep mosquitoes out. But who could sleep—with uncles and aunts singing, spinning ghost stories, and telling magical tales of life back in Mexico?

Cesar thought the whole world belonged to his family. The eighty acres of their ranch were an island in the shimmering Arizona desert, and the starry skies were all their own.

Many years earlier, Cesar's grandfather had built their spacious adobe house to last forever, with walls eighteen inches thick. A vegetable garden, cows, and chickens supplied all the food they could want. With hundreds of cousins on farms nearby, there was always someone to play with. Cesar's best friend was his brother Richard; they never spent a day apart.

222

Cesar was so happy at home that he was a little afraid when school started. On his first day, he grabbed the seat next to his older sister, Rita. The teacher moved him to another seat—and Cesar flew out the door and ran home. It took three days of coaxing for him to return to school and take his place with the other first graders.

Cesar was stubborn, but he was not a fighter. His mother cautioned her children against fighting, urging them to use their minds and mouths to work out conflicts.

Then, in 1937, the summer Cesar was ten, the trees around the ranch began to wilt. The sun baked the farm soil rock hard. A drought was choking the life out of Arizona. Without water for the crops, the Chavez family couldn't make money to pay its bills.

There came a day when Cesar's mother couldn't stop crying. In a daze, Cesar watched his father strap their possessions onto the roof of their old car. After a long struggle, the family no longer owned the ranch. They had no choice but to join the hundreds of thousands of people fleeing to the green valleys of California to look for work.

Cesar's old life had vanished. Now he and his family were migrants—working on other people's farms, crisscrossing California, picking whatever fruits and vegetables were in season.

When the Chavez family arrived at the first of their new homes in California, they found a battered old shed. Its doors were missing and garbage covered the dirt floor. Cold, damp air seeped into their bedding and clothes. They shared water and outdoor toilets with a dozen other families, and overcrowding made everything filthy. The neighbors were constantly fighting, and the noise upset Cesar. He had no place to play games with Richard. Meals were sometimes made of dandelion greens gathered along the road.

Cesar swallowed his bitter homesickness and worked alongside his family. He was small and not very strong, but still a fierce worker. Nearly every crop caused torment. Yanking out beets broke the skin between his thumb and index finger. Grapevines sprayed with bug-killing chemicals made his eyes sting and his lungs wheeze. Lettuce had to be the worst. Thinning lettuce all day with a short-handled hoe would make hot spasms shoot through his back. Farm chores on someone else's farm instead of on his own felt like a form of slavery.

The Chavez family talked constantly of saving enough money to buy back their ranch. But by each sundown, the whole family had earned as little as thirty cents for the day's work. As the years blurred together, they spoke of the ranch less and less.

The towns weren't much better than the fields. WHITE TRADE ONLY signs were displayed in many stores and restaurants. None of the thirty-five schools Cesar attended over the years seemed like a safe place, either. Once, after Cesar broke the rule about speaking English at all times, a teacher hung a sign on him that read, I AM A CLOWN. I SPEAK SPANISH. He came to hate school because of the conflicts, though he liked to learn. Even he considered his eighth-grade graduation a miracle. After eighth grade he dropped out to work in the fields full-time.

His lack of schooling embarrassed Cesar for the rest of his life, but as a teenager he just wanted to put food on his family's table. As he worked, it disturbed him that landowners treated their workers more like farm tools than human beings. They provided no clean drinking water, rest periods, or access to bathrooms. Anyone who complained was fired, beaten up, or sometimes even murdered.

So, like other migrant workers, Cesar was afraid and suspicious whenever outsiders showed up to try to help. How could they know about feeling so powerless? Who could battle such odds?

Yet Cesar had never forgotten his old life in Arizona and the jolt he'd felt when it was turned upside down. Farmwork did not have to be this miserable.

Reluctantly, he started paying attention to the outsiders. He began to think that maybe there was hope. And in his early twenties, he decided to dedicate the rest of his life to fighting for change.

Again he crisscrossed California, this time to talk people into joining his fight. At first, out of every hundred workers he talked to, perhaps one would agree with him. One by one—this was how he started.

At the first meeting Cesar organized, a dozen women gathered. He sat quietly in a corner. After twenty minutes, everyone started

wondering when the organizer would show up. Cesar thought he might die of embarrassment.

"Well, I'm the organizer," he said—and forced himself to keep talking, hoping to inspire respect with his new suit and the mustache he was trying to grow. The women listened politely, and he was sure they did so out of pity.

EN EL AÑO SESENTA Y DOS, CON ESFUERZO Y DESATINO

SE PRINCIPIO UNA CAMPAÑA EN FAVOR DEL CAMPESINO....

But despite his shyness, Cesar showed a knack for solving problems. People trusted him. With workers he was endlessly patient and compassionate. With landowners he was stubborn, demanding, and single-minded. He was learning to be a fighter.

In a fight for justice, he told everyone, truth was a better weapon than violence. "Nonviolence," he said, "takes more guts." It meant using imagination to find ways to overcome powerlessness.

More and more people listened.

One night, 150 people poured into an old abandoned theater in Fresno. At this first meeting of the National Farm Workers Association, Cesar unveiled its flag—a bold black eagle, the sacred bird of the Aztec Indians.

La Causa—The Cause—was born.

It was time to rebel, and the place was Delano. Here, in the heart of the lush San Joaquin Valley, brilliant green vineyards reached toward every horizon. Poorly paid workers hunched over grapevines for most of each year. Then, in 1965, the vineyard owners cut their pay even further.

Cesar chose to fight just one of the forty landowners, hopeful that others would get the message. As plump grapes drooped, thousands of workers walked off that company's field in a strike, or *huelga*.

Grapes, when ripe, do not last long.

The company fought back with everything from punches to bullets. Cesar refused to respond with violence. Violence would only hurt *La Causa*.

Instead, he organized a march—a march of more than three hundred miles. He and his supporters would walk from Delano to the state capitol in Sacramento to ask for the government's help.

Cesar and sixty-seven others started out one morning. Their first obstacle was the Delano police force, thirty of whose members locked arms to prevent the group from crossing the street. After three hours of arguing—in public—the chief of police backed down. Joyous marchers headed north under the sizzling sun. Their rallying cry was *Sí Se Puede*, or "Yes, It Can Be Done."

The first night, they reached Ducor. The marchers slept outside the tiny cabin of the only person who would welcome them.

Single file they continued, covering an average of fifteen miles a day. They inched their way through the San Joaquin Valley, while the unharvested grapes in Delano turned white with mold. Cesar developed painful blisters right away. He and many others had blood seeping out of their shoes.

The word spread. Along the way, farmworkers offered food and drink as the marchers passed by. When the sun set, marchers lit candles and kept going.

Shelter was no longer a problem. Supporters began welcoming them each night with feasts. Every night was a rally. "Our pilgrimage is the match," one speaker shouted, "that will light our cause for all farmworkers to see what is happening here."

Another cried, "We seek our basic, God-given rights as human beings . . . ¡Viva La Causa!"

Eager supporters would keep the marchers up half the night talking about change. Every morning, the line of marchers swelled, Cesar always in the lead.

On the ninth day, hundreds marched through Fresno.

The long, peaceful march was a shock to people unaware of how California farmworkers had to live. Now students, public officials, religious leaders, and citizens from everywhere offered help. For the grape company, the publicity was becoming unbearable.

And on the vines, the grapes continued to rot.

In Modesto, on the fifteenth day, an exhilarated crowd celebrated Cesar's thirty-eighth birthday. Two days later, five thousand people met the marchers in Stockton with flowers, guitars, and accordions.

That evening, Cesar received a message that he was sure was a prank. But in case it was true, he left the march and had someone drive him all through the night to a mansion in wealthy Beverly Hills. Officials from the grape company were waiting for him. They were ready to recognize the authority of the National Farm Workers Association, promising a contract with a pay raise and better conditions.

Cesar rushed back to join the march.

On Easter Sunday, when the marchers arrived in Sacramento, the parade was ten-thousand-people strong.

From the steps of the state capitol building, the joyous announcement was made to the public: Cesar Chavez had just signed the first contract for farmworkers in American history.

The parade erupted into a giant fiesta. Crowds swarmed the steps, some people cheering, many weeping. Prancing horses carried men in mariachi outfits. Everyone sang and waved flowers or flags. They made a place of honor for the fifty-seven marchers who had walked the entire journey.

Speaker after speaker, addressing the audience in Spanish and in English, took the microphone. "You cannot close your eyes and your ears to us any longer," cried one. "You cannot pretend that we do not exist."

The crowd celebrated until the sky was full of stars.

The march had taken its toll. Cesar's leg was swollen, and he was running a high fever. Gently he reminded everyone that the battle was not over: "It is well to remember there must be courage but also that in victory there must be humility."

Much more work lay ahead, but the victory was stunning. Some of the wealthiest people in the country had been forced to recognize some of the poorest as human beings. Cesar Chavez had won this fight—without violence—and he would never be powerless again.

Objectives
• Provide evidence from the text to demonstrate understanding.
• Read independently for a sustained period of time and paraphrase the reading.

Envision It! Retell

Think Critically

1. Think about Cesar Chavez's early life, before he led the march from Delano to Sacramento. What resources outside himself and within himself helped him to become a leader? What experiences have you had that give you some qualities of a leader? **Text to Self**

2. Biographies tell not only about a person's life but also about conditions that surrounded that life. What do this author and illustrator tell you about conditions in the lives of migrant workers? **Think Like an Author**

3. On page 227, the author writes, "Poorly paid workers hunched over grapevines for most of the year." Is this a statement of fact or of opinion? Give support for your answer.
   Fact and Opinion

4. In what order are the events of Chavez's life told? Point out one benefit of this order.
   Text Structure

5. **Look Back and Write** The march grew from sixty-eight people to a parade of ten thousand. Look back at pages 228–230 and make a list of the many types of people who learned of the march and gave it their support.

   TEST PRACTICE Extended Response

232

Meet the Author and the Illustrator

Kathleen Krull and Yuyi Morales

Kathleen Krull says, "When I was fifteen, I was fired from my part-time job at the library. The reason? I was reading too much while I was supposed to be working." Today she is a full-time writer of books for young people and lives in San Diego with her husband. "As a child," she says, "I thought books were the most important thing in the world, and that perception is actually more intense now. I'm grateful, for so many reasons, to be able to work in a vital and exhilarating field: preserving literacy. One of its benefits is that I can't be fired. Especially for reading too much!"

Yuyi Morales is an artist, writer, puppet maker, and Brazilian folk dancer. She lives in California with her husband, son, and cat. Ms. Morales says, "I was born in the city of flowers, Xalapa, Mexico. When I was a child I spent most of the time thinking about extraterrestrials and waiting for them to come in their UFOs to take me away. I practiced to be an acrobat too—and broke many things at home. Then I grew up and became an artist and a writer. Oh, well."

Other books: *Just a Minute: A Trickster Tale and Counting Book* written and illustrated by Yuyi Morales and *The Boy on Fairfield Street* by Kathleen Krull

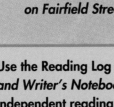
Use the Reading Log in the *Reader's and Writer's Notebook* to record your independent reading.

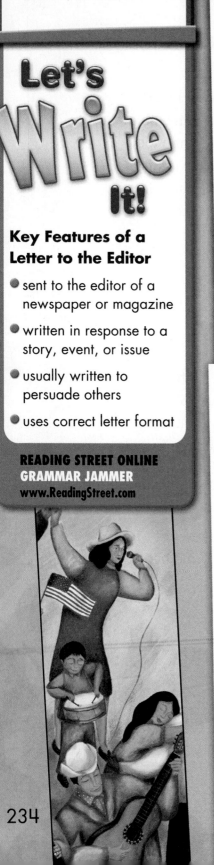

Objectives
● Understand the key features of a letter to the editor. ● Write a letter to the editor. ● Use adjectives and articles correctly. ● Understand features of persuasion.

Let's Write It!

Key Features of a Letter to the Editor

● sent to the editor of a newspaper or magazine

● written in response to a story, event, or issue

● usually written to persuade others

● uses correct letter format

READING STREET ONLINE
GRAMMAR JAMMER
www.ReadingStreet.com

Persuasive

Letter to the Editor

A **letter to the editor** gives an opinion on a story, issue, or event and is written to a newspaper or magazine editor. The student model on the next page is an example of a letter to the editor.

Writing Prompt Think about an issue in your community you feel strongly about. Now write a letter to the editor expressing and supporting your opinion.

Writer's Checklist

Remember, you should . . .

☑ write about an issue.

☑ include a greeting and a closing.

☑ write clear statements that will convince others of your position.

☑ include support to make your position believable.

☑ choose words, such as strong adjectives, that will persuade others.

234

January 14, 20__

To the Editor:

Most everyone agrees that we need a new shopping center. However, I am alarmed that people want the Stone House on Magnolia Lane demolished to make space for the development.

The Stone House is part of the earliest days of history here, and there are many stories in our town about events in this house. The first mayor of the town lived there. Important original documents are displayed in the room where they were signed!

The Stone House represents our town's past. Demolition of this historic structure would be a mistake. Once it is ripped down, it can never be replaced. I strongly urge the developers of the new shopping center to search for a new site. I also ask all residents to sign our petition on this issue.

Sincerely,

Emma Long

City of Oakwood

Writing Trait Word Choice The writer uses precise language to persuade the reader.

Genre A **letter to the editor** clearly expresses an opinion.

Adjectives and articles are used correctly.

Conventions

Adjectives and Articles

Remember Adjectives describe nouns or pronouns, and tell *what kind? How many? Which one?* (The wind was **warm; several** workers rested; Curtis lived in **that** house.) A, an, and the are **articles.** An article is used before nouns or other adjectives.

235

Objectives
● Examine features of poetry.
● Examine how poets create vivid images in their poems. ● Make connections between and among texts.

Genre
Poetry

● A poem is a carefully crafted composition that is arranged in lines. Some poems have lines that rhyme, while others do not.

● Poetry that does not rhyme and is "free" of any fixed pattern is called free verse.

● Poetry often expresses the poet's serious, deep thoughts on a subject.

● Poetry often makes readers think about a new or unexpected way of looking at human experiences.

● Read "Fieldworkers" and "Farmworkers" and consider how much information and feeling come across in the short space of these two poems.

Fieldworkers
by Leobardo V. Cortéz

Early,
when the sun comes out,
lumps move throughout the field like
clockwork every sunrise,
until the moon comes.

Their bronze hands
wave
like
rifles in a war.

Fighting
for survival
a new tomorrow
for our children. . . .

The white vests
our innocence
purity
and wealth. . . .

Come child, leave your life
    upon the land.
I am
the slave of my children.

I am
their owner as well.
Yes!

I am
the *campesino*
in the fields. . . .

Farmworkers

by Alma Flor Ada

Farmworkers is the name we give
to the people who work the land,
who harvest the fields,
united beneath one sky.

Thank you, farmworker,
for the fruits your hands have
   brought me.
I will grow stronger and kinder
as I eat what you have grown.

Let's Think About...

What serious, deep thoughts are the poets expressing in these two poems? **Poetry**

Let's Think About...

Reading Across Texts Which poem reflects the life and struggles of Cesar Chavez and his family? Whose voice do we hear in the other poem?

Writing Across Texts Write what you think Cesar Chavez would think of these two poems about the workers who harvest food.

237

Let's Learn It!

READING STREET ONLINE
ONLINE STUDENT EDITION
www.ReadingStreet.com

Vocabulary

Homonyms

Context Clues Remember that if you think you know a word's meaning, but the meaning doesn't make sense in the sentence, the word might be a homonym—two or more words that are spelled the same but have different meanings. Use nearby words and phrases to figure out which meaning makes sense.

Practice It! Read the sentences below. Use context clues to figure out the correct meaning of the homonyms *bank, pitcher, batter,* and *plate.* Then think of another meaning for each word that does not make sense here.

• They sat near the *bank* of the river and had a picnic.

• The *pitcher* threw the baseball to the *batter,* who stood at home *plate* in the ballpark.

Fluency

Appropriate Phrasing

Reading with appropriate phrasing means grouping words together. Let punctuation cues guide you: group words set off by commas or semicolons or dashes; come to a full stop at the end of a sentence.

Practice It! With a partner, practice reading aloud the three paragraphs on page 222 of *Harvesting Hope: The Story of Cesar Chavez.* How can you use appropriate phrasing to make sense of what you are reading? Give your partner feedback on phrasing to help comprehension.

Listening and Speaking

When you give a presentation, speak loudly and clearly and use visuals to help make your points.

Analyze an Editorial Cartoon

Newspapers and news magazines run editorial cartoons to point attention to and sometimes make fun of important people and what they've done.

Practice It! With a partner, choose an editorial cartoon from a newspaper or magazine. Evaluate the cartoon by answering these questions: What person or group is the target of the cartoon? Which current event is the cartoon about? What is the cartoonist's opinion about this person and event? Share your analyses with the class.

Tips

Listening . . .

• Draw conclusions about what the speaker says.

• Ask appropriate questions.

Speaking . . .

• Hold up the cartoon while your partner reads your analysis of it.

• Speak clearly and distinctly.

• Invite questions afterwards.

Teamwork . . .

• Write down your analysis and follow it for your presentation.

• Talk about how you and your partner agree and disagree with the editorial cartoon you chose.

239

Objectives
• Listen to and interpret a speaker's message and ask questions.
• Describe the phenomena explained in origin myths from various cultures.

Let's Talk About

Natural Changes

- Share any stories you know that explain something about nature.

- Describe how Earth was shaped by the movement of the glaciers.

- Ask questions that prehistoric people might have had about natural phenomena.

READING STREET ONLINE
CONCEPT TALK VIDEO
www.ReadingStreet.com

241

Envision It! | Skill Strategy

Skill

Strategy

Comprehension Skill

Cause and Effect

• A cause is what makes something happen. An effect is something that can happen as the result of a cause. Clue words such as *since, thus, as a result, therefore,* and *consequently* point to cause-and-effect relationships.

• Sometimes an effect has more than one cause; sometimes one cause has more than one effect.

• When a cause is not directly stated, you must think about why something happened.

• Use a graphic organizer like the one below to identify cause and effect as you read the tall tale "Super Smart."

Comprehension Strategy

Story Structure

Active readers pay attention to the story structure of fiction. In most writing, a story has a beginning, when characters and the plot are introduced; a middle, when problems or conflicts are introduced; and an end or climax, when the problems or conflicts are resolved. Authors may also use story incidents to foreshadow or hint at future events.

Super Smart

Long ago and far away lived Super Smart. The day she was born, her mother said, "Here are six diapers."

"Here are three more," said her father. When the baby held up nine tiny fingers, he said, "She is super smart!" And that is how she got her name.

Skill Describe what earned Super Smart her name.

The next day, her father started to read her a story. When he pointed to a picture, Super Smart read the whole page out loud. She read book after book, so fast that her mother and father kept running out of books.

Super Smart's parents were glad when she was old enough to go to school. They were tired of buying books. But the first week of school, Super Smart read all the books in the school.

Next, Super Smart started reading her way through the library. In a month, she had read all the books in the library.

"That's okay," said Super Smart. "These books are too easy anyway. I will write books for smart people so I will have something to read."

Skill Why did Super Smart start writing books?

So Super Smart started writing books. She wrote so many that a whole new bigger library had to be built. Unfortunately, nobody else was smart enough to read her books. And that is why none of her books are read today.

Strategy What did you learn at the beginning, middle, and end of this story?

Your Turn!

Need a Review? See the *Envision It! Handbook* for help with cause and effect and story structure.

Ready to Try It? Use what you've learned about cause and effect as you read *The River That Went to the Sky.*

densest

eaves

moisture

expanse

ventured

Vocabulary Strategy for

🎯 Synonyms

Context Clues Synonyms are two or more words that mean almost the same thing. An author may use a synonym near a difficult word to help you understand the difficult word's meaning.

Choose one of the Words to Know that is unfamiliar to you and follow these steps.

1. Read the words and sentences around the word.

2. Look for clues that indicate the unfamiliar word has a synonym. A synonym is often preceded by the word *or* or *like,* and it may be set off by commas.

3. If you find a synonym, try using it in place of the unfamiliar word. This will help you understand the meaning.

4. If this does not help you understand the word, read on or look up the word in the glossary or a dictionary.

Read "Tropical Rain Forest." Use context clues to identify synonyms for unfamiliar words or, if you can't find them on your own, consult a thesaurus and a dictionary.

Words to Write Reread "Tropical Rain Forest." Imagine an animal living in a tropical rain forest. Write a paragraph describing a typical day in its life. Use words from the Words to Know list as you write.

Tropical Rain Forest

The tropical rain forest is a green super-city. We think of cities as being crowded places, but rain forests have the densest, or most crowded, populations of living things. A city may grow to hold many millions of people, but the world's rain forests contain nearly half the world's species, or kinds, of plants as well as a huge variety of animals.

Those who have ventured into the rain forest know that its vast expanse, or area, includes towering trees and miles of long vines. Under the eaves of these giants, many kinds of ferns, mosses, flowers, and shrubs grow. Because it gets so much moisture—from as little as 80 inches to as much as 250 inches of rainfall each year—and warmth, a tropical rain forest is always lush and green.

Of course, animals of all kinds love it there—fish, frogs, birds, snakes, and monkeys, to name a few. Insects, however, are by far the most plentiful animals in the rain forest.

Your Turn!

❙❙ Need a Review? For help using synonyms, see *Words!*

▶ Ready to Try It? Read *The River That Went to the Sky* on pp. 246–255.

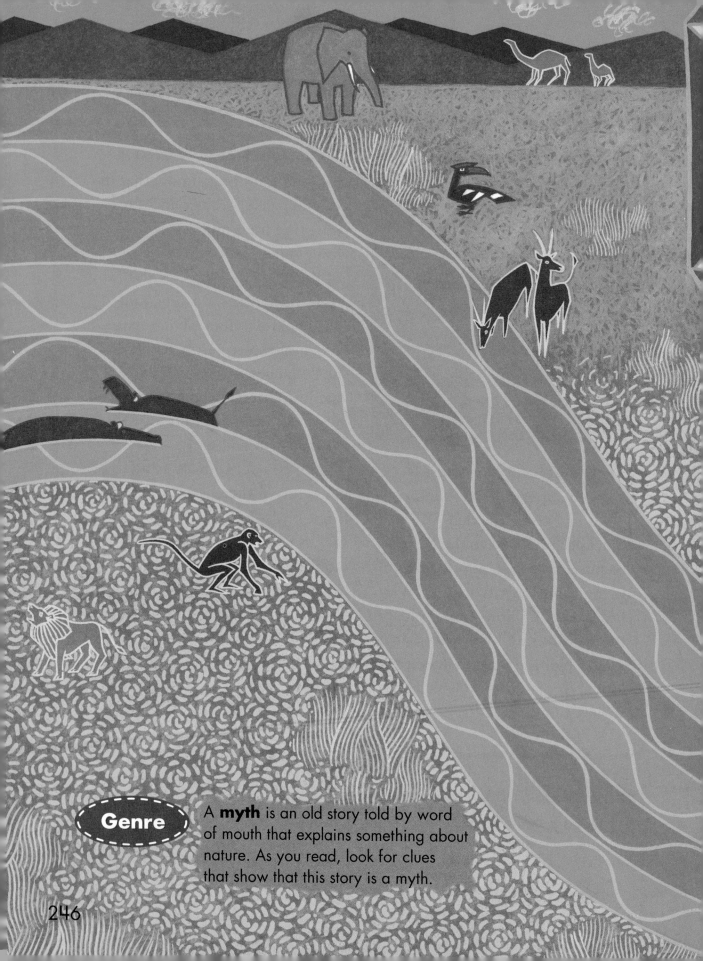

Genre

A **myth** is an old story told by word of mouth that explains something about nature. As you read, look for clues that show that this story is a myth.

246

The River That Went to the Sky

A Story from Malawi

retold by Kasiya Makaka Phiri
illustrated by Stéphan Daigle

Question of the Week
How can stories be used to explain the workings of nature?

Once there was a River. It ran from one side of the great continent to the other, and it was so wide it looked like a lake, and the land around it was rich. All the animals that lived there had plenty of everything. Grass to graze, fruit to eat, nuts to crack, roots to chew, bark to nibble, and leaves to eat. The animals ambled all day long, eating a little, stopping, gazing into the distance, eating a little more, and going on slowly, for there was no hurry. The great vast River meandered across the land avoiding all the mountains, choosing only the plains and the valleys but always spreading wide, wide across the land. It rolled gently from one side of the vast continent and went to sleep and glided on the night tide to the other side. Backward and forward. It felt good and made happy noises on the banks, like the sound of calabashes filling with water, one gulp at a time.

On the banks grew the low grasses that like to trail their roots in cool river water. With them grew the papyrus and bulrushes. Behind them grew those grasses that like to smell the water every day and hear the happy sounds of the River. Water trees stood knee-deep in the water, looking toward the grasses of the low plains that gave way to ankle-high grass, then knee-high grass, all the way to the towering elephant grass. Then came the tall trees of the woods, beyond which were the high plains and foothills of great mountains. The high plains were covered in shorter grasses where the swift wind blew, keeping everything down except in the sheltered folds of the rolling ridges. In these hidden valleys were groves of rare trees and flowers and many other plants.

So everything was all right, until one day the River, gliding sleepily, looked up and saw the stars in the night sky.

"What is that?" said the River in a sleepy voice.

Hyena, who happened to be nearby taking a sip of water, looked up and said, "What's what, where?"

"Up there with the many eyes," said the sleepy River.

"That is the night sky," Hyena said and went on his way.

"Oh, how I wish I could go to the sky," said the River, sighing as it fell asleep.

The grass with the roots in the water heard this and whispered: "The River wants to go to the sky."

The whisper went on, to the papyrus, to the reeds, to the short plain grass, and to the knee-high grass.

"The River wants to go to the sky!"

"The River . . ."

" . . . wants to . . ."

" . . . go to . . ."

" . . . the sky. . . ."

The whisper went very fast until it was at the edge of the woods that are hedged by bushes guarding the foothills of the great mountains and the high plains.

"The River wants to go to the sky," said a bush, and the trees whispered from trunk to branch to leaf to leaf to leaf like a gentle stir in an invisible breeze all the way to the wind-swept high plains where the grass lay low below the swift wind.

The wind was quick at picking up whispers from the lower plains, so it snapped the whisper up and dragged it over the high plains up to the mountains and over the peaks, where nothing grew because it was too cold. Away into the sky the wind carried the whisper.

"Shoosh-whoosh, whoosh-whoosh, the River wants to go to the sky."

The night sky heard it, the stars heard it, and early the following day before dawn, just as it was eating its breakfast ready to start the day, the Sun heard it.

"Very well, I'll visit the River today," said the Sun.

The River woke up very early, and soon after, the Sun came to visit.

"I hear you want to go to the sky, meandering River?" said the Sun.

"Yes! Oh, to walk the blue and see the twinkling eyes," the River sighed.

"Very well," said the Sun. "I can help you up, but you'll have to find your way down."

"Down! It looks so beautiful up there, I won't want to find my way down."

Gazelle, who happened to be taking a drink just then, sprang up and ran to Elephant and said, "The Sun is going to take the great River up to the sky, and she says she'll never come back here again!"

Elephant thought for a while, then raised her trunk and blew a message into the air. The wind, who was always quick at picking up messages, snapped it up, and everywhere it blew, the animals and the plants heard it.

The trees were the first to react. They gathered together into the densest forest ever and talked over the matter for days and days. The gathering of trees and creepers became a jungle, but the grasses, thinking it was too dark under the eaves of those huge trees, wandered out onto the plains, and they were so happy they rocked in the wind singing in their throaty voices. They spread as far as the eye could see. Some small thorn trees and bushes came out and dotted the grassy plains, and this became the savanna.

When the animals gathered they too talked for days and days.

"This is a serious matter," said Elephant.

"It is time to migrate to faraway places," said Rhino. Saying so, he put down his head and followed his nose South. South, South, always South. That started the exodus, and animals wandered in all directions. Great Gorilla and Brainy Chimpanzee, feeling that they did not want to go too far, simply went into the jungle. Tree Pangolin, Leopard, Gabon Viper, and Royal Antelope did the same.

Elephant led a whole delegation South following the rhinoceros. Buffalo, Lion, Giraffe, Gazelle, Hyena, Zebra, Cheetah, and many others wandered South and roamed the grasslands. But rock-climbing Barbary Sheep, Camel, Addax, Sand Cat, Desert Hedgehog, Fennec Fox, Jerboa, Sand Grouse, and many others remained exactly where they were.

Meanwhile, the Sun had gathered all its strength. It sent its hottest rays to heat the River, and slowly, oh so slowly you could not see what was happening, the River started to lift in particles too tiny for the eye to see. Up, up, up they went until they were so high that it felt cold. Then the tiny particles of the River huddled together and formed white fluffy clouds of all sizes. They were so happy to be floating in the air, and they waited in excitement for the spectacle of the night sky when they would walk among the many winking stars.

Sure enough, in the evening, the night sky prepared to lay out the best winking stars for the visiting clouds to walk among, and as it got darker the stars winked and twinkled and sparkled.

"Oh, isn't this wonderful!" said a cloud. "Simply stupendous!"

Whoosh! A gust of wind came in.

"You're sitting on my bit of sky ledge," the wind said.

"Oh, I beg your pardon," said the cloud, and she moved over to one side.

Whoosh! Gusts of wind came over and over again, here and everywhere. They claimed parts of the sky where the clouds were. Sometimes they came while the clouds were trying to get some sleep, and they would shake them awake and push them over.

Now, pushing and shoving is about the only thing that the gentle River would not stand. And all the clouds remembered the peaceful days of being water down on Earth. They remembered the gentle flow in one direction and the gliding back of the tide, and a small cloud said, "I want to go home."

Yes. They all wanted to go home. But how? The wind, so quick at picking up conversations, snapped up the news of the clouds trying to go home, and it gathered all its sisters, cousins, and brothers.

WWHHOOOSSSHH!!

They carried the clouds high and made them feel colder, and as the clouds huddled together they grew heavy and began to fall as rain. Down below, the Sun was still burning out any manner of moisture that remained in the river bed.

But it rained. It rained all day long and all night long. It rained everywhere but never in the old river bed. It rained in Abyssinia and formed the Blue Nile. It rained and rained and formed the White Nile and Lake Victoria and Lake Tanganyika and Lake Malawi and Lake Chad, Lake Turkana, and many small lakes besides. It rained and rained and formed the Shire River. It rained and formed the Zambezi. It rained some more and the Limpopo, the Orange, the Niger, the Luangwa, and many, many other rivers were born. It rained heavily and lightly, day and night, and if you put your hands over your ears and moved them on and off, you could hear something like a song but not quite a song. Something like words but not quite like words:

"I am the River, the River that went to the sky for a walk. I am the River, the River that went to the sky for a walk."

It rained and rained everywhere but never in the place where the River once lived. If any of the drops ventured anywhere near that place, the Sun bore down on them and sent them back into the sky. And it is true. If you go to the great continent of Africa today you will see the vast expanse of sand where the meandering River lived. Sand everywhere, even in places where grass had been plenty. To this day the Wildebeest have not stopped running away from the Sun, following their noses to wetter places where the grass would be as it used to be once upon a time, a long time ago, on the great continent of Africa.

255

Objectives
• Provide evidence from the text to demonstrate understanding.
• Read independently for a sustained period of time and paraphrase the reading.

Envision It! | Retell

Think Critically

1. Think of an area you know or have studied that dried up, became flooded, or otherwise changed. How were the plants, animals, and people affected? Did the change lead to migrations? **Text to World**

2. The description of African topography is real. Read about the River and its surroundings on page 248. Draw a diagram showing the setting where the story begins. **Think Like an Author**

3. On page 249, the River first whispers, "Oh, how I wish I could go to the sky." How does the whisper finally reach the Sun? **Cause and Effect**

4. Story events are usually told in sequence. Create a graphic organizer that shows the sequence of events after the disappearance of the River. **Story Structure**

5. Look Back and Write A turning point in the story is when the River wanted to go home. Why? Look on pages 253–254 and write your answer. Provide evidence to support what you write.

TEST PRACTICE Extended Response

Kasiya Makaka Phiri

Kasiya Makaka Phiri is a poet, a playwright, and a storyteller. He says that *The River That Went to the Sky* was inspired by many experiences—"the Limpopo River, a flight over the Sahara, the migration of wildlife on the plains of East Africa, and the great spectacle of the transition from the dry to the wet season." Mr. Phiri tells new stories and retells old ones. He tries out his stories on his three daughters, and later he tells the stories in front of an audience. Born in Zimbabwe and educated in Malawi, Mr. Phiri now lives in Wisconsin. He says that collecting and publishing African stories is "a great support for the evolution of our African culture in these days of rockets, lasers, and bombs."

Other African tales: *The Lion's Whiskers and Other Ethiopian Tales* and *Tales from Africa*

Use the Reading Log in the *Reader's and Writer's Notebook* to record your independent reading.

Key Features of a Tall Tale

● may be based on real or fictional characters and events

● has larger-than-life characters

● includes exaggerated deeds and events

READING STREET ONLINE
GRAMMAR JAMMER
www.ReadingStreet.com

Tall Tale

A **tall tale** is a greatly exaggerated story of real, imaginary, or impossible acts. They may be based on the life of a real person or made-up characters. The student model on the next page is an example of a tall tale.

Writing Prompt Write a tall tale about a larger-than-life character and his or her adventures.

Writer's Checklist

Remember, you should ...

☑ write about a larger-than-life character.

☑ include exaggerated or impossible actions and events.

☑ use a lively, or animated, tone.

☑ use demonstrative adjectives correctly.

258

Lightning and Diana

Long ago, in the Wild West, lived a horse named Lightning. Why was he named Lightning? That's how fast that horse could run!

Lightning belonged to Diana, who also moved with frightening speed. In the morning, they rounded up cattle in Texas. At noon, they picked berries in California. Diana's hands were a blur as they moved.

One morning, as they raced down a brushy Texas road, Diana spotted two masked bandits crouching in some bushes. One, who had a bow and arrow, said, "This arrow won't make any noise. Nobody will come after us."

Just then, a sheriff and his deputies trotted by on their horses. The bandit in the bushes shot an arrow straight at the sheriff. Lightning raced forward. Diana reached out and caught that arrow just as it was about to hit the sheriff.

Before the sheriff could figure out what was happening, Lightning and Diana were in California, picking berries.

Genre
A **tall tale** uses characters and events that are exaggerated or larger than life.

**Writing Trait
Voice** The tale has a lively, informal tone.

Demonstrative adjectives are used correctly.

Conventions

Demonstrative Adjectives

Remember The adjectives *this, that, these,* and *those* are called **demonstrative adjectives.** They describe which one or which ones. *This* and *that* modify singular nouns. *These* and *those* modify plural nouns.

Social Studies in Reading

Genre
Tall Tale

● A tall tale is a greatly exaggerated, usually humorous account of a superhuman character.

● Tall tales are a form of folk literature.

● While some tall tales are based on lives or undertakings of real people, many use realistic details to tell about fictitious people.

● Tall tales often center on the culture of nineteenth-century frontier Americans and make light of their hardships.

● Read "Pecos Bill and the Cyclone" and see which details make this tall tale seem almost believable.

Pecos Bill *and the* Cyclone

from *American Tall Tales*
by Mary Pope Osborne

Once Bill settled down with the gang, his true genius revealed itself. With his gang's help, he put together the biggest ranch in the Southwest. He used New Mexico as a corral and Arizona as a pasture. He invented tarantulas and scorpions as practical jokes. He also invented roping. Some say his rope was exactly as long as the equator; others argue it was two feet shorter.

Things were going fine for Bill until Texas began to suffer the worst drought in its history. It was so dry that all the rivers turned as powdery as biscuit flour. The parched grass was catching fire everywhere. For a while Bill and his gang managed to lasso water from the Rio Grande. When that river dried up, they lassoed water from the Gulf of Mexico.

No matter what he did, though, Bill couldn't get enough water to stay ahead of the drought. All his horses and cows were starting to dry up and blow away like balls of tumbleweed. It was horrible.

Just when the end seemed near, the sky turned to a deep shade of purple. From the distant mountains came a terrible roar. The cattle began to stampede, and a huge black funnel of a cyclone appeared, heading straight for Bill's ranch.

The rest of the gang shouted "Help!" and ran.

But Pecos Bill wasn't scared in the least. "Yahoo!" he hollered, and he swung his lariat and lassoed that cyclone around its neck.

Bill held on tight as he got sucked up into the middle of the swirling cloud. He grabbed the cyclone by the ears and pulled himself onto her back. Then he let out a whoop and headed that twister across Texas.

The mighty cyclone bucked, arched, and screamed like a wild bronco. But Pecos Bill just held on with his legs and used his strong hands to wring the rain out of her wind. He wrung out rain that flooded Texas, New Mexico, and Arizona, until finally he slid off the shriveled-up funnel and fell into California. The Earth sank about two hundred feet below sea level in the spot where Bill landed, creating the area known today as Death Valley.

"There. That little waterin' should hold things for a while," he said, brushing himself off.

After his cyclone ride, no horse was too wild for Pecos Bill.

Let's **Think** About...

What are some exaggerated or impossible deeds described in this tale? **Tall Tale**

Let's **Think** About...

Reading Across Texts Both the myth *The River That Went to the Sky* and this tall tale tell about land or water formations that actually exist. What are they?

Writing Across Texts Make a chart that lists the formations you read about in the myth and in this tall tale about Pecos Bill.

Objectives

- Read aloud grade-level stories with expression.
- Use context clues to identify a synonym for an unfamiliar word.
- Describe how various cultures used origin myths to explain and understand the world around them.
- Tell a story as an organized presentation that communicates your ideas effectively.

Let's Learn It!

Vocabulary

Synonyms

Context Clues When you come to a word you do not know, see if you can find a synonym, or another word with almost the same meaning, that could take its place. Read the words and sentences around the word you don't know. Here's a clue: a synonym may be preceded by the word *or* or *like* and may be set off by commas.

Practice It! Find the word *stupendous* in paragraph 4, page 253. There is a synonym near it. What does the word *wonderful* mean? Try using it in place of *stupendous*. If you are not sure that the two words have similar meanings, check a dictionary or a thesaurus.

Fluency

Expression

When you read with expression, you bring the characters in a story to life. Change your tone of voice as you read to reflect each character's feelings or personality. You can express surprise and excitement, anger, or frustration with your voice and rate.

Practice It! With a partner, practice reading aloud the top half of page 250 in *The River That Went to the Sky: A Story from Malawi*. Change the speed, volume, and expression of your voice to follow the mood of the story. Be sure to give each other feedback on your reading.

Listening and Speaking

When you tell a story, speak clearly, use specific details, and follow a plot carefully.

Storytelling

Storytelling is a time-honored way of sharing information orally. People have often told stories about dramatic natural events. A plot and vivid details make stories come to life for an audience.

Practice It!

With a partner, choose a natural phenomenon such as lightning, a landform, or eclipses and write a story to explain where the phenomenon came from and how it happens. One person will tell the story to the class; the other will illustrate it.

Tips

Listening . . .

- Listen carefully to hear if the plot of the story makes sense.

- Face the speaker and look at the illustration.

Speaking . . .

- Be sure that details of the plot are in sequence and make sense.

- Speak clearly and at a pace that matches the tone of the story.

- Share the illustration that explains your story with the class.

Teamwork . . .

- Toss a coin to see who tells the story. Write it together.

263

Objectives
- Listen to and interpret a speaker's message and ask questions.
- Identify the main ideas and supporting ideas in the speaker's message.

Oral Vocabulary

Let's Talk About

Pursuing Resources

- Describe the qualities that make a resource precious.

- Express opinions about why people always seem to have sought resources that they considered valuable.

- Ask questions about resources of the Earth and how they are used.

READING STREET ONLINE
CONCEPT TALK VIDEO
www.ReadingStreet.com

265

Objectives
- Summarize the main ideas and supporting details in a text.
- Use text features and graphics to gain an overview and locate information.

Envision It! | Skill Strategy

Skill

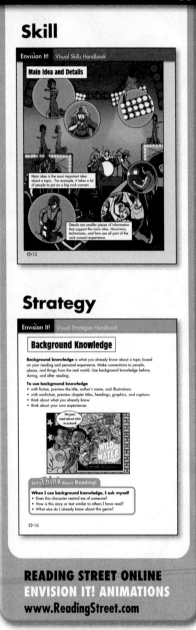

Envision It! Visual Skills Handbook

Main Idea and Details

Main idea is the most important idea about a topic. For example, it takes a lot of people to put on a big rock concert.

Details are smaller pieces of information that support the main idea. Musicians, technicians, and fans are all part of the rock concert experience.

EI·12

Strategy

Envision It! Visual Strategies Handbook

Background Knowledge

Background knowledge is what you already know about a topic based on your reading and personal experience. Make connections to people, places, and things from the real world. Use background knowledge before, during, and after reading.

To use background knowledge
- with fiction, preview the title, author's name, and illustrations
- with nonfiction, preview chapter titles, headings, graphics, and captions
- think about what you already know
- think about your own experiences

We just read about this in school!

WILD WATER

Let's Think About Reading!

When I use background knowledge, I ask myself
- Does this character remind me of someone?
- How is this story or text similar to others I have read?
- What else do I already know about this genre?

EI·16

READING STREET ONLINE
ENVISION IT! ANIMATIONS
www.ReadingStreet.com

Comprehension Skill

Main Idea and Details

- The main idea is the most important idea about a topic. Details are less important pieces of information that tell more about the main idea.

- Sometimes an author states the main idea of a paragraph or an entire article in a single sentence at the beginning or the end or, rarely, in the middle of the writing.

- The topic of a paragraph can usually be stated in a word or two. Look at the first sentence to find out what the paragraph will be about.

- Use a graphic organizer like the one below to identify the main idea and supporting details of "Metals" on page 267.

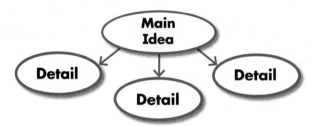

Comprehension Strategy

Background Knowledge

Good readers use what they already know to understand what they are reading. As you read about metals, think about what you already know about these substances. Making these connections will help you become a more active reader.

266

METALS

WHAT ARE METALS? Some substances, such as gold, iron, aluminum, and silver, are called metals. They are good conductors, meaning that it is easy for heat or electricity to flow through them. Metals are also malleable, which means they can be shaped and made flat.

ARE THERE MANY METALS? There are many different metals on Earth. In fact, three-fourths of all of the chemical substances humans know about are metals. Many, such as iron, are found in the Earth's crust.

WHAT TYPES OF METALS ARE THERE? Metals are grouped in three categories based on their characteristics. There are alkali metals, alkaline-earth metals, and transition metals. Alkali metals, such as sodium, dissolve in water. The molecules in these metals often join with other elements to form new substances. Alkaline-earth metals also dissolve in water, and the new substances they form are often found in nature. Calcium, which is found in your bones, is an alkaline-earth metal. Transition metals are the largest group of metals. Most metals that are used in everyday life, such as copper and iron, are transition metals. These metals are hard, strong, and shiny.

Strategy Consider what you already know about metals as you read this paragraph. What metals have you seen? What did they look like? What did they feel like?

Skill The topic of this paragraph is the quantity of metals. What is the main idea of the paragraph?

Skill What is the main idea of this paragraph? What is one detail about each kind of metal?

Your Turn!

❙❙ Need a Review? See the *Envision It! Handbook* for help with main idea and details and background knowledge.

▶ Ready to Try It? Use what you've learned about main idea and details as you read *Gold*.

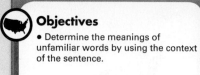

Objectives
• Determine the meanings of unfamiliar words by using the context of the sentence.

Envision It! | Words to Know

corrode

engulfed

hoard

characteristic

exploit

extract

READING STREET ONLINE
PICTURE IT! ANIMATIONS
www.ReadingStreet.com

Vocabulary Strategy for

🎯 Unfamiliar Words

Context Clues If you find a word you do not know, check the context, or the words and sentences around the unfamiliar word. Often an author provides clues that suggest the meaning of a word.

1. Reread the sentence in which the unfamiliar word appears. Look for a specific clue to the word's meaning.

2. Think about the overall meaning of the sentence in which the unfamiliar word appears.

3. If you need more help, reread other sentences near the sentence with the unfamiliar word. They may contain enough information to suggest the word's meaning.

4. Try your meaning in the original sentence. Does it make sense? If it doesn't, consult the glossary or a dictionary.

Read "All That Glitters." Use context clues to figure out the meanings of unfamiliar words.

Words to Write Reread "All That Glitters." Then look closely at a piece of jewelry and write a description of it. Use as many words from the Words to Know list as you can.

All That Glitters

Gold and silver are the metals most often used for making jewelry. Both have a characteristic shine. Because they reflect light, people have long been drawn to both metals. However, you may know that silver will corrode. This means that its atoms mix with oxygen. Eventually, a coat of tarnish appears on the surface. The process eventually eats away the outer layer of silver. Gold does not corrode.

Both metals must be mined. That is, it is necessary to extract them from the Earth. This can only be done where they are found in a concentrated form. If the metal is not found in pure chunks, it must somehow be pulled out of the ore in which it is found.

Many people are drawn to places where large pockets of ore are discovered. Gold and silver miners hope to exploit, or profit from, the rich veins of metal. For centuries, people have wanted to gather hoards of the stuff. A stockpile of gold and silver tells the world, "I am powerful and rich!" Even usually kind people can be engulfed by greed and selfishness at the thought of getting all that gold and silver!

Your Turn!

▮▮ Need a Review? For help with context clues, see *Words!*

▶ Ready to Try It? Read *Gold* on pp. 270–279.

gold

Question of the Week
How do we decide the value of different resources?

Genre

Expository text explains the nature of an object or idea. As you read, look for explanations of the nature, the rarity, and the many, varied uses of gold.

gold

by Sarah Angliss

What Is Gold?

Glistening bright yellow, gold is a heavy metal that is treasured in every country of the world.

Almost all metals have a characteristic luster (shininess)—that is, they reflect light in a mirrorlike way. Gold is special because its luster never fades. That is because gold does not react with air, water, or any ordinary chemical. In other words, it doesn't corrode. Roman coins, masks from ancient Egypt, decorated books from Persia, and other golden treasures from the ancient world shine as brilliantly now as they did the day they were made.

Gold excites people all over the world. The gold jewelry that people own is often among their most valued possessions.

Melting Pots

At room temperature, gold is solid. Gold melts at 1943°F (1062°C). It is often heated to this temperature so that it can be poured into molds.

Gold is 19.3 times denser than water and 3 times denser than iron. Density means the mass of a substance that fills a given volume. It is usually measured in grams per cubic meter. So, one cubic meter of pure gold is 19.3 times heavier than one cubic meter of water. Imagine this: if you could just manage to lift a pail of water, you would need nineteen friends to help you lift that pail if it were filled with gold instead.

Despite its great density, pure gold is soft enough to cut with a knife. This makes gold the perfect metal for intricate jewelry, artwork, and many industrial components.

This gold has been heated until it has melted and is now being poured so that it can be shaped into bars.

Did You Know?

THE FORTY-NINERS

Gold fever swept through California in 1849, the year after traces of the metal were discovered there. More than 100,000 "forty-niners" flooded into the area from Europe and the United States, hoping to find their fortune there. The old picture above, from the 1850s, shows prospectors panning for gold during the California Gold Rush.

Nuggets of gold such as this are usually found in veins of the mineral quartz. Often, the gold is combined with another precious metal—silver.

Many prospectors have been misled by this very believable look-alike for gold. This is not a gold nugget but a sample of pyrite, a mineral rich in iron and sulfur rather than gold. It is commonly referred to as "fool's gold."

Where Gold Is Found

Gold is extremely rare, which is one of the many reasons why we value it so highly. The proportion of Earth's crust that is made of gold is only five-billionths.

As gold reacts with very few other chemicals, gold prospectors (people who search for gold) usually find it in its pure form. Occasionally, they come across gold that has combined with the metals bismuth, tellurium, or selenium.

Prospectors usually extract tiny crystals of gold, just a few millimeters in size. If they are very lucky, they may come across larger lumps of gold, known as nuggets. Gold is most often found in veins of a mineral called quartz. Sometimes it is discovered in loose chunks that pepper sand or gravel. These chunks are called placer deposits. They form when gold breaks free from rocks that have eroded (worn away). Running water, wind, or rain can erode rocks like this over millions of years.

275

The leading areas for goldmining include South Africa, Russia, the United States, Canada, Australia, Brazil, and China. The single most productive area is the Transvaal Province of South Africa, a country that now produces over a quarter of the world's annual gold production of 3,300 tons (3,000 tonnes).

Wealth Beneath the Waves

The oceans, which cover about three-quarters of Earth's surface, contain a much higher proportion of gold than the land. On average, one cubic foot (0.09 m³) of ocean is between 1,000 and 50,000 times more likely to contain gold than one cubic foot of Earth's crust.

Rich Oceans but Poor Returns

Some eighty years ago, when people thought that there was more gold in seawater than there really is, German scientist Fritz Haber (1868–1934) was asked to find a way to extract the oceans' gold. His government wanted gold to pay the debts it had built up by the end of World War I (1914–1918).

DidYou Know?

A RIVETING STORY

The design of jeans may well have been perfected during the Gold Rush of 1849. At that time, people needed hard-wearing trousers with pockets that could safely store nuggets of gold. People made their trousers of rugged denim and put metal rivets around the pockets to ensure that their seams would not break.

276

In fact, the proportion of gold in seawater is a mere ten parts per trillion, so Haber succeeded only in showing that it would cost more to extract the gold than the gold would be worth.

Searching for Gold

As traces of gold have been found and used by many ancient civilizations, it is impossible to say who first discovered this metal. But historic treasures and records that survive to this day show that many early peoples had a passion for gold. Cities have been founded and expeditions and wars started by people scrabbling for more of this precious metal.

Early gold prospectors, such as those in Persia and ancient Egypt, probably panned for gold. Using river water, they would wash sand or gravel through a sieve. Any lumps of gold would be left behind in their sieve for them to collect.

Over the centuries, people have also developed the technology to dig gold out of solid rock. In the sixteenth century, the Spanish invaders of South America used slave labor to mine vast amounts of gold, changing the world economy forever. The population of states such

This astronaut's tether is his lifeline. It contains strands of gold that are guaranteed never to corrode. That means the tether should not snap and cause the astronaut to drift off into space.

as Nevada mushroomed in the nineteenth century as people rushed there to exploit newly discovered reserves of gold.

Gold mining is still big business, especially in South Africa. Today, gold prospectors use satellite technology and chemical rock analysis to search for new reserves. They can blast gold from rock using high-pressure water. They can even extract gold economically from low-grade ores (rocks that contain very small amounts of the metal). Gold can be dissolved from these rocks using the chemical potassium cyanide.

Precious Properties

Gold catches our eye and is attractive to many people because it shines so brilliantly. People also like it because it is so rare and precious. But gold is valued for more than its scarcity and beauty. It has several other unusual properties that make it a perfect metal for many tasks.

Most metals, such as iron and copper, corrode over time. Corrosion happens when a metal combines with another element—usually the gas oxygen in the air—to form a compound that covers the metal's surface as a dull film. Gold objects never corrode. That is why they still look new even centuries after they were made. In fact, gold does not react in any way with water, air, and most acids, or with any other common substance.

Because it is easy to form gold into elaborate shapes, this precious metal has been used in sacred and important works of art in every region of the world—the example above is a piece of pre-Columbian art.

Stamped to show its authenticity, 45 percent of the world's gold is kept under lock and key in bank vaults as bars of gold bullion.

A LITTLE GOES A LONG WAY

A cube of gold the size of a plum could be beaten to form a sheet of gold leaf that could cover a tennis court, or it could be stretched to form a wire nearly 2 miles (3.2 km) long. Less than 1/250,000 in. (1/10,000 mm) thick, gold leaf can be folded and torn as easily as paper.

Bend Me, Shape Me

Pure gold is extremely malleable, which means that it is soft enough to bend or beat into many different shapes. You can beat a lump of gold with a hammer, for example, to turn it into a thin, flexible sheet of "gold leaf."

Gold is also very ductile. This means that it can be easily stretched into extremely fine wire, especially when first softened by heat.

Gold is an excellent thermal and electrical conductor—in other words, it lets heat and electricity flow through it very easily. Only silver and copper are more effective conductors of heat and electricity than gold.

Gold has these properties because of the way its atoms, the tiny particles that make it up, are arranged. Compared to most metals, gold has atoms that are bonded together very loosely. This means that they are able to slide past each other easily when only a tiny force is applied to them—for instance, when you try to bend or stretch a lump of gold.

With so many special properties, it is no wonder that gold can be put to so many different uses.

Objectives
• Provide evidence from the text to demonstrate understanding.
• Read independently for a sustained period of time and paraphrase the reading.

Envision It! | Retell

Think Critically

1. Why shouldn't we use gold—rather than coins and bills—as money for purchases we make every day? Text to World

2. The author writes about the fact that gold is noncorrosive. Why do you think she included this information in the selection? Think Like an Author

3. On page 275, the author states that one of the reasons gold is precious is because it is so rare. What detail in the passage supports this main idea? Is this statement supported by details in the selection? Main Idea and Details

4. How did the *Did You Know?* sidebars help you call upon your background knowledge to understand this selection? Background Knowledge

5. **Look Back and Write** Why would or wouldn't gold prospectors be wiser to look for gold in the sea than in the hills? Read from page 276 to the top of 278; then write a clear answer. Provide evidence to support your answer.

TEST PRACTICE Extended Response

Meet the Author

Sarah Angliss

Sarah Angliss was trained in electroacoustics, music, and evolutionary robotics. She specializes in creating original sound installations, exhibits, and live performances that mix cutting-edge science with vintage sound technology and little-known stories from the history of science. Included among her installations is a soundpiece in the Reptile House of the London Zoo and another in the Butterfly House, which responds to the flight of butterflies. She says, "When I'm not working with sound, I'm usually dreaming up new exhibits and galleries, digging out facts and stories from archives, editing video for use in theater shows, presenting live events . . . or writing books and articles on science."

Ms. Angliss, the author of numerous hands-on books about science for young people, including those on this page, also plays the musical saw.

Other books by Sarah Angliss: *Future Files: Cosmic Journeys* and *Hands-On Science: Electricity and Magnets*

Reading Log
Use the Reading Log in the *Reader's and Writer's Notebook* to record your independent reading.

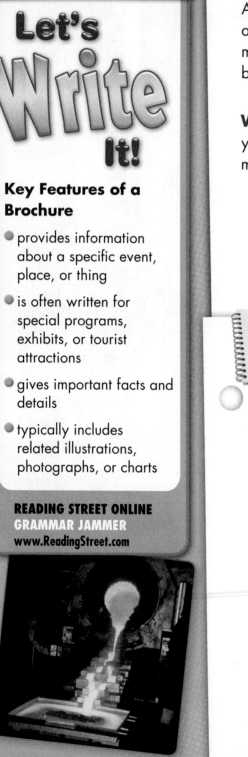

Let's Write It!

Key Features of a Brochure

● provides information about a specific event, place, or thing

● is often written for special programs, exhibits, or tourist attractions

● gives important facts and details

● typically includes related illustrations, photographs, or charts

READING STREET ONLINE
GRAMMAR JAMMER
www.ReadingStreet.com

Brochure

A **brochure** gives interesting facts and details about an event, a place, or thing. The student model on the next page is an example of a brochure.

Writing Prompt Think about something that you think is valuable. Write a brochure for a museum exhibit that features this item.

Writer's Checklist

Remember, you should ...

✓ write a brochure for a museum exhibit.

✓ separate varying topics by subheads.

✓ provide visual images that draw in readers.

✓ use a variety of sentence types, such as questions and commands.

282

"Quilting Through History" at the Cooper Museum

The Cooper Museum of Lafayette invites you to "Quilting Through History," open now through June 28. See quilts from many eras in our largest exhibit of the year.

Underground Railroad Quilt

This Civil War-era quilt was found in Pennsylvania. The quilt patterns were used to send signals on the Underground Railroad. This is one of the best, most detailed quilts we have ever featured.

Charm Quilts or Beggar Quilts

These interesting and unique quilts use many different kinds of fabric. They will dazzle you with their vibrant colors!

Want to make your own quilt? Visit our Wednesday Quilting Bee. Supplies are included with a $15 entrance fee. The museum is open 10 a.m.-5 p.m., Tuesday-Sunday.

Genre
This **brochure** includes facts and details about an event.

Comparative and superlative adjectives are used correctly.

Writing Trait Word Choice
A variety of sentence types help transition ideas and grab readers' attention.

Conventions

Comparative and Superlative Adjectives

Remember A **comparative adjective** is used to compare two people, places, things, or groups (e.g., *better*). A **superlative adjective** is used to compare three or more people, places, things, or groups (e.g., *best*).

21st Century Skills
INTERNET GUY

Online Sources What is the first thing to do at a new Web site? Find out who wrote the information. Use the "About This Site" button. Can you believe what you find there?

- On Internet Web sites, you can find reference sources such as atlases, encyclopedias, and dictionaries. They look like printed sources and usually follow a formal organization.

- Some sites give you several different reference sources in one place.

- Sites that end with *.gov* or *.edu* may be more reliable than *.com* sites. (*.com* stands for "commercial.")

- Read "The California Gold Rush" and notice the Web pages that Pablo chose. Do they look reliable?

The California Gold Rush

Pablo learned a lot about gold in the selection *Gold*. But he was also interested in the California Gold Rush and the famous "forty-niners." He decided to find out more by going to an online reference source run by the United States Department of State.

Pablo sees that there are several reference sources on this site—biographies, fast facts, almanacs, dictionaries, encyclopedias, sources of quotations, as well as other Web sites. He clicks on one of the encyclopedia links.

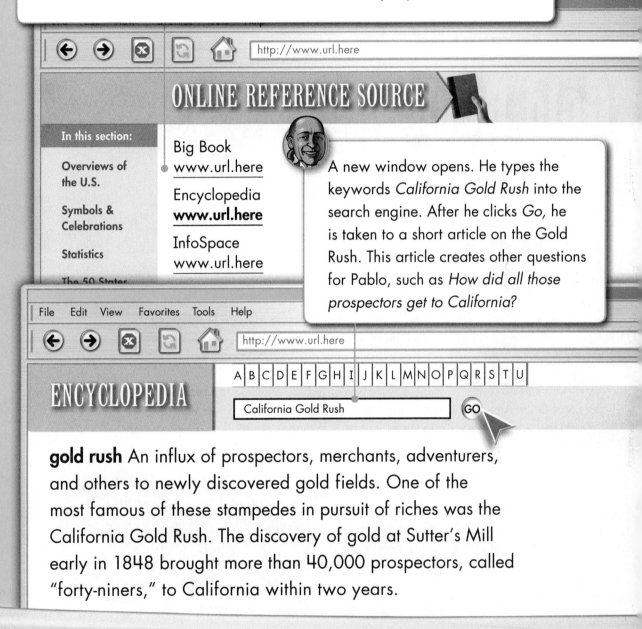

http://www.url.here

ONLINE REFERENCE SOURCE

In this section:

Overviews of the U.S.

Symbols & Celebrations

Statistics

The 50 States

Big Book
www.url.here

Encyclopedia
www.url.here

InfoSpace
www.url.here

A new window opens. He types the keywords *California Gold Rush* into the search engine. After he clicks *Go*, he is taken to a short article on the Gold Rush. This article creates other questions for Pablo, such as *How did all those prospectors get to California?*

File   Edit   View   Favorites   Tools   Help

http://www.url.here

A B C D E F G H I J K L M N O P Q R S T U

ENCYCLOPEDIA

California Gold Rush   GO

gold rush An influx of prospectors, merchants, adventurers, and others to newly discovered gold fields. One of the most famous of these stampedes in pursuit of riches was the California Gold Rush. The discovery of gold at Sutter's Mill early in 1848 brought more than 40,000 prospectors, called "forty-niners," to California within two years.

Pablo types in *forty-niners* and searches again. He finds this Web site from a state university. This is what he reads:

Edit View Favorites Tools Help

http://www.url.here

The Gold Rush

"The reports of the gold regions are as encouraging here as they were back in Massachusetts. Just imagine yourself seeing me return with $10,000 to $100,000."
— **ANONYMOUS FORTY-NINER**

The Journey

The departing gold-seekers, called "forty-niners" for the year, 1849, faced an immediate problem. California was far away. There was no railroad to whisk them west, no river to float them to California. Instead, the journey would be a painful test of endurance.

There were two miserable choices. The sea route around the tip of South America often took more than six months. The sea route was favored by gold-seekers from the Eastern states, but on a ship seasickness was rampant, and food was often full of bugs or rancid. Water stored for months on a ship was almost impossible to drink.

For Americans who lived in the Central states, there was another way west: the Oregon-California Trail. The overland road was much shorter than the sea route, but it wasn't faster. Most had no idea how severe the overland journey would be.

All they could think about was gold as they plodded alongside covered wagons at two miles per hour—for up to six months.

The real danger of the overland journey was the lack of water. At some points there were no water resources at all, and some people would die of thirst. A number of people in California heard of this, and they came out with just about anything filled with water. They would sell the water for $1 or more a glass. The price for water could go as high as $100 per drink. Those without money were sometimes left to die. It was a lesson in supply and demand in frontier California.

286

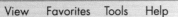
Gold Rush

On the same university Web site, Pablo comes across a link to *Fun Facts about the Gold Rush*. This is what he finds:

Weird Ways West

A California-bound airline in 1849? Don't laugh; it almost happened. Rufus Porter, founder of *Scientific American* magazine, planned to fly forty-niners west on propeller-driven balloons. He advertised the expedition, and two hundred brave souls signed up for the trip. But the "airline" never got off the ground.

Then there was the "wind wagon," sort of a cross between a sailboat and a wagon. A prototype was built, and for a brief moment it barreled across the plains at the advertised 15 miles per hour. Then it went out of control and crashed. The inventor—Frederick "Wind Wagon" Thomas—kept trying for years to make his invention work, but he never succeeded.

Others took another approach, making the trip with only a wheelbarrow. It's hard to imagine pushing a fully loaded wheelbarrow for 2,000 miles, but several dozen attempted the trip. For a time, they could outpace everything on the trail, but human endurance has its limits. No one is quite sure if any of them made it all the way with their wheelbarrows.

Why all the weird contraptions? Everyone was in a big hurry to get West—to strike it rich.

Frederick Thomas's "wind wagon"

---

for more practice

www.ReadingStreet.com
Use online reference sources to research the California Gold Rush.

**21st Century Skills
Online Activity**
Log on and follow the step-by-step directions for using online reference sources to find out more about the California Gold Rush.

Let's
Learn
It!

Vocabulary

Unfamiliar Words

Context Clues Surrounding words, phrases, and sentences may give clues to the meaning of an unfamiliar word. If the nearby words and phrases do not provide a definition for the unfamiliar word, predict a meaning for it. Try out the meaning to see if it makes sense. If it doesn't, consult a dictionary to find out more.

Practice It! Look at the word *luster* in paragraph 2, page 272, of *Gold*. Notice that the word next to it provides its definition. This is one example of a context clue. Now look at paragraph 3 on page 277, at the word *sieve*. Use context clues to find what a sieve is like.

Fluency

Rate

When you read aloud, read at a rate, or speed, that is appropriate for what you are reading. Try to read at a rate that people naturally use for everyday speech. When you are reading complicated text, preview what you are about to read for unfamiliar words or ideas.

Practice It! With a partner, practice reading aloud from *Gold*, page 278, beginning at "Precious Properties." Adjust the rate at which you read to the text. Because these two paragraphs are technical, you may want to slow down to be sure you understand. Give your partner feedback.

Listening and Speaking

When giving an informational speech, maintain eye contact and speak clearly, with confidence.

Informational Speech

In a speech, a speaker gives a formal talk to an audience for a specific purpose. An informational speech is intended to give listeners facts about a topic.

Practice It! Research and prepare an informational speech about a natural resource and its value. Explain why it has this value and what factors shape the value of any resource. Use note cards to stay organized. Rehearse your speech with a partner. Then give it to the class.

Tips

Listening . . .

- Listen attentively to the speaker.
- Determine the speaker's main ideas.
- Ask relevant questions.

Speaking . . .

- Speak clearly and with confidence.
- Use note cards to stay on topic.
- Make eye contact.
- Explain your topic adequately.

Teamwork . . .

- Ask for honest feedback from your partner to improve your speech.
- Accept and adopt your partner's valid suggestions.

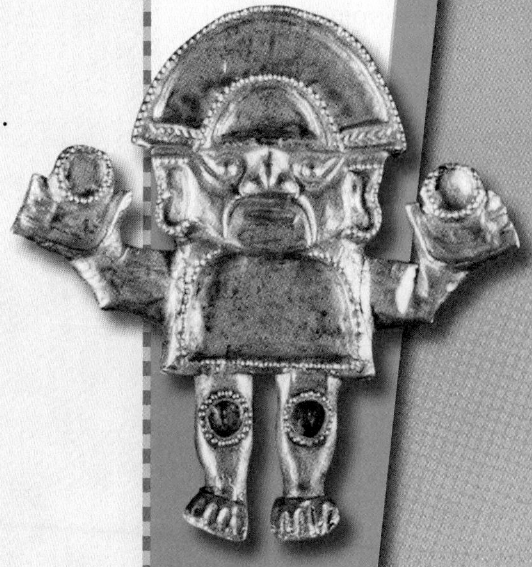

Oral Vocabulary

Let's Talk About

Preserving Resources

- Describe ways that people can save resources.

- Share what you know about alternative energy.

- Express opinions about why it's important to preserve resources.

READING STREET ONLINE
CONCEPT TALK VIDEO
www.ReadingStreet.com

290

Objectives
● Analyze how the organization of a text, such as sequential order, affects the way ideas are related.
● Understand how to use the strategy of monitor and clarify.

Envision It! | Skill Strategy

Skill

Strategy

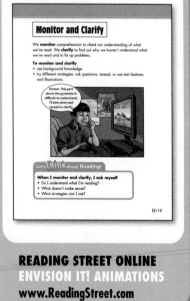

Comprehension Skill
🎯 Sequence

- Sequence refers to the order of events or the steps in a process.

- Dates, times, and clue words such as *first, next, then,* and *last* can help you determine sequence.

- Sometimes a text will present events out of order. In that case, you can read on, review, or reread in order to learn the correct sequence.

- Use a graphic organizer like the one below to show the sequence of important events in "Weather Watch" on page 293.

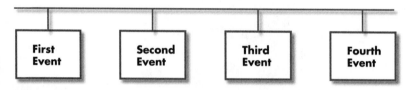

| First Event | Second Event | Third Event | Fourth Event |

Comprehension Strategy
🎯 Monitor and Clarify

One strategy good readers use to get back on track when they are confused is to keep reading. Confusion is often cleared up when you've read the entire section or text. If you are still confused, go back to the confusing section and see if it helps to reread the text.

WEATHER WATCH

Early on Saturday morning, August 10, we listened closely to the weather forecaster. A hurricane brewed fiercely in the Gulf, and we wanted to know if we might have to evacuate. Weather watches stated that we should pay careful attention but that there was no need to leave our home at that point.

By that night, the hurricane had not changed direction. Mom said that we should buy canned goods, water, and batteries for our flashlights and radios and then hunker down at home and continue to listen to the weather. We headed for the grocery store.

On Sunday afternoon, August 11, the hurricane had changed course just slightly, but we weren't in the clear yet. We loaded our supplies in a big box and put them near the back door so we could quickly put them into the car, if necessary. Then we went to fill our gas tank. We wanted to be ready to evacuate if the hurricane wobbled back our way.

Early Monday morning, we learned that the hurricane had veered away from land and we would not have to evacuate. We took the supplies out of the box near the back door, sighed a big sigh of relief, and headed out to see a movie.

Strategy If you do not understand what is happening with the weather, continue to read in order to clarify.

Skill How does this part of the passage help you figure out the sequence of events?

Skill What are clue words that help you determine the sequence of events? How do they help you?

Your Turn!

⏸ **Need a Review?** See the *Envision It! Handbook* for help with sequencing and monitoring and clarifying.

▷ **Ready to Try It?** Use what you've learned about sequencing as you read *Greensburg Goes Green.*

293

Envision It! Words to Know

emissions

forecasters

3 DAY FORECAST
TUE   WED   THU
80°   83°   8

turbines

consequences

ferocious

incubator

sustainable

READING STREET ONLINE
VOCABULARY ACTIVITIES
www.ReadingStreet.com

Vocabulary Strategy for

🎯 Unknown Words

Dictionary/Glossary When you come across a word you don't know and can't use context clues to figure out the word's meaning, use a dictionary or glossary for help.

Choose one of the Words to Know and follow these steps.

1. Open a dictionary or turn to the glossary at the back of this book.

2. Find the entry for the word. Entries in both places are in alphabetical order.

3. Read all the meanings given for the word.

4. Choose the meaning that makes the best sense in the sentence.

Read "An Environmentally Friendly Vacation." Use a dictionary or the glossary to help you determine the meanings of this week's Words to Know.

Words to Write Reread "An Environmentally Friendly Vacation." Find any other unknown words in the selection. Using a dictionary, find and write definitions for those unknown words.

An Environmentally Friendly Vacation

My mother had a great idea for our vacation this year—an ecotourism trip to Costa Rica! Mom explained that ecotourism is environmentally friendly traveling. Costa Rica is a country in Central America that has a lot of ecotourism. Mom found a hotel there that is sustainable, which means it is able to serve its guests without harmful consequences to the environment. The more Mom told me about the hotel, the more excited I became. It is on a hill on the edge of the jungle. The hotel gets all its electricity from solar panels and wind turbines that look like big metal windmills made with huge airplane propellers. We will get around on bicycles instead of in cars, so we won't cause any greenhouse-gas emissions.

At the hotel, we will learn about the local culture and the plants and animals in the jungle. Mom read that sometimes the hotel workers find abandoned toucan eggs, and they keep them warm and hatch them in incubators! I'd love to know what a toucan chick looks like. It's a good thing I'm taking my camera.

I am so excited about our trip that I get on the Internet every day to look up the weather in Costa Rica. A big, ferocious storm has passed, and the forecasters are saying that next week will be sunny and warm. Mom planned our vacation carefully, and I can't help thinking that she even planned the weather!

Your Turn!

Need a Review? For help using a dictionary/glossary to determine the meanings of unknown words, see *Words!*

Ready to Try It? Read *Greensburg Goes Green* on pp. 296–313.

GREENSBURG GOES GREEN

GREENSBURG
GOES GREEN

by Susan Nelson

Genre   **Expository text** is nonfiction that explains the natural or social world, using facts and graphics to help convey ideas more directly to the reader.

Question of the Week

How are people rethinking Earth's resources?

May 4, 2007, started out as a typical spring day in Greensburg, in southwestern Kansas.

Greensburg, population 1,400, is the main town in Kiowa County. It's located six hours from Topeka, the state capital, and just an hour away from the Oklahoma state line.

In that part of the United States, the Earth is so flat you can see the horizon in any direction. Every few hours a train whistles its way across the fertile farmland where the nation's wheat and other grains are grown.

On that sunny Friday, flowering trees and white yucca plants were in bloom. Birds sang. A few thousand cedar and other trees stood taller than anything else in town except for a half dozen church steeples, the water tower, and the six-story concrete grain elevator along Highway 54, just north of the town's twin stoplights.

As usual, parents dropped off their children at Delmer Day Elementary/Junior High School. Teenagers drove to Greensburg High School. Wherever they went, Greensburg residents recognized the people they passed. The people of Greensburg knew their neighbors.

As the day unfolded, the air grew humid. More clouds than usual formed in the sky. The wind picked up. Weather reports predicted thunderstorms for the evening. Because it had been so dry, rain would be welcome.

The clouds grew thicker. Forecasters spoke of severe weather coming. There would be heavy thunderstorms, they said, and very likely a tornado.

Three views of Greensburg, Kansas,
before May 4, 2007

But Kansas is a land of many tornadoes. Greensburg lies right in "Tornado Alley," where many of the United States's 1,200 tornadoes occur each year.

Most of the tornadoes that Greensburg had known might knock down an old barn or hen house, kick up a lot of dust in the fields, or even blow limbs from trees. Those tornadoes had meant taking shelter and then, after an hour or so, going back to life as usual. This time, however, would be different.

By 7:00 that evening, it looked like rain. At 8:00 it began to pour. By 9:00 a ferocious wind was blowing trees sideways. Forecasters now said that tornadoes had been spotted in Oklahoma and were moving north toward Kansas.

At 9:15 Greensburg's tornado sirens began to wail. Storm chasers, scientists and concerned citizens who track storms, had spotted a tornado outside town. The tornado was huge and wedge-shaped, they said. And it was moving straight toward Greensburg.

MORE ON TORNADOES

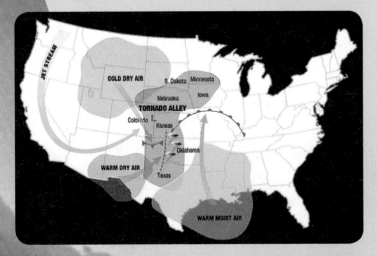

Tornadoes, nature's most violent storms, form when warm, humid air rushing up from the southern United States collides with cooler, dry air pushing down from Canada. When these opposite winds move fast enough, severe thunderstorms called "super cells" can be formed. Sometimes one of these super cells becomes a tornado.

Most of the world's tornadoes occur in the United States in the central Great Plains states, between the Rocky Mountains and the Appalachian Mountains. This swath is known as "Tornado Alley." It stretches from Texas north through parts of Oklahoma, Kansas, Nebraska, Iowa, and South Dakota. Nearly 1200 confirmed tornadoes touch down each year.

Tornado "season" usually begins in the late winter in the southeastern United States. It moves to the central states between March and May and then moves farther north as the weather warms. The season is usually over by late summer.

When a tornado touches the Earth, its cycling, twisting air can pick up anything in its path—even cars or trucks and houses. A twister, as tornadoes are also called, often forms a funnel cloud. This cloud dances along the Earth and grows dark with the soil and debris it picks up.

Most tornadoes sputter out, or dissipate, and disappear with little or no damage. But a few do not.

This time, instead of sounding only for a few minutes, the sheriff decided to leave the sirens on. The prediction now was that Greensburg was about to take a direct hit from this tornado.

Townspeople quickly went underground. Some climbed into their outdoor storm cellars, but most went down to their basements, where many had a television or radio to track the storm upstairs. There they went to the strongest wall away from windows and crawled under something sturdy, perhaps also covering their heads with pillows or blankets. Not many people thought about putting on boots or gathering up family treasures. They had all seen tornadoes before.

Outside, hailstones as big as golf balls bounced off anything they hit. The wind knocked down telephone poles and trees. Roofs lifted up from houses, and buildings were blown from their foundations. Lightning flashed on and off, showing the sinister, dark wedge moving steadily across the night sky.

At 9:45 the sirens stopped. The city's electrical power station had been hit. Suddenly it was silent. Next came a drop in pressure that made people's ears pop, as if they were in a plane coming in for a landing.

Then, as the tornado raged above them, came the sounds: like ice cubes going around in a blender, or a locomotive overhead, or the roar of a huge waterfall. Windows shattered. Heavy objects, even cars and trucks, were picked up and slammed into walls. The bark was scraped off of the few trees that were still standing. And then it was silent again.

But not for long. After the "eye" passed, the rest of the tornado tore over the same path. By the time it had ground its way across Greensburg, the town was no more.

The people of Greensburg slowly came out of their safe places. Some climbed basement stairs and found themselves standing in empty darkness and bewilderment: their houses were gone. Others found just a part of their homes, maybe a wall or bookshelf or stairway, still in place—or maybe a neighbor's car or pickup in their kitchen.

As they made their ways outside, residents found that rescue workers had arrived from nearby towns with fire trucks and ambulances. They had come to Greensburg expecting the worst. On foot, through deep rainwater and using two-way radios, rescuers walked yard to yard, calling out to find people who might need help.

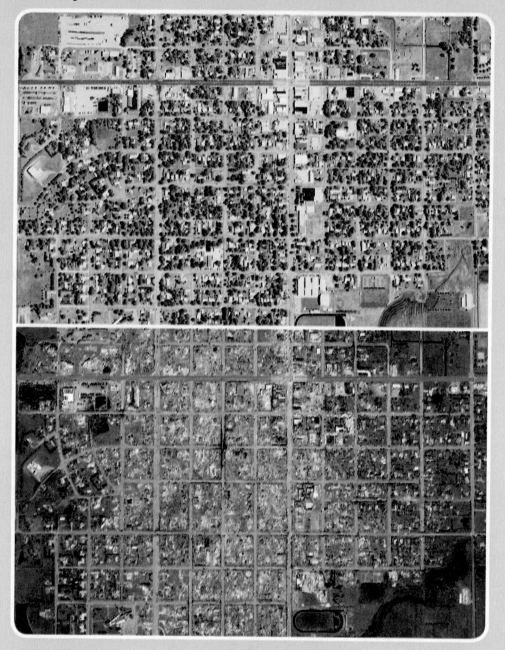

THE ENHANCED FUJITA TORNADO SCALE

Named for scientist Tetsuya "Ted" Fujita, the power of tornadoes is ranked on an "enhanced Fujita" (EF) scale:

CATEGORY	WINDSPEED	% OF ALL TORNADOES	DAMAGE
EF 0	65–85 mph	53.5%	Light
EF 1	86–110 mph	31.6%	Moderate
EF 2	111–135 mph	10.7%	Considerable
EF 3	136–165 mph	3.4%	Severe
EF 4	166–200 mph	.7%	Devastating
EF 5	> 200 mph	< .1%	Total Destruction

Farmers whose property had been spared drove tractors and front-loaders into town. They knew that trees and all sorts of other debris would need to be moved so that rescue vehicles could get through.

Until batteries ran down, residents used flashlights or the light from their cell phones to find their ways. There was no telephone service: the cell phone tower had been blown down, and land-line service was out as well.

The town's only supermarket was still partly standing, so residents were directed to it. It became the hub of rescue and recovery. Lists were made of residents so that they could be accounted for. Buses pulled up to carry survivors to shelters in schools in nearby towns. Families that lived nearby took in friends and families.

It wasn't until daybreak that rescue workers and Greensburg's leaders saw the full consequences of the night before. The tornado that had struck was an EF 5—the most serious category of tornado and the most destructive.

Greensburg's tornado had been clocked at 205 miles per hour. It was 1.7 miles wide; Kansas tornadoes average 75 yards across. Its path of destruction was 22 miles long; Kansas tornadoes average between 1 and 4 miles long.

Ninety-five percent of the town of Greensburg was demolished. Homes and businesses, the stoplights and fairgrounds, schools and gas stations—all had vanished except for a wall or a stairway here or there. Street signs had been wrenched out and had disappeared; the trees and steeples were gone. The water tower lay crumpled, and other landmarks were nowhere to be seen. Only the grain elevator was standing.

The air smelled of cedar and tree sap. The ground was covered with debris and toothpick-shaped splinters of what had been buildings and trees and people's worldly possessions.

Eleven people lost their lives. About ninety were treated in area hospitals; Greensburg's hospital had been destroyed. If not for the accurate warnings that people had heeded, the numbers would have been much higher.

Relief workers began to pour into Greensburg. The Kansas National Guard arrived, as did kind strangers, volunteers who had come to help the people of Greensburg sort through what was left and clean what could be saved. Together they raked debris into piles that were shoveled into dump trucks headed for the town's landfill. There the fires of what had been Greensburg burned nonstop for three-and-a-half months.

On Wednesday, May 9th, President George W. Bush flew to Greensburg. He walked what was left of the streets and saw the damage, and he declared the town a national disaster area. That allowed the Federal Emergency Management Agency (FEMA) to arrange for temporary housing and other government assistance.

But something was happening in Greensburg even before it was officially declared a disaster area. On Monday, just three days after the storm, many residents gathered in what remained of the county courthouse. They wondered about the future. Would everyone move away? Or would people stay to rebuild their town?

Before long, it was suggested that Greensburg should take advantage of its name and rebuild as a "green" town. People would have to start from scratch anyway — and what better way to do it?

Going green would mean using far less oil and natural gas than before. It would mean generating electricity by using turbines—propellers that spin a shaft connected to a generator— to capture the wind. It would mean capturing the sun with solar panels for heat and harnessing geothermal energy from the Earth.

Buildings in the United States consume about 70 percent of all electricity used and about 40 percent of other energy consumed. They emit nearly 40 percent of the nation's carbon dioxide (CO_2) emissions, and they use about 40 percent of all raw materials. In addition, buildings generate about 30 percent of the nation's waste and consume more than 10 percent of its drinkable water.

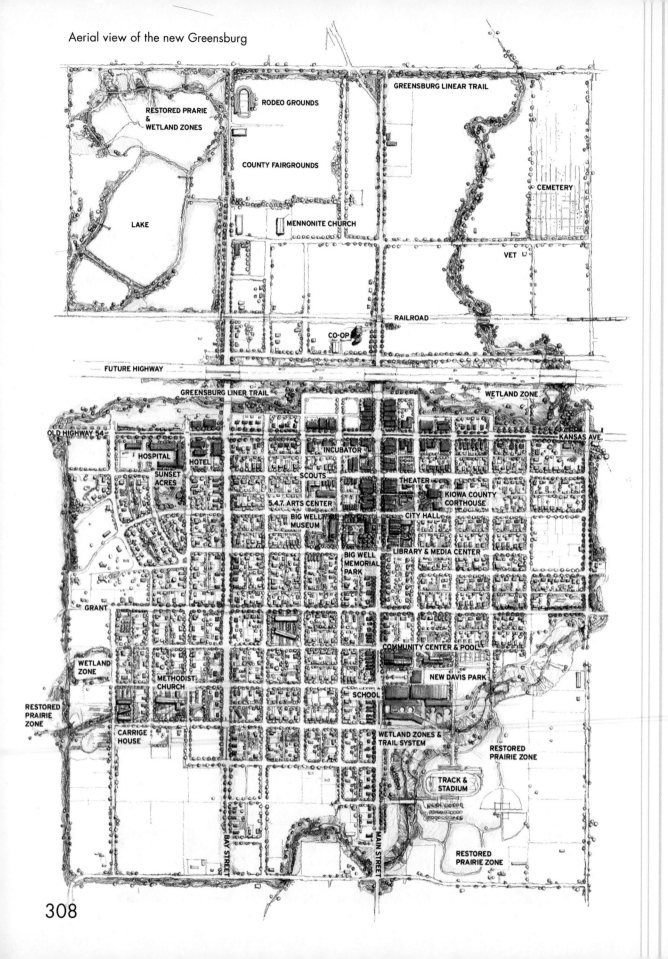

Aerial view of the new Greensburg

RESTORED PRARIE & WETLAND ZONES

RODEO GROUNDS

GREENSBURG LINEAR TRAIL

COUNTY FAIRGROUNDS

CEMETERY

LAKE

MENNONITE CHURCH

VET

RAILROAD

CO-OP

FUTURE HIGHWAY

GREENSBURG LINER TRAIL

WETLAND ZONE

OLD HIGHWAY 54

KANSAS AVE.

HOSPITAL

HOTEL

INCUBATOR

SUNSET ACRES

SCOUTS

THEATER

KIOWA COUNTY CORTHOUSE

5.4.7. ARTS CENTER

BIG WELL MUSEUM

CITY HALL

LIBRARY & MEDIA CENTER

BIG WELL MEMORIAL PARK

GRANT

WETLAND ZONE

COMMUNITY CENTER & POOL

NEW DAVIS PARK

METHODIST CHURCH

RESTORED PRAIRIE ZONE

SCHOOL

CARRIGE HOUSE

WETLAND ZONES & TRAIL SYSTEM

RESTORED PRAIRIE ZONE

TRACK & STADIUM

BAY STREET

MAIN STREET

RESTORED PRAIRIE ZONE

The idea began to catch on. Town meetings were held every week, first in a large tent and then in a quickly constructed gymnasium, to make a plan for rebuilding. News stories and soon even a television series appeared. They said that yes, people in Greensburg had lost nearly everything. But here was a small Kansas town that was determined to rebuild itself as the first all-green town in the world.

Though the cost of rebuilding would be high, townspeople knew that there could be many benefits to going green. They would be helping the environment by protecting ecosystems and biodiversity, improving air and water quality, reducing solid waste, and conserving natural resources.

They could also realize economic benefits. If Greensburg rebuilt green, companies that wanted to go green might locate there, which could mean many more jobs.

Town leaders and residents grew excited about the possibilities. High school students talked about coming back to Greensburg after they finished their education. Before the tornado, many had thought they would have to leave home to find work.

In the meantime, even though there were almost no houses yet built in Greensburg, schools opened in August, in trailers. Students came every day, from their FEMA trailers or from temporary homes in nearby towns.

On May 19, 2008, after a year's worth of meetings, the residents of Greensburg voted to adopt a Sustainable Comprehensive Plan. Following the plan would make Greensburg the greenest town in the United States and perhaps on Earth. But how would a town go green?

Greensburg's new Business Incubator

First of all, the plan calls for all city-owned buildings to be self-sufficient: they will generate their own energy and make the wisest possible use of natural resources. Also, houses will be built using the newest energy-saving methods. Corporations around the United States quickly donated money and such green supplies as water-saving shower heads.

The high school formed a Green Club, organized by Greensburg GreenTown, a nonprofit organization. For more than a year after the tornado, club members picked up rubble throughout the town. They planted trees in one of the town's parks and oversaw Christmas trees turned into mulch to help the newly planted trees thrive. The Green Club recycles paper and plastics at the schools and has run light-bulb exchanges, trading incandescent bulbs for donated energy-efficient compact fluorescents.

The plan for the town emphasizes walking instead of driving to the shops and businesses and other features of the new downtown. Bicycle racks were built outside the GreenTown office, and the staff began to ride donated, refurbished bikes. It was a new idea that slowly caught on.

Greensburg's plan also includes a wind farm with turbines large enough to provide electricity to power the town. When winds generate more energy than the town needs, Greensburg will sell the excess energy to other communities.

Further, the plan provides that all city-owned buildings will be built to meet the highest levels of environmental standards. The U.S. Green Building Council, a nonprofit organization, started a program in 2000 called Leadership in Energy and Environmental Design, or LEED. LEED standards measure a building's location, water efficiency, energy and atmosphere, materials and resources, indoor environmental quality, and innovation and design.

Abundant greenery along downtown streets, above, and the 5.4.7 Arts Center, the first LEED Platinum building in Kansas

Architects and builders apply for LEED certification for new and existing buildings. Independent reviewers study their plans and then award points based on how well the buildings in question meet these six standards. The highest of the ratings is Platinum. The town decided that all of its city structures would be built LEED Platinum.

Greensburg's first Platinum building, also the first Platinum building in the state of Kansas, is the town's art center. Named for the date of the tornado, the 5.4.7 Arts Center has three small wind turbines, solar panels, and geothermal heating and cooling. Skylights and a wall of windows on the sunnier, south side of the building reduce the need for daytime electric lights.

Next to be built Platinum was another modern-looking structure for a dozen new businesses, including the first new restaurant after the tornado. This building is Greensburg's Business Incubator. Its purpose is to provide a place to "hatch" and grow small businesses, much as other incubators hatch and then support new chicks. Later, when the new businesses are successful, they move on to their own buildings and allow other new businesses to move into the incubator and start the process again.

City leaders know that bringing new businesses to Greensburg is necessary if the town is to grow. People expect that the town's population may exceed 1,400 by 2012.

The anchor of the new Greensburg is its Platinum-rated school. Students from kindergarten through twelfth grade will have solar panels and south-facing windows to provide affordable energy. Rainwater will be captured and reused. Skylights will make classrooms so bright that electric lights will only turn on — automatically — when it is too cloudy outside to provide enough light.

Going green means not wasting resources in other ways too. Greensburg's plan calls for the new school to share space with a media center containing the town's library, the Kansas State University Extension Service, and a museum. The city also decided that one new downtown auditorium would be used both by the school and by a movie theater on weekends.

The vision of the city also includes an eco-museum that people from around the world can visit when they want to see how a green town really operates. Included are a "chain of homes" tour and model green bed-and-breakfasts.

Though the cost of rebuilding is indeed high, townspeople recognize the many benefits to going green. They are definitely helping the environment by conserving natural resources, improving air and water quality, and reducing waste. They will realize economic benefits that come with reduced operating costs of their new buildings.

In addition, the health of residents of Greensburg will improve from making walking and bicycling a part of everyday activities. All of this will add to the overall quality of life.

So the people of Greensburg are working together to turn tragedy to triumph. The utter devastation of their town offered them a tremendous opportunity to create a uniquely green environment. And they are as determined to succeed as Kansas sunflowers were to bloom again among the town's ruins.

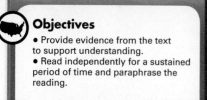

Objectives

● Provide evidence from the text to support understanding.
● Read independently for a sustained period of time and paraphrase the reading.

Envision It! Retell

READING STREET ONLINE
STORY SORT
www.ReadingStreet.com

Think Critically

1. The selection includes the Enhanced Fujita Scale. How is this scale important in parts of the world where there are many tornadoes? **Text to World**

2. The writer begins the selection by telling you about how peaceful life seemed on May 4 in Greensburg. Why do you think she begins the selection this way? **Think Like an Author**

3. Create a time line to show the major events in Greensburg from May 4, 2007, through May 19, 2008. **Sequence**

4. If, as you are reading, you are not sure about different kinds of "green" technology, what can you do to help yourself understand what you are reading? **Monitor and Clarify**

5. Look Back and Write How did Greensburg "go green"? Could other places follow this model? Before responding, reread pages 307–313. Provide evidence to support your answer.

TEST PRACTICE Extended Response

Meet the Author

Susan Nelson

Susan Nelson has been a journalist for the *Chicago Tribune* and other newspapers, a writer and editor with the United States Environmental Protection Agency, a magazine and book editor, and a teacher of students from kindergarten to college. Her newspaper and magazine articles have covered many topics, including the aftermath of earthquakes that devastated Guatemala in 1976. She likes to travel to places as varied as Turkey, Central America, and North Africa. She was born in South Bend, Indiana, and spent some of her growing-up summers with relatives in Kansas, in a town less than half the size of Greensburg. She goes green as much as possible in her own life, in Chicago. She says, "Curiosity is the best friend any writer can have!"

Other books about going green: *Planet Earth: 25 Environmental Projects You Can Build* and *Earth Watch: Protecting Our Planet*

Use the Reading Log in the *Reader's and Writer's Notebook* to record your independent reading.

Let's Write It!

Key Features of a Cause-and-Effect Essay

● includes a central idea in the topic sentence

● gives reasons and explanations for an event or situation

● identifies causes (reasons or explanations of why or how something happened) and effects (what happened as a result of that event or situation)

● often includes clue words such as *because*, *since*, *so that*, and *therefore*

READING STREET ONLINE
GRAMMAR JAMMER
www.ReadingStreet.com

Cause-and-Effect Essay

A **cause-and-effect essay** is a nonfiction composition that explains why an action or event happened and tells what occurred as a result. The student model on the next page is an example of a cause-and-effect essay.

Writing Prompt Write a cause-and-effect essay that describes one or more effects humans have on the environment.

Writer's Checklist

Remember, you should ...

✓ state the problem or situation in a topic sentence.

✓ explain the specific causes of that problem or situation in your body paragraphs.

✓ check for correct punctuation.

✓ include a strong conclusion.

Why Town River Is So Polluted

It is important to look closely at the reasons Town River is so polluted. What are the factors that have made it the most polluted river in the state?

One contributor to the pollution is a company near the river that makes tires. For years, they were dumping unused pieces of tires into the river. This caused fish to die, which upset the local ecosystem. Since no one seemed to pay attention, the dumping never stopped.

Also, people seem to **more frequently** throw trash from their car windows when driving by the river. Because there are not many tickets issued for this offense, people keep littering. There have not been enough tickets issued to **more efficiently** curb this habit.

Finally, some chemicals leaked out of big bins stored on the far end of the river's edge. Since no one removed the bins, the chemicals kept leaking into the river.

Due to these actions, Town River needs a big cleanup. Our town can help fix the problem if we work together.

Writing Trait Conventions
The essay is properly punctuated.

Comparative and superlative adverbs are used correctly.

Genre
This **cause-and-effect essay** identifies a problem and explains its causes.

Conventions

Comparative and Superlative Adverbs

Remember An adverb tells how, when, or where something happens. **Comparative adverbs** compare two actions and are usually formed by adding *-er: quieter*. **Superlative adverbs** compare three or more actions and are usually formed by adding *-est: quietest*.

317

Social Studies in Reading

Genre
Journal

- A journal, or diary, is one person's record of personal events and thoughts.

- A journal is an example of literary nonfiction because its author is writing a form of autobiography.

- The writer of a journal usually tells events in chronological order.

- The words "journal" and "diary" come from the French and Spanish words for "day"—*jour* and *dia*, respectively.

- Read "Green Journal" and see how these passages are different from other forms of nonfiction.

Green Journal

April 18th

Today we elected Zoe and Mike to run our anti-litter campaign. We'll work during Science class next week to pick up papers and other trash that blows around the school. The hardware store is giving us trash bags and two rakes. Mr. Davis, the engineer, will let us use his brooms. We're supposed to bring old gloves from home.

In Math today Mrs. Copenhaver showed us how to read an electric meter. Our meter is in the backyard, but some kids' meters are in their basements. We're going to write down the numbers from the dials this week to get a "baseline" reading. Then we'll write them down next month to see how many kilowatt hours we've used. That's how electric bills are figured. We'll see who burns up the most hours —and the fewest.

To keep kilowatt hours low:
- turn out lights
- use fans, not air conditioner all the time
- for winter, put up plastic over windows and turn down heat. (Wear more clothes!)

April 30th

Big news today—I got to go with Mrs. C. to the metals recycling center. The guy there weighed all the aluminum cans we collected—we got $18 for them, for the Tree Fund. Last year's 6th graders earned enough to buy two new maple trees that are planted in front of the school. We're aiming for two and maybe some flower bulbs too. Any extra money goes for paint for the picnic tables and benches.

I get to go with Mrs. C. and the Earth Club next week to the animal shelter. We'll take the newspapers we get every other Monday for Social Studies and then collect in a special box. The shelter uses our newspapers to line cages.

I wonder if Mom might let me get a kitten. . . .

Let's **Think** About...

Why do you think this student is keeping a journal of green activities?
Journal

Let's **Think** About...

Reading Across Texts What green activities do the people in Greensburg and this student's journal tell about?

Writing Across Texts Make a Venn diagram showing the green activities both places have in common.

READING STREET ONLINE
ONLINE STUDENT EDITION
www.ReadingStreet.com

Vocabulary

Unknown Words

Dictionary/Glossary When you come across a word you don't know and can't figure out from context clues, use a dictionary or glossary to look it up. Along with the definition, you can also find the word's part of speech, syllabication, and pronunciation.

Practice It! Identify three words you don't know from *Greensburg Goes Green*. Look up each word in a dictionary or in the glossary at the back of this book. Write down the part of speech and the definition that best fits the word as it is used in the text.

Fluency

Accuracy

When you read with accuracy, you read without errors or mispronunciations. You can increase your reading accuracy by previewing and identifying unfamiliar words before you begin to read aloud.

Practice It! With a partner, practice reading aloud from the "More on Tornadoes" sidebar on page 301 of *Greensburg Goes Green*. Alternate paragraphs, and listen for any words you might misread or mispronounce. Give your partner feedback and listen to what he or she says to you.

Listening and Speaking

In a persuasive speech, be sure to explain both the problem and the solution you suggest.

Persuasive Speech

A persuasive speech is a formal talk given for the purpose of persuading the audience to think or act in a way the speaker explains and supports.

Practice It! Research local recycling practices. Then write a speech that tries to persuade listeners that they and the local town or city should recycle more. Tell why, and use facts and examples. With a partner, rehearse your speech. Then present it to the class.

Tips

Listening . . .

- Pay attention to the speaker.

- Listen carefully to be sure that the speaker uses facts, not opinions.

Speaking . . .

- Use note cards to organize your ideas and stay focused.

- Use language that helps you persuade.

- Make eye contact.

Teamwork . . .

- Ask for suggestions from your partner and other students, and consider their ideas.

Objectives
● Evaluate the effects of sensory details and imagery in poems.
● Understand the features of free verse poetry.

Poetry

- Poets usually write about some form of nature or the nature of people or things.

- Poetry can take many forms. It can rhyme or not or follow a regular rhythm— meter—or not. But all poetry uses imagery and **sensory details** to let readers experience things in a different way.

- **Free verse poems** are free of regular rhymes and regular meter. Their power lies in repetition, vivid imagery, sensory details, and topics that interest the reader.

- Read the following four poems and choose the one that you think best describes nature or the nature of people.

For the Earth Day Contest

by Bobbi Katz

Someday there may be no "away"
to throw stuff anymore,
so we better all start thinking
and we better know the score.
We better ask some questions
about the things we choose:
Do we want a certain something
to use
    and use
      and use?
When it's broken, small, or empty,
will that be that something's end?

Can we fix it?
  Can we fill it?
    Can we give it to a friend?
Can we make that something something else
  or will that something be
    just a use-it-one-time-toss-it-out,
      a trash-it—1-2-3?
The garbage trucks
  roll
    down
      the streets
when it is garbage day.
But where will they be rolling to
when there is no "away"?

Pods Pop and Grin

by James Berry

Strong strong sun, in that look
you have, lands ripen
fruits, trees, people.

Lands love the flame of your gaze.
Lands hide some warmth
of sun-eye for darkness.

All for you pods pop and grin.
Bananas hurry up and grow.
Coconut becomes water and oil.

Palm trees try to fly to you
but just dance everywhere.
Silk leaves of bamboo rustle wild.

And when the rain finished falling
winds shake diamonds from branches
that again feel your eye.

Strong strong sun, in you
lands keep ripening
fruits, trees, people.

Birds go on tuning up
and don't care at all—
more blood berries are coming.

Your look strokes up all
summertime. We hear streams running.
You come back every day.

Let's **Think** About…

What three elements make "Pods Pop and Grin" a poem in free verse?

Let's **Think** About…

Poems often tell about a form of nature. Of these two poems, which is your favorite, and why?

maggie and milly
and molly and may . . .

by e. e. cummings

maggie and milly and molly and may
went down to the beach (to play one day)

and maggie discovered a shell that sang
so sweetly she couldn't remember her troubles, and

milly befriended a stranded star
whose rays five languid fingers were;

and molly was chased by a horrible thing
which raced sideways while blowing bubbles: and

may came home with a smooth round stone
as small as a world and as large as alone.

For whatever we lose (like a you or a me)
it's always ourselves we find in the sea

Maple Talk

by Lilian Moore

Plant us.
Let our roots go
deeply down.
We'll hold the soil
when rain tugs
at the earth.

Plant us.
You will better know
how seasons come
and go.

Watch for
    our leaves unfurling
    in spring green,

    our leafy roofs of summer
    over pools of shade,

    our sunset red and gold
    igniting autumn's blaze.

When cold winds
leave us bare
we'll show you treetop nests
where songbirds hid
their young.

And when
in early spring
the sweet sap flows again,
have syrup for your pancakes!

Plant us.

Exploring Cultures

In what ways does one culture affect another?

Let's **Think** About **Reading!**

Objectives
● Listen to and interpret a speaker's message and ask questions.

Oral Vocabulary

Let's Talk About

Imagination

● Ask questions about why imagination is important.

● Describe the ways that Don Quixote tries to pursue his dream of becoming a knight.

● Express ways that artists of many types— musicians, painters, writers, for example— use their imaginations.

**READING STREET ONLINE
BIG QUESTION VIDEO
www.ReadingStreet.com**

You've learned
2 5 0
Amazing Words
so far this year!

Objectives
● Draw conclusions about texts and evaluate how well the author achieves his or her purpose. ● Understand how to use the questioning strategy to comprehend text.

Envision It! | Skill Strategy

Skill

Strategy

Comprehension Skill

🎯 Author's Purpose

- Authors have different reasons for writing. They may write to persuade, inform, entertain, or express thoughts and feelings. They may have more than one purpose for writing.

- Study what the author writes to help you figure out his or her purpose for writing.

- Adjust the way you read based on the author's purpose. If the purpose is to entertain, you may read faster. If the purpose is to inform, you may want to read more slowly.

- Use a graphic organizer like the one below to determine the author's purpose for writing "Gina's Adventures in Italy" on page 331.

Comprehension Strategy

🎯 Questioning

Active readers ask frequent questions before, during, and after reading. You can ask a literal question, which can be answered by looking at or recalling information directly from the text. Inferential or interpretive questions may lead you to do more thinking, discussion, or even research about what you are reading.

Gina's Adventures in Italy

My sister Gina has always been unique. She repeatedly showed this during the summer we spent in Italy.

In Florence, Gina was admiring a row of scooters parked on the sidewalk. In typical Gina fashion, she accidentally bumped into one, and they all fell like a row of dominoes. Later I suggested we go see Michelangelo's famous sculpture, *David*. "David who? Do we know this fellow?" Gina asked. As always, I gave up trying to explain and just took her there. She loved it.

Our next stop was Rome. I had always wanted to see the Trevi Fountain, the gorgeous old fountain that many tourists wade in on hot days. Gina had obviously heard about this because, as we walked toward the fountain, I saw her donning a bathing cap and swim goggles. "What are you doing?" I asked.

"I read that you can go in. I'm having a swim!" she said. I watched as she galloped to the fountain and jumped in. Other tourists watched the strange scene with amazement. "Man, I wish I had my flippers!" Gina said as she came up for air.

Strategy What questions can you ask before reading that will help you understand this story?

Skill How do you know that the purpose of this paragraph is to entertain you by describing some silly situations, rather than to inform you about scooters in Florence or the works of Michelangelo?

Skill Which details in this paragraph tell you that its purpose is to entertain you?

Your Turn!

 **Need a Review?** See the *Envision It! Handbook* for help with author's purpose and questioning.

Let's Think About...

▶ **Ready to Try It?** Use what you've learned about author's purpose as you read *Don Quixote and the Windmills*.

lance

misfortune

squire

quests

renewed

renowned

resound

Vocabulary Strategy for

⬤ **Prefixes *re-* and *mis-***

Word Structure When you come across a word you do not know, one way to figure out its meaning is to understand the meanings of its parts. An affix— a prefix or suffix—is a syllable added to a base word that changes the base word's meaning. The prefix *re-* means "again" or "back," as in *retell* and *recall*. The prefix *mis-* means "bad" or "wrong," as in *misbehave* or *misspell*.

Choose one of the Words to Know and follow these steps.

1. Identify the prefix.

2. Cover the prefix and look at the base word. Think about its meaning.

3. Uncover the prefix and identify its meaning.

4. Add the prefix's meaning to the meaning of the base word.

5. Check the context. Does this meaning make sense in this sentence?

Read "Knights of Old." Look for words that have prefixes. Use the prefixes to help you figure out the meanings of the words.

Words to Write Reread "Knights of Old." Imagine that you are watching two knights battle. Describe the scene. Use as many words from the Words to Know list as you can.

KNIGHTS OF OLD

Medieval knights were actually soldiers, not just the brave heroes of adventure stories. Stories tell us that knights went on quests. A knight might fight an evil beast or save a fair lady whom misfortune had placed in danger. In spite of great hardship, he always renewed his devotion and carried on. One of the most renowned of these legendary knights was Lancelot.

Real knights did go through a ceremony in which they promised to use their weapons for noble causes and high ideals. A boy who was to become a knight first served as a squire. At 15 or 16 he became the personal servant of a knight. He trained hard and rode with his master into battle. Knights wore heavy armor and used a lance as well as a sword to fight.

Knights sometimes fought in tournaments, which at first were much like battles. The air would resound with the clanging of swords. Over time, the contests changed. Pairs of knights would square off and try to unseat each other using blunt lances. Today, fights similar to these are sometimes re-created for educational and entertainment purposes.

Your Turn!

⏸ **Need a Review?** For help with prefixes, see *Words!*

Let's **Think** About...

▶ **Ready to Try It?** Read *Don Quixote and the Windmills* on pp. 334–345.

333

Question of the Week
How can stories from the past influence our imaginations?

Classic historical fiction is fiction that is written about a time in the past. As you read, look for clues that indicate this story takes place in another time period.

DON QUIXOTE AND THE WINDMILLS

retold and adapted by Eric A. Kimmel

illustrations by Leonard Everett Fisher

Let's
Think
About
Reading!

re you one who loves old stories? Does your heart
beat faster when you hear tales of knights in armor?
Of castles and dragons? Of ogres, sorcerers, and damsels in
distress?

Beware! Those tales can drive you mad. It happened to a certain Spanish gentleman who lived four centuries ago in the province of La Mancha.

Señor Quexada was his name. He had a tall, lean figure and wore a woeful expression on his face, as if his heart held some secret sorrow.

Indeed, it did. Señor Quexada longed to live in days gone by, when gallant knights battled for the honor of ladies fair. Books of their adventures filled his library. *Amadis of Gaul, The Mirror of Chivalry,* and *The Exploits of Esplandián* were but a few of the volumes that tumbled from his shelves.

Let's Think About...

Why does the author warn "Beware!"? What does he mean by tales that "can drive you mad"?

Questioning

337

Señor Quexada buried himself in these books. He read all day and far into the night, until his mind snapped. "Señor Quexada is no more," he announced to his astonished household. "I am the renowned knight and champion Don Quixote de la Mancha."

In the attic he found a rusty suit of armor, his grandfather's sword, a round leather shield, and an antique lance. His helmet was a foot soldier's steel cap that lacked a visor. Don Quixote made one out of paperboard and tied it on with ribbons. It would serve until he won himself a proper helmet on the field of battle.

Let's Think About...

What does knowing that Señor Quexada had all these items in his attic tell the reader? **Inferring**

A knight must have a noble steed. Don Quixote owned a nag as tall and bony as himself. He named the horse Rocinante, which means "Nag No More."

A knight must also have a squire, a faithful companion to share his quests. Don Quixote invited Sancho Panza, a short, fat farmer from the neighborhood, to accompany him. "Come with me, Sancho," Don Quixote said. "Within a week I will conquer an island and make you king of it."

"That will be no bad thing," Sancho replied. "If I were king of an island, my wife would be queen, and all my children princes and princesses." So Sancho agreed to come along. Although he was not as crackbrained as Don Quixote, he certainly saw no harm in seeing a bit of the world.

Finally, a knight must have a fair lady to whom he has pledged his loyalty and his life. "A knight without a lady is like a tree without leaves or fruit, a body without a soul," Don Quixote explained to Sancho. After considering all the damsels in the district, he chose a pretty farm girl—Aldonza Lorenzo—from the village of Toboso.

Don Quixote rechristened his lady as he had rechristened his horse. He called her "Dulcinea," meaning "Sweetness." The very word breathed music and enchantment.

"Dulcinea of Toboso . . . Dulcinea . . . Dulcinea . . ." The knight's heart overflowed with devotion as he whispered the sacred name.

Let's Think About...

What are the three requirements Don Quixote de la Mancha decides a knight must have? **Summarize**

One moonless night, while everyone in town lay asleep, Don Quixote and Sancho set forth. By dawn they were miles away. Don Quixote rode ahead, scanning the plain for ogres and sorcerers. Sancho followed on his little donkey, munching his breakfast of bread and cheese.

Don Quixote halted. "Fortune has favored our quest, good Sancho. Can you see what lies yonder? There stand the monstrous giants who have plagued this countryside long enough. I intend to strike them down and claim their wealth as our just reward."

Sancho squinted into the distance. "Giants, Master? What are you talking about? I see no giants."

"There they are. Straight ahead. Can't you see them? They have four arms, each one more than six miles long."

"Oh, Master, you are mistaken. Those aren't giants. They're windmills. What you call arms are really sails to catch the wind. The wind turns the sails and makes the millstones go round and round."

"It is plain you know nothing at all," Don Quixote replied. "I say those are giants, whether or not you recognize them as such. I intend to slay them. If you are frightened, you may hide yourself away and say your prayers while I challenge them to mortal combat."

Having said this, Don Quixote lowered his visor and put his spurs to Rocinante. He galloped across the plain to do battle with the windmills.

"Take to your heels, cowardly giants! Know that it is I, the noble Don Quixote, Knight of La Mancha, who am attacking you!"

"Master! They are only windmills!" Sancho called after him.

The wind picked up. The sails billowed. The great arms of the windmills began to turn.

Let's Think About...

What is Don Quixote trying to accomplish on his quest for ogres, sorcerers, and giants?
◉ Questioning

Let's Think About...

What can you do to understand what is happening when Don Quixote attacks the windmills?
Monitor and Clarify

Let's **Think** About...

What specific information does the author tell about Don Quixote's battle with the windmill? What does the image of Sancho Panza suggest about him?

🔍 **Questioning**

Don Quixote laughed with scorn. "Do you think to frighten me? Though you have more arms than the giant Briareus, I will still make an end of you!" He lifted his eyes toward heaven. "Beautiful damsel, Dulcinea of Toboso, in your honor do I claim the victory. If I am to die, let it be with your sweet name upon my lips."

Shouting defiance, he charged at the nearest windmill.

His lance pierced the canvas sail and became tangled in the ropes. Attempting to pull free, Don Quixote became caught as well. The windmill's rumbling arm dragged him out of the saddle, carrying him higher and higher.

Don Quixote drew his sword. "Release me, Giant, before you feel the sharp sting of my blade!" He slashed at the ropes. The windmill's arm swept past its zenith. It began hurtling toward the ground at an ever-increasing speed.

Sancho trotted up on his donkey. "Master, I will save you!" He grasped Don Quixote's ankle when the knight swept by. The faithful squire found himself pulled off his donkey and carried aloft with his master.

"Do not fear, good Sancho. I feel the giant weakening. I will soon make an end of this villain." Don Quixote hacked at the ropes with renewed vigor.

Sancho saw the cords begin to fray. "Master! Spare the poor giant a few moments of life. At least until he brings us closer to the ground."

"Giant, in the name of my lady, Dulcinea of Toboso, I command you to yield or die."

Don Quixote made one last thrust. The ropes parted. The sail blew away. Don Quixote, with Sancho clinging to his ankle, plunged straight down. Together they would have perished, knight and squire, dashed to a hundred pieces, had the sail of the following arm not caught them and sent them rolling across the plain.

Let's Think About...

What saved Don Quixote and Sancho from perishing at the windmill?
Important Ideas

343

They tumbled to a stop at Rocinante's feet. Sancho felt himself all over for broken bones. "Ay, Master!" he groaned. "Why didn't you listen to me? I tried to warn you. Could you not see that they were only windmills? Whatever possessed you to attack them?"

Don Quixote dusted off his battered armor. He tied the crushed visor back onto his helmet. "Be silent, Sancho. Your words reveal your ignorance. You know nothing about these matters. It is true that the giants now have the appearance of windmills. This is because they were bewitched by my enemy, the wizard Frestón. At the last moment, he transformed the giants into windmills to deprive me of the glorious victory that

Let's Think About...

How does Don Quixote retell the story of the windmills he has just done battle with? **Summarize**

was rightfully mine. Never fear, Sancho. We will meet him again. All the power of his magic arts will not save him when he feels the edge of my mighty sword."

"I hope so," said Sancho as he pushed Don Quixote back onto Rocinante. "Another tumble like this and we will all go home in pieces."

Don Quixote took the reins in hand. "Never fear, faithful Sancho. The road to victory is often paved with misfortune. A true knight never complains. Follow me, and I promise we will dip our arms up to the elbow in what common people call 'adventures.' Our names and the stories of our matchless deeds will resound through the ages."

"Ay, Master! When I hear you say those words, I can almost believe they are true. Perhaps I really will have my island someday."

"Of course you will, Sancho. Why would you ever doubt it?"

Sancho mounted his donkey and went trotting after Rocinante, vowing to follow Don Quixote wherever fortune's winds might carry him.

Let's **Think** About...

What is the main idea of the story of Don Quixote?
Important Ideas

Objectives
● Provide evidence from the text to demonstrate understanding.
● Read independently for a sustained period of time and paraphrase the reading.

Envision It! Retell

Think Critically

1. Have you ever wished your life had more adventure? If you were to imagine a new identity and new adventures, who would you be and where in the world would you go? **Text to World**

2. Reread the first paragraph. Examine the illustrations of Don Quixote attacking windmills. How can you tell that the author and illustrator had fun with their jobs? **Think Like an Author**

3. Why did the author retell this classic story? What was he trying to accomplish? Was he successful? Explain. **Author's Purpose**

4. Did the story give you all the information you wanted about Don Quixote? Did it leave unanswered questions? What might you ask the author about the story if you could? **Questioning**

5. **Look Back and Write** Don Quixote finally realizes that he has battled windmills, but he still believes they are really his mortal enemies. Read pages 344–345 for his explanation. Then predict what he and Sancho Panza will do next. Provide evidence from the text to support your answer.

TEST PRACTICE | Extended Response

ERIC A. KIMMEL AND LEONARD EVERETT FISHER

Eric A. Kimmel, who was born in Brooklyn, New York, now travels throughout the world visiting schools to tell stories and talk about his books. His first love is sharing stories from different countries and cultures. He says, "I don't have any set routine for writing other than I think about the story a lot before I actually sit down at my desk. Most of the work is done before I write the first word. The real work of creating a story comes in the thinking. The rest is just a matter of revision." Mr. Kimmel's interests range from bluegrass music to horses. He lives with his wife, a dog, a cat, and a tankful of tropical fish in Portland, Oregon.

Leonard Everett Fisher was just two years old when he added his own touches to a painting his father had left on an easel. Although he ruined the painting, young Leonard was given his own small studio in a hall closet, complete with worktable, crayons, paper, and pencils. Today he is a painter, illustrator, educator, and the author of more than two hundred books. His illustrations have won many awards. Mr. Fisher lives with his wife in Westport, Connecticut.

Other books: *The Adventures of Hershel of Ostropol*, retold by Eric A. Kimmel, and *William Tell*, illustrated by Leonard Everett Fisher

Use the Reading Log in the *Reader's and Writer's Notebook* to record your independent reading.

347

Let's Write It!

Key Features of a Parody

● imitates a familiar story's plot, style, and language

● changes some details of the original story for comic effect

● style of original writer may be imitated

READING STREET ONLINE
GRAMMAR JAMMER
www.ReadingStreet.com

Narrative

Parody

A **parody** retells a familiar story in a new and comical way. Readers should be able to recognize the story on which the parody is based. The student model on the next page is an example of a parody.

Writing Prompt Think about the characters and events in *Don Quixote and the Windmills*. Write a parody of the story.

Writer's Checklist

Remember, you should . . .

☑ retell the story in a new and funny way.

☑ keep some of the story's original details.

☑ use sensory details to create the setting.

☑ use some of the original author's style, tone, and language.

Parody of <u>Don Quixote and the Windmills</u>

Señor Quexada was a gentleman who lived in El Paso, Texas. Señor Quexada dreamed of living like the stories he read, where brave knights rescued <u>fair</u> ladies from danger.

To live his dream, Señor Quexada changed his name to Don Quixote, the name a <u>renowned</u> knight would have. Then he set off on a quest to win the admiration of the <u>pretty</u> girl who worked at the local farmer's market, Aldonza Lorenzo.

Arriving at the market, Don Quixote was <u>very</u> alarmed to see Aldonza, whom he dubbed "Dulcinea," using a stick to fight off dozens of slithering snakes.

"I'll save you, my fair lady!" Don Quixote bellowed, and he grabbed the stick from Dulcinea.

"What are you doing?" Dulcinea cried, confused.

Then Don Quixote looked down and realized he was holding a string kitchen mop <u>with a wooden handle</u>—there were no snakes, after all!

Genre
A **parody** imitates a familiar story or style for comic effect.

Writing Trait Focus/Ideas
Ideas are focused and sensory details grab the reader's attention.

Modifiers are used correctly.

Conventions

Modifiers

Remember A **modifier** is an adjective, adverb, or prepositional phrase that tells more about, or modifies, other words. To avoid confusion, place modifiers close to the words they modify. (*Every knight needs a lady, **fair** and **sweet**.*)

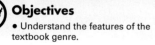
Genre
Textbook Entry

● A textbook entry is an excerpt from a book used in classrooms to teach facts, provide information, and offer explanations about a particular subject.

● The information in textbooks has been well researched for accuracy.

● Textbooks are generally written as expository or informational text, but may feature examples of other kinds of writing.

● Textbooks often use illustrations to organize information in a visual way.

● Read "Feudalism" and decide how this textbook entry differs from *Don Quixote and the Windmills.*

Feudalism

from *Scott Foresman Social Studies: The World*

During the Middle Ages, Europe had few strong central governments. People formed their own system to meet their need for protection and justice. **Feudalism** was a political, social, and economic system that began in the 800s. It provided the needed protection for people.

Feudalism resembled a social structure. At the top was the **monarch**, a king or queen who was the supreme ruler. The next level included lords who pledged their loyalty to the monarch and military support in the event of a war or conflict. In return, the monarch granted the lord an estate.

The lord owned the land. He also received a large percentage of the crops produced on the land and received all the income from the crops. He collected taxes, maintained order, enforced laws, and protected the serfs. **Serfs** were the people who lived on the land and farmed it.

Many lords had **knights**, or warriors trained and prepared to fight on horseback. Knights were supposed to have deep faith, be ready to die for the church, give to all, and stand against injustice.

serf

lord

Feudalism Declines

Serfs, who are sometimes called peasants, formed the base of the society in the Middle Ages. Unlike kings, lords, and knights, who were bound to be faithful to one another, serfs had no such loyalty to anyone. Serfs were not slaves, yet could not become knights. They could not be bought or sold separate from the land. Even so, serfs were tied to the land they worked and could not leave it without the lord's permission.

As time passed, some lords had many faithful knights, therefore building up much military power. These lords became independent of the monarch, who originally granted the land to them. The lords substituted payment in money for actual military support. By the 1400s, feudalism had begun to decline.

monarch

lords

knights

serfs, or peasants

In feudalism, peasants made up 90 percent of the population. Monarchs, lords, and the church had all the power and wealth.

church

castle or manor house

knight

Let's Think About...

What features of a textbook does this selection have, and how can these features help you understand the text? **Textbook**

Let's Think About...

Reading Across Texts You read about knights in the article "Feudalism." If Señor Quexada, or Don Quixote, were really a knight, do you think he would have been a good one?

Writing Across Texts Write your answer about Don Quixote.

Let's Learn It!

READING STREET ONLINE
ONLINE STUDENT EDITION
www.ReadingStreet.com

Vocabulary

Prefixes *re-* and *mis-*

Word Structure When you find a word you do not know, see if the word begins with a prefix. For example, the prefix *re-* usually adds the meaning "again" to a word, as in *rewrite,* or "back," as in *repay.* The prefix *mis-* means "bad" or "wrong," as in *mislead* or *mispronounce.*

Practice It! Find the word *rechristened* on page 339. What does the prefix *re-* mean? What does the base word *christened* mean? Use the meaning of the prefix and the meaning of the base word to determine the meaning of the word. Explain to a partner why the prefix is important to the meaning of the word.

Fluency

Expression

Use different tones of voice to show emotion as you read. Reading with expression can show the unfolding of a story and the way the characters speak and even think. Be guided by punctuation cues—pause at a comma, pause longer at a dash or semicolon or colon, and stop at a period or other end mark.

Practice It! With a partner, practice reading aloud page 341 of *Don Quixote and the Windmills.* Vary the tone, pitch, and volume of your voice to express the actions, emotions, and moods in the sentences. Place emphasis on important words.

Listening and Speaking

Make contributions and keep the discussion going for a book review.

Book Review

A book review is a summary of a book that tells its strengths and its weaknesses. A reviewer uses examples to make points about the book and may recommend it or not.

Practice It! With a small group, write and present a review about another classic book you have read. If you wish, compare it to *Don Quixote and the Windmills*. Discuss your reactions to your classic book and decide if you would recommend it to friends.

Tips

Listening . . .

- Listen to and interpret the speaker's message about the reviewed book.

- Determine the main idea and supporting details about the book.

Speaking . . .

- To make a comparison, use comparative and superlative adjectives (*good, better, best*).

- Identify personal opinions in your review.

- Quote from the book for examples.

Teamwork . . .

- Consider the opinions of group members who may disagree.

Oral Vocabulary

Let's Talk About

Ancient Greece

● Share what you know about the influence of ancient Greece on United States politics.

● Describe how the Olympics began and then how they were started again.

● Ask questions about daily life in ancient Greece.

READING STREET ONLINE
CONCEPT TALK VIDEO
www.ReadingStreet.com

355

Objectives

• Use text features and graphics to gain an overview and to locate information in the text. • Interpret information in maps, charts, illustrations, graphs, time lines, tables, and diagrams.

Envision It! | Skill Strategy

Skill

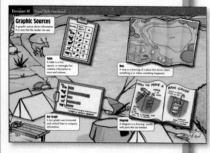

Strategy

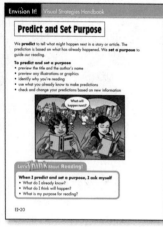

Comprehension Skill

Graphic Sources

• Graphic sources include maps, charts, diagrams, and other visual presentations of information.

• While reading, study the information in the graphic sources and ask: What does this information tell me about this topic? How does this graphic connect to what I'm reading in the text?

• A graphic organizer like the one below can help to organize ideas based on "GREECE: Land and Climate" on page 357. This chart suggests the kind of clothing that ancient Greeks might have worn year-round.

Greek Clothing		
Clothing type	**Indoor**	**Outdoor**
Regular clothing	tunic	tunic
Heavier clothing		cloak
On feet	shoeless	sandals
On head	hatless	veil or hat

Comprehension Strategy

Predict and Set Purpose

Active readers try to predict what they will learn when they read a nonfiction text. Previewing an article is a good way to predict what you will be reading and to establish a purpose for reading it. Establishing a purpose for reading something can help you comprehend it better.

GREECE: Land and Climate

Greece is a country in Europe. It is made up of a mainland and more than 2,000 islands that have a total area of 50,949 square miles. While Greece is known as a rocky place with many mountains, it also has some level ground.

The Land Because Greece touches the Mediterranean, Ionian, and Aegean Seas, it has a great deal of coastline. In fact, there is only one small area in all of Greece that is farther than fifty miles from the coast.

Several mountain ranges run across the country, forming many narrow valleys. Some of the tallest mountains in Greece are Mt. Smolikas (8,652 feet), Mt. Orvilos (7,287 feet), and Mt. Parnassus (8,061 feet).

The Climate Greece has a comfortable climate. Warm southern winds blow on Greece during the winter months. The average January temperature in Thessaloniki, in the north, is 43°F, while Athens, farther south, averages 50°F, and Iraklion, even farther south, averages 54°F. In the summer it is dry and hot all over Greece. The normal July temperature is 80°F.

THE LAND OF GREECE

= mountains
= lowlands

Strategy The title will help you predict what the selection is about. Read the title and then set a purpose for reading based on what you think the selection is about.

Skill Refer to the pie chart to choose the best answer.
a) Greece has more lowlands than mountains.
b) Most of Greece's land is mountainous.
c) Greeks like the mountains.

Skill Does the information in the pie chart relate to the information presented in this paragraph of the text? Why or why not?

Your Turn!

⏸ **Need a Review?** See the *Envision It! Handbook* for help with graphic sources and predicting and setting a purpose.

▶ **Ready to Try It?** Use what you've learned about graphic sources as you read *Ancient Greece*.

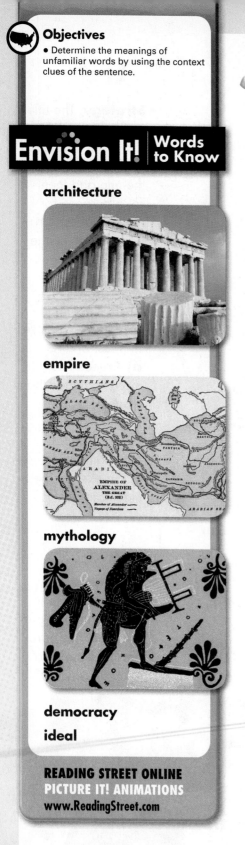

Envision It! | Words to Know

architecture

empire

mythology

democracy

ideal

Vocabulary Strategy for
Unfamiliar Words

Context Clues When you come across a word you do not recognize, sometimes you can use context clues—the words and sentences around an unfamiliar word—to help you figure out the meaning of the word.

Choose one of the Words to Know and follow these steps.

1. Read the words and sentences around the unfamiliar word. The author may give you a definition of the word or suggest a relationship that can help you predict the word's meaning.

2. If you find no clues, say to yourself what you think the sentence that contains the word means.

3. Predict a meaning for the unfamiliar word.

4. Try your predicted meaning in the sentence. Does it make sense?

5. If necessary, consult the glossary or a dictionary.

Read "Lessons from the Past." Use context clues to help you determine the meanings of unfamiliar words.

Words to Write Reread "Lessons from the Past." In which past era would you most like to have lived? Write a journal entry telling about this era and why you admire it. Use words from the Words to Know list in your journal entry.

LESSONS *from the* PAST

Human beings have always asked themselves: How should we live? What way of life is best? We can study the past to try to answer these questions. By asking still more questions (What kind of government has been best? When have people been happiest?), we can learn from the past. We can try to comprehend what would make up the ideal, or perfect, way of life.

Ancient civilizations have sent us messages. Their literature and histories communicate how people lived and felt. Every civilization has its mythology—a body of stories that explain the workings of the world and religion. These tales, filled with struggle, show us what ancestors believed to be the meaning of life. However, they express little happiness or contentment.

The empire was a common type of government in many past civiliza-tions. The strong rule of a single person might lead to astounding art, architecture, and invention. But most subjects were not free to enjoy these boons. Over thousands of years, humans have moved away from government with a single, all-powerful ruler toward democracy. We have come to believe that each person should be free and have a voice in how his or her community is governed.

Your Turn!

❚❚ Need a Review? For help with context clues, see *Words!*

▶ Ready to Try It? Read *Ancient Greece* on pp. 360–375.

How have ancient cultures influenced modern ones?

Expository text explains the nature of something. Look for facts about the nature of ancient Greece as you read.

ANCIENT GREECE

by Kim Covert

CHAPTER 1

THE ANCIENT OLYMPICS

Twenty runners get into position on the starting line. A trumpeter sounds the start of the race. Sand flies up as the runners race down the 210-yard (192-meter) track. The crowd cheers as the runners cross the finish line. The judges place a wreath of olive leaves on the winner's head.

Later, horse-drawn chariots line up on an oval track. At the sound of the trumpet, each driver urges his horses forward. In the first turn, a driver cuts in front of another chariot. The two chariots run into each other and tip over. The horses and drivers crash to the ground. Several more chariots fall in the pileup. Many horses and drivers are hurt. The drivers who missed the wreck bolt to the finish line. The owner of the winning chariot receives a wreath of olive leaves.

Footraces and chariot races were part of the Olympic games of ancient Greece. Wrestling, boxing, and the pentathlon were other events. The pentathlon included javelin, discus, long jump, running, and wrestling.

The first recorded Olympics were held in 776 B.C. The games took place in Olympia, a town in western Greece. They honored the Greek god Zeus. In Greek mythology, Zeus was the ruler of all the Olympian gods.

For one thousand years, the Olympic games were held every four years. Before each Olympics, the Greeks stopped all warfare. No wars could be fought just before, during, or just after the

CHARIOT RACE This is a scene on a vase from the 500s B.C. It shows a chariot race, one of the ancient Olympic events.

games. Wars were stopped so athletes and people coming to watch could travel to and from the games safely.

The modern Olympics are one of many traditions developed in Greece. Ancient Greece is often called the cradle of Western civilization. It was the birthplace of many modern ideas. Greek ideas are found in today's governments, art, architecture, and literature. They are also seen in science, drama, and athletics.

CHAPTER 2

EARLY GREEKS

The Minoans

The first civilization in Greece formed on the island of Crete. The Minoans lived from 2200 to 1450 B.C. They built a huge port on Crete and a large fleet of ships. Their ships allowed them to trade with people in other areas.

The Minoans also built palaces. They covered the palace walls with paintings. The paintings show peaceful, happy people. The Minoans built their largest palace at Knossos. The palace honored King Minos. In Greek mythology, Minos was a son of Zeus.

RUINS OF A MINOAN PALACE at Knossos can be seen today. Sir Arthur Evans discovered the ruins in the early 1900s.

The Mycenaeans

By about 1600 B.C., the Mycenaeans had settled in cities on the Greek mainland. A king ruled each city. Mycenaeans built huge walls around their palaces. Paintings, gold, and jewels decorated their palaces.

The Mycenaeans were great warriors. Around 1450 B.C., the Mycenaeans invaded Crete. They conquered the Minoans, who disappeared from history at this time.

According to legend, around 1220 B.C. the Mycenaeans conquered Troy. This city was on the northwestern coast of Asia Minor. Today this area includes the country of Turkey. Stories about the Trojan War have lasted to the present day.

Few Mycenaeans remained in Crete or Greece by 1200 B.C. Their palaces on the mainland were destroyed. Historians believe they were invaded by another civilization. Soon after, the Dorians took over Crete. They came from northern Greece.

The Trojan War

According to legend, the Mycenaeans attacked the city of Troy to rescue Helen. She was the wife of King Menelaus of Sparta. A Trojan prince had kidnapped her.

The tall walls around Troy kept the Greeks out for ten years. Finally, the Greeks built a huge, hollow wooden horse. They gave it to the Trojans as a gift. The Trojans dragged the horse into Troy. They did not know that Greek warriors were hiding inside. That night, the warriors climbed out and opened the city's gates. The Greek army then defeated the Trojans.

Around 750 B.C., two long poems about the Trojan War were written. *The Iliad* describes the long struggle between Greek and Trojan soldiers. *The Odyssey* tells the story of the hero Odysseus. He suffers

TROJAN HORSE

many difficulties while trying to get home after the Trojan War. Historians disagree about who wrote the poems. Many people believe the Greek poet Homer wrote them.

The Dark Age

Historians know little about Greece from 1100 to 800 B.C. During this time, Greece was a land of small farming villages. These villages had little contact with one another. Historians call this period the Dark Age.

Around 800 B.C., the Greeks appeared in history again. They built new colonies in parts of Europe and Africa. They traded with western Asia and learned to make iron objects. With iron, the Greeks could more easily make tools for farming and other tasks.

The Phoenicians lived across the Mediterranean Sea. The Greeks traded with the Phoenicians and learned their alphabet and system of writing. They also learned about Phoenician art and shipbuilding. This progress helped end the Dark Age.

CHAPTER 3

THE RISE OF GREECE

By the end of the Dark Age, the Greeks had built many villages. Many villages centered around a high hilltop, called an acropolis. The farms and villages surrounding each acropolis joined to form a city-state. Each city-state ruled itself and had its own customs. By 700 B.C., hundreds of independent city-states had formed. The two most powerful city-states were Athens and Sparta.

MACEDONIA

ASIA MINOR

Troy

Aegean Sea

Athens

Olympia

Marathon

PELOPONNESUS

Piraeus

Sparta

N
W   E
S

**ANCIENT GREECE
500 B.C.–336 B.C.**

Athens and Sparta

Athens was a city-state located slightly inland from the Aegean Sea. Athens built a port city called Piraeus. This port allowed Athens to launch its powerful navy and trade ships. Long walls joined Athens and Piraeus.

Athenians welcomed new ideas and customs. Athenians believed that a city-state should serve all of its citizens. They created a new type of government called a democracy. Each free male citizen in Athens could vote on laws and choose leaders. Women and slaves could not vote. An assembly made governmental decisions.

Sparta was located 150 miles (241 kilometers) from Athens. Mountains around Sparta protected the city-state. Spartans were different from Athenians. Spartans wanted no contact with outsiders. They were against change.

Sparta's government was also different from Athens's government. Two kings and a council of elders ruled Sparta. Only rich people served on the council.

Each Greek city-state formed an army. In Athens, men between ages seventeen and fifty-nine were required to serve in the military.

Sparta's society was based on the military. Every adult male was a full-time soldier. Soldiers were not allowed to work at other jobs.

PIRAEUS Ships sailed from Athens's port, Piraeus. Long walls connected Piraeus to Athens.

The Persian Wars

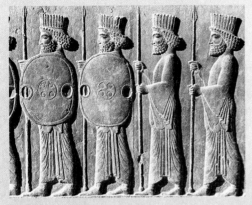

PERSIAN GUARDS c. 5th century B.C.

Persia was a large empire east of Greece. The Persians' territory covered much of Asia and the Middle East. King Darius I of Persia wanted to rule Greece. In 490 B.C., Darius's army landed at the village of Marathon, northwest of Athens. An army of 10,000 Athenians marched to Marathon to face 60,000 Persians. Athens defeated them in a surprise victory.

Ten years later, Darius's son Xerxes returned to Greece. He brought an army of 200,000 men. Athens and Sparta led a united army of all Greek city-states. After fighting for a year, the Greeks defeated Persia. Their victory in 479 B.C. kept the Persians from taking over Europe.

The Golden Age of Athens

After the Persian Wars, Athens entered its Golden Age. During this period, Athens reached its peak of power. The Greeks enjoyed great achievements in art, science, and government during this time.

Pericles was the leader of Athens from 461 to 429 B.C. He supported democracy. He also started a system of payment for government service. The earlier system did not pay government workers. Only rich people could afford to serve in the government. The new system of payment allowed anyone to earn a living by working at a government job.

Pericles planned to make Athens a model for other cities. He helped build a strong navy. Athens became wealthy through trade with other lands. Athens was also a model for art and culture. The government supported the work of architects, artists, and writers.

This sculpture of Pericles shows him wearing a helmet because he was a general.

CHAPTER 4

FALL FROM POWER

**Coin featuring
Alexander the Great**

After the Greeks beat Persia, many Greek city-states joined together. They agreed to protect each other. This alliance was known as the Delian League. Delian League members contributed ships or money to the league. They kept the money in the Delian League treasury.

People in Athens began taking the league's money. Athens's government made decisions for the league. Athens used the money to build temples and new colonies. Athens built a large and powerful empire throughout the Mediterranean.

The Peloponnesian War

For many years, Sparta and Athens were rivals. The two city-states did not trust each other. Athens wanted to spread democracy, freedom, and self-rule.

Sparta was afraid that Athens's power would reach too far. Other Greek city-states also were unhappy with Athens. They were upset that Athens was taking money from the Delian League.

In 431 B.C., Sparta declared war on Athens. For twenty-seven years, Athens and Sparta and their allies fought in the Peloponnesian War. Athens finally surrendered in 404 B.C.

Alexander the Great

In 359 B.C., Philip II became the king of Macedonia. Philip wanted to rule the Persian Empire. He asked the Greeks to help him defeat Persia. In return, he would let them govern themselves. In 336 B.C., before Philip could organize an attack on Persia, he was killed. His son, Alexander, became king at age twenty. A strong military leader, he became known as Alexander the Great.

ALEXANDER THE GREAT This statue was created between the 1st and 2nd centuries B.C.

In 334 B.C., Alexander led an army of Macedonians and Greeks. They attacked Persia. In three years, he defeated the Persian king.

Alexander's army later conquered Egypt, western Persia, and western India. He also conquered the countries now known as Afghanistan and Pakistan. Alexander founded many military colonies in the lands he conquered. These settlements helped provide supplies to his armies.

After his death in 323 B.C., Alexander's generals fought to control his empire. They divided Greece into three kingdoms.

The Hellenistic Age

The Greek language was spoken in Alexander's colonies. The colonists copied Greek architecture, law, and art. They studied Greek science and philosophy. The most famous city Alexander founded was Alexandria, Egypt. It became the world's most important center of trade and learning.

After Alexander's death, the power of the Greek city-states faded. But the rulers of Greek kingdoms promoted Greek culture. Elements of Greek culture spread from southern present-day France to what is now northern Afghanistan. This period is known as the Hellenistic Age.

The Roman Empire

Around 275 B.C., the Romans defeated the Hellenistic King Pyrrhus in Italy. Rome gradually took over other kingdoms. It conquered Sicily in 241 B.C. and Spain in 201 B.C. Rome began conquering other areas. By 31 B.C., Rome defeated the last Greek kingdom. It was the end of the Hellenistic Age.

THIS STATUE OF THE GODDESS ATHENA is an example of art from the Hellenistic Age.

After conquering the Greeks, the Roman Empire grew. The Romans adopted the best ideas of the people they conquered. The Romans used Greek styles in literature and architecture. They modeled many public buildings after Greek temples. The Romans based their government on some of Greece's democratic ideas. Rome fell in the A.D. 400s. The

GREEK INFLUENCE Part of Roman Emperor Hadrian's villa uses Greek columns.

Visigoths, a tribe from Germany in northern Europe, defeated the last Roman emperor. Rome's influence faded.

Europeans once again took interest in Greek culture in the A.D. 1400s and 1500s. This period was known as the Renaissance. Classical ideas of ancient Greece influenced artists, writers, and architects. For three hundred years after the Renaissance, Europe developed colonies around the world. The Europeans spread these classical ideas to the colonies. Greek culture continued to thrive.

CHAPTER 5

LASTING ACHIEVEMENTS

The ancient Greeks made lasting contributions to art, architecture, science, and medicine. They also developed drama, literature, and philosophy. Their ideas still influence the modern world.

Architecture and Art

Greek water jug from 530 B.C. showing women filling vases at a fountain

The Greeks built many structures that still stand today. Temples are the most famous of their buildings. Most of the temples have a similar design. The buildings are rectangular with columns holding up the sloping roof. Modern architects base many of their designs on Greek styles.

The most famous example of Greek architecture is the Parthenon. Completed in 432 B.C., this temple honored the goddess Athena. She was the goddess of war and wisdom.

The Greeks created their own forms of sculpture, pottery, and painting. They were the first to sculpt human statues in a natural style. Greek statues usually showed perfect bodies. Earlier statues had looked stiff and unnatural. Athenians made the most valued pottery of the ancient Western world. They painted their pots with pictures of gods, heroes, and ordinary people. Greek artists decorated buildings with beautiful paintings called frescoes. These wall paintings on plaster showed scenes from Greek myths.

Sculptures of women support the roof on this porch of the Erechtheum, a temple on the Acropolis in Athens.

Science and Medicine

Ancient Greeks were among the first to use logic to explain the world around them. They wanted to discover the reasons why things worked.

Anaxagoras was an early Greek astronomer. He learned that the moon did not make its own light. Instead, Anaxagoras believed that the moon's light was a reflection from the sun.

Archimedes was an inventor and mathematician. He discovered the principle of a lever. Archimedes created a complicated set of levers and pulleys. He used them to lift a large ship from water to land by himself.

Hippocrates was a Greek doctor. He is often called the father of medicine. He developed the Hippocratic oath, a promise to heal the sick. Today, many medical students take this oath when they become doctors.

ARCHIMEDES

PARTHENON
The most famous example
of Greek architecture

Menander with theatrical masks

Drama and Literature

The ancient Greeks created drama. The earliest Greek plays were religious ceremonies. A chorus sang and acted out stories about the gods. Later, dramas told legends of Greek heroes. Many plays were about gods. Other plays told about the Persian Wars.

The Greeks were the Western world's first writers of history. Around 450 B.C., Herodotus explored the Mediterranean region. He wrote long reports of wars, geography, customs, and legends. Herodotus is often called the father of history.

Aesop is one of the most famous Greek writers. Historians believe Aesop was a Greek slave who had been freed. In the 500s B.C., Aesop wrote hundreds of fables. These short stories about animals taught a lesson. Aesop's fables include "The Tortoise and the Hare" and "The Fox and the Grapes." Many of Aesop's fables are still told today.

Philosophy

Early Greek philosophers studied life, death, and other mysteries of the natural world. Socrates was the most famous philosopher from Athens. He was one of the first to study ethics. He taught students by asking questions, rather than giving them answers. This teaching method is now known as the Socratic method.

Plato was a student of Socrates. In his book *The Republic*, Plato describes his ideas for an ideal government. He also founded a school called the Academy.

Plato's most famous student was Aristotle. Aristotle became a great philosopher and scientist. He developed a scientific system to help understand the world. The ideas of Socrates, Plato, and Aristotle are still discussed today.

Plato and Aristotle, from exterior of belltower of Santa Maria del Flore in Florence

Daily Life in Ancient Greece

Most people in ancient Greece were farmers. Their farms were usually small and run by one family. Often, slaves helped them.

Men and women lived in separate parts of the house. The women had a special room. There, they played with their children, spun thread, and sewed. The men often held parties in the men's area. Slaves brought them food and drink. At the center of each home was an outdoor courtyard. There, children played games.

Each day people filled the market-place, or *agora*. People came to shop, meet friends, and do business. Farmers brought their goods to market on donkeys. Pottery, cloth, and jewelry were also sold there.

When they became adults, children brought their toys to the temple. Girls did this before they married. Boys did this around age fourteen. Children offered their toys to the Greek gods Apollo and Artemis and then took part in a ceremony that welcomed them to adult life.

SOCRATES

CHAPTER 6

GREEK INFLUENCE TODAY

Greece has influenced many modern governments. Democracy is now a common form of government. Ancient Greeks developed political speeches, debates, and voting. Trial by jury is another system created by the Greeks. A jury is a group of people who listens to and decides a court case.

The ancient Greeks believed in the rights of the male citizen. Aristotle wrote that the pursuit of happiness was important. When the Thirteen Colonies in North America separated from Great Britain, the colonists created the Declaration of Independence. This document borrowed Aristotle's idea. It states that people have the right to life, liberty, and the pursuit of happiness.

Often, government buildings also have Greek influence. Court buildings, capitols, and presidential homes have all used Greek architecture.

Every day, people take part in activities invented by the ancient Greeks. They read novels, attend plays, or exercise in a public gym. Athletes wrestle, box, and compete in track-and-field events. Philosophers explore the meaning of life. Scientists search for logical answers to problems. Ideas from ancient Greece continue to influence modern life.

Greek architecture influenced the U. S. Supreme Court building in Washington, D. C.

EQUAL JUSTICE UNDER LAW

Envision It! Retell

Think Critically

1. How was daily life in ancient Greece like your life today? How was it different? Text to Self

2. Much of *Ancient Greece* tells about the different periods and conquests of ancient Greece or Greek leaders. But Chapter 5 discusses the arts and other lasting achievements. Why do you think the author thought it was important to include this information? Think Like an Author

3. How do the photos, drawings, and map add to the depth of your understanding of the text? Graphic Sources

4. How do the chapter titles and headings help you predict what you will read next and set a purpose for your reading? Predict and Set Purpose

5. **Look Back and Write** What does the term "the Golden Age of Athens" mean? When was the Golden Age of Athens? Look back at page 367 and write a summary of this particular period in Greek history. Provide evidence to support your answer.

TEST PRACTICE Extended Response

Meet the Author

KIM COVERT

Kim Covert has written many nonfiction books, but she says that *Ancient Greece* is her favorite. She did extensive research because "When writing about events that occurred thousands of years ago, it's especially important to use accurate sources. I based my research on books written by historians and archaeologists who specialize in ancient Greece." As a child, Ms. Covert lived in many different places. "My father was a pilot in the Air Force, and our family moved frequently when I was growing up. We lived in Japan, England, Germany, and many states in the U.S." After college, Ms. Covert taught at international schools in Japan and Hong Kong and continued to travel to many other places, including China, Russia, Europe, Australia, and New Zealand. She visited Greece several years ago and says, "Greece is one of the countries I'd most like to visit again." She lives in Minnesota with her two teenage children.

Other books about ancient Greece:
Ancient Greece and
Ancient Greek Children

Use the Reading Log in the *Reader's and Writer's Notebook* to record your independent reading.

Key Features of Notes

- include most important facts and dates

- paraphrase, or restate, information in one's own words

- cite, or name, original source(s)

READING STREET ONLINE
GRAMMAR JAMMER
www.ReadingStreet.com

Notes

Notes are taken from a source to record main topics and important details in the writer's own words. The student model on the next page is an example of notes.

Writing Prompt Think about one interesting section of *Ancient Greece*. Now take notes on that section, including main topics and important details.

Writer's Checklist

Remember, you should . . .

✓ cite the author and title of work.

✓ include only the most important ideas and details in your notes.

✓ tell information in your own words.

✓ use quotation marks around any text you copy verbatim, and attribute it to the original source.

Ancient Greece by Kim Covert

Chapter 5, "Lasting Achievements"

The ancient Greeks still influence our world.

1. Architecture and Art

Many structures still exist from ancient Greece today.

Temples—rectangular buildings with columns (Parthenon)

Greeks created a style of sculpture **and** paintings.

2. Science and Medicine

Famous thinkers include:

Anaxagoras—moon's light reflected from sun

Archimedes—lever **and** pulleys

Hippocrates—"father of medicine"

3. Drama and Literature

Early—religious ceremonies; later—heroes, gods, wars

Aesop—fables; Herodotus—"father of history"

4. Philosophy

Study of life, death, **and** other mysteries of world

Socrates—famous philosopher from Athens

Genre Notes include main topics and details from a text.

Writing Trait Focus/Ideas The most important ideas are paraphrased.

Conjunctions are used correctly.

Conventions

Conjunctions

Remember A **conjunction** is a word such as *and, but, or, because, if, then,* and *although* used to join words, phrases, or sentences.

Social Studies in Reading

Genre
Expository Text

- Expository text is a form of nonfiction.

- Expository text tells and explains facts and information about real people, events, and things.

- Expository texts often contain graphics such as photographs, charts, and other images that tell more about the topic.

- Read "Relighting the Flame." As you read about how the modern Olympics came to be, think about what you already know about the Olympic games.

RELIGHTING THE FLAME

BY JESSE ROGERS

THE ANCIENT GAMES

The first Olympic games were held in 776 B.C. on the plains of Olympia, Greece. Athletes from all over the ancient Greek world came to compete in a stadium that could hold 40,000 spectators. The games were dedicated to Greece's Olympian gods. The winners became instant celebrities and were portrayed on pottery and in sculptures.

The games continued until the Romans invaded and occupied Greece. The new rulers refused to honor this Greek tradition, and in A.D. 393, the games were disbanded.

Greek athletes became famous after winning an event in the ancient Olympics. Greek athletes are still strong competitors in the modern Olympics.

THE MODERN GAMES

For some 1,500 years, there were no Olympic games. They resumed in 1896, when Baron Pierre de Coubertin of France organized the first modern Olympics. After that, the official Olympic games were held in a different nation every four years.

To honor the original games, the 1896 Olympics were held in Greece's capital city of Athens. A white marble stadium was built with room for 60,000 spectators. Most of the athletes came from Germany, France, and Greece. For ten days, they competed in sports such as cycling, fencing, gymnastics, wrestling, swimming, weightlifting, and tennis. Today, Olympic athletes are sponsored by the nations they represent, but in the 1896 games most competitors had to pay their own way. Only men were allowed to compete, because Baron de Coubertin felt that allowing women would be "impractical, uninteresting, unaesthetic, and incorrect."

The games began on April 6 with 60,000 spectators filling the new stadium. The prize for first place was a silver medal and a crown of olive branches, while second-place winners received a bronze medal and a laurel crown.

Let's **Think** About...

How does the carving on page 380 show that the Olympic games were important in ancient times?
Expository Text

The Olympic rings are the symbol of the Olympic games and appear on the Olympic flag. The Olympic flag was designed by Baron Pierre de Coubertin and was first flown in 1920.

THE FIRST MARATHON

The 1896 games marked the first time the marathon event was run. This long-distance footrace honored the Greek soldier Philippides. In 490 B.C., tradition says, he ran 40 kilometers, about 25 miles, to Athens to deliver the triumphant news that Greece had defeated the Persian army. Shortly after his arrival in Athens, it was said, Philippides fell to the ground and died of exhaustion. The Olympic contestants had to run the same exhausting distance that Philippides did.

Spyridon Louis, a Greek shepherd, was one of the contestants in this first marathon. Because he was an unknown and started at such a slow pace, no one took much notice of him. It was unseasonably hot that April, and the other racers soon began to wither in the heat. In the last ten kilometers, many runners fell back, but Louis surged ahead.

Spyridon Louis

When he ran into the stadium at the finish, the cheers were deafening. It was as if Philippides himself had returned. Louis won the race in a time of 2 hours, 58 minutes, and 50 seconds. From then on, he would always be a champion, part of Greek Olympic history.

Let's **Think** About...

How do the photos and captions help you understand the excitement that Olympic athletes feel? **Expository Text**

Athletes from all over the world compete in the Olympics to jump higher, swim faster, run faster, and be stronger.

"Faster, Higher, Stronger"

In 1900, the second Olympic games were held in Paris, France. Some 1,000 athletes from twenty-four countries competed. For the first time, women athletes were allowed, but only eleven and only in lawn tennis and golf. Gradually, over the years, women would participate in more and more Olympic events, but not without a struggle.

In 1904, the games moved to the U.S. city of St. Louis, Missouri. Attendance was disappointing. St. Louis was difficult to get to, and a war between Russia and Japan had made some countries uneasy about attending. Only 650 athletes representing twelve countries competed in the 1904 Olympics.

In 1924, the Winter Olympics were established. These games are also held every four years, and they feature winter sports such as skiing, bobsledding, and skating.

Today the Olympics are more popular than ever. The advent of television makes the Olympics available the world over. Now millions of people can watch the best athletes in the world compete to be faster, higher, and stronger.

Olympic Summer Games

Athens	1896
Paris	1900
St. Louis	1904
London	1908
Stockholm	1912
Antwerp	1920
Paris	1924
Amsterdam	1928
Los Angeles	1932
Berlin	1936
London	1948
Helsinki	1952
Melbourne	1956
Rome	1960
Tokyo	1964
Mexico City	1968
Munich	1972
Montreal	1976
Moscow	1980
Los Angeles	1984
Seoul	1988
Barcelona	1992
Atlanta	1996
Sydney	2000
Athens	2004
Beijing	2008
London	2012

The Olympic motto is *Citius, Altius, Fortius,* which is Latin for "Faster, Higher, Stronger."

Let's Think About...

Reading Across Texts What are the most important differences between the ancient and modern Olympic games? Use what you read in *Ancient Greece* and this selection to answer.

Writing Across Texts Which Olympic games would you have preferred to attend—ancient or modern? Why? Use information from *Ancient Greece* and this selection as you write.

Vocabulary

Unfamiliar Words

Context Clues Remember that nearby words and phrases, or context, can help you learn the meaning of an unfamiliar word. If you don't find good clues, predict a meaning for the unfamiliar word. Then try the meaning to see if it makes sense in the sentence. Finally, a dictionary or glossary can tell you more information.

Practice It! Find how the word *acropolis* is defined for you on page 365 in Chapter 3 of *Ancient Greece.* Look for other unfamiliar words in the selection and see if you can discover their meanings from their contexts. If an unfamiliar word is highlighted, you will find it in the glossary at the back of this book.

Fluency

Rate

Remember that when you read aloud, you should read at a speed that fits the text. Reading more quickly can add energy and excitement; reading more slowly can add emphasis. The idea is to read at a rate that imitates the flow of everyday speech.

Practice It! With a partner, practice reading aloud page 366 of *Ancient Greece.* Focus on reading at an appropriate rate and adding either emphasis or energy to what you are reading. Take turns reading, and offer each other feedback.

Listening and Speaking

Get Ready For High School

When you participate in a listening and speaking activity, always take turns and listen carefully.

Analyzing Art

When you analyze art, you examine such things as when and where the art object was made, who the artist was, the purpose (functional or not), materials used, colors, and other details that make this object different from others you have seen.

Practice It! In a small group, choose one ancient Greek art object such as a water jug, or urn, like the one pictured below. Individually research that style of art on the Internet or in an encyclopedia. Write about what you find. Then share written reports in your group.

Tips

Listening . . .

- Face each speaker.
- Listen attentively and take notes.
- Think of art you have seen as you listen.

Speaking . . .

- Take turns speaking.
- Stay on the topic you chose to speak about.

Teamwork . . .

- Do your share of the research and writing.
- Acknowledge others' ideas and the research and writing they have done.

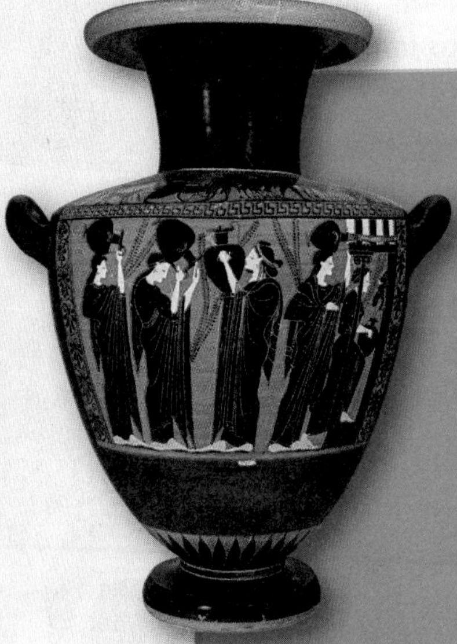

Objectives
• Listen to and interpret a speaker's
message and ask questions.

Oral Vocabulary

Let's Talk About

Customs

- Describe customs you know about from another culture.

- Ask questions about how different customs can make the world more interesting.

- Express opinions about what the term "melting pot" means in the United States.

READING STREET ONLINE
CONCEPT TALK VIDEO
www.ReadingStreet.com

387

Objectives

● Analyze how the organization of a text, such as compare-and-contrast, affects the way ideas are related.

Comprehension Skill

Compare and Contrast

When you compare and contrast, you tell how two or more things are alike or different.

- Clue words such as *like, similarly,* and *both* can show comparison. Clue words such as *unlike, on the other hand,* and *however* can indicate contrast.

- Sometimes writers do not use clue words.

- Use a graphic organizer like the one below to compare and contrast Mrs. Wallen and Mrs. Casa in "My Fifth-Grade Teachers."

Comprehension Strategy

Inferring

Authors do not always tell readers everything about the characters, setting, and events in a story. For better understanding, readers need to infer, or figure out on their own, what is not stated directly. Use details from the text and from your own experiences to make inferences about the ideas, themes, and lessons of a written work as you read.

388

My Fifth-Grade Teachers

When I was in fifth grade, our school combined two classes together in one extra-large classroom. We were co-taught by two teachers, Mrs. Wallen and Mrs. Casa.

Mrs. Wallen was very strict. She had clear procedures for everything, from how you stood in line to how you raised your hand. She tended to be serious and curt. But she expected a lot from us and made sure we learned everything we were supposed to learn. Mrs. Wallen's appearance was flawless. Her blond hair was always perfectly done. Her clothes were always carefully pressed, and her posture was always perfect. She was like a well-dressed statue.

Mrs. Casa, on the other hand, was a lot softer. She had a wonderful sense of humor and enjoyed a little playful banter during lessons. However, if we ever got out of control or lost our focus, she would very strongly bring us back to attention. She was inconsistent at enforcing the rules but always insisted that we work hard, pay attention, and learn. Well-dressed and pretty, she was a welcome sight each morning.

Despite their differences, Mrs. Casa and Mrs. Wallen worked well together. They were both great teachers, and I learned a lot that year.

Skill When the author says Mrs. Wallen is *like a well-dressed statue,* in what way are a statue and Mrs. Wallen alike?
a) They both have perfect posture.
b) They both are made of stone.
c) They both are very strict.

Skill In what ways are the two teachers alike and different? Look back at the descriptions of each. Do you see any clue words that might help you compare and contrast them?

Strategy With which teacher would you expect the students to have more fun? What details from the story tell you? How does your own experience support your inference?

Your Turn!

❙❙ Need a Review? See the *Envision It! Handbook* for help with comparing and contrasting and inferring.

▶ Ready to Try It? Use what you've learned about comparing and contrasting as you read *The All-American Slurp.*

relish

revolting

unison

disgraced

progress

promoted

retreat

Vocabulary Strategy for

⟳ Multiple-Meaning Words

Context Clues Some words have more than one meaning. You can use words and sentences near a multiple-meaning word to figure out which meaning the author is using.

Choose one of the Words to Know and follow these steps.

1. Read the sentences near the word in question.

2. Think about the different meanings the word may have. For example, *drum* can be a musical instrument, a metal container, or the act of tapping one's fingers.

3. Decide which meaning makes sense in this sentence: He began to *drum* his fingers on the desk.

4. Reread the sentence, replacing the word with the meaning you chose.

5. If this meaning seems right, read on. If not, try another meaning.

Read "A Party for Mom." Use context clues and your knowledge to decide which meaning a multiple-meaning word has in the article. For example, does *relish* mean "a liking for something" or "a food eaten with other foods to add flavor"?

Words to Write Reread "A Party for Mom." Describe a family party or special event that you have enjoyed. Use words from the Words to Know list.

A Party for Mom

When Mom was promoted at work, our family had a party to celebrate. We were all proud of her progress in the company. She had been employed at Merritt Controls for only three years, and she had been made a manager.

I hoped Dad wasn't planning to serve any revolting foods, such as avocado or broccoli, at the party. Of all the foods I dislike, those are my least favorite. To my relief, my parents put me in charge of the chips, dip, and relish trays. My orders were to be sure that there were plenty of eye-popping green, red, and orange colors on those trays. The pickles were green. I added green food coloring to pep them up! Maraschino cherries were red, and cheese curls added an orange-yellow color. When I saw my parents' shock, I knew I had disgraced myself.

"That's not what we meant!" they sputtered in unison. They had wanted peppers, cherry tomatoes, and carrots. Then the doorbell rang. It was too late to change the trays. I beat a retreat to my room then and there. Later, I found out that because the trays were so interesting and different, they turned out to be a big hit with all the guests.

Your Turn!

⏸ Need a Review? For help using context clues with multiple-meaning words, see *Words!*

▶ **Ready to Try It?** Read *The All-American Slurp* on pp. 392–407.

The All★American Slurp

by Lensey Namioka
illustrated by Stephane Jorisch

Genre

Realistic fiction stories are made-up stories about things that could really happen. As you read, notice the moments that seem realistic.

Question of the Week
How can we understand and appreciate our cultural differences?

The first time our family was invited out to dinner in America, we disgraced ourselves while eating celery. We had emigrated to this country from China, and during our early days here we had a hard time with American table manners.

In China we never ate celery raw, or any other kind of vegetable raw. We always had to disinfect the vegetables in boiling water first. When we were presented with our first relish tray, the raw celery caught us unprepared.

We had been invited to dinner by our neighbors, the Gleasons. After arriving at the house, we shook hands with our hosts and packed ourselves into a sofa. As our family of four sat stiffly in a row, my younger brother and I stole glances at our parents for a clue as to what to do next.

Mrs. Gleason offered the relish tray to Mother. The tray looked pretty, with its tiny red radishes, curly sticks of carrots, and long, slender stalks of pale green celery. "Do try some of the celery, Mrs. Lin," she said. "It's from a local farmer, and it's sweet."

Mother picked up one of the green stalks, and Father followed suit. Then I picked up a stalk, and my brother did too. So there we sat, each with a stalk of celery in our right hand.

Mrs. Gleason kept smiling. "Would you like to try some of the dip, Mrs. Lin? It's my own recipe: sour cream and onion flakes, with a dash of Tabasco® sauce."

Most Chinese don't care for dairy products, and in those days I wasn't even ready to drink fresh milk. Sour cream sounded perfectly revolting. Our family shook our heads in unison.

Mrs. Gleason went off with the relish tray to the other guests, and we carefully watched to see what they did. Everyone seemed to eat the raw vegetables quite happily.

Mother took a bite of her celery. *Crunch*. "It's not bad!" she whispered.

Father took a bite of his celery. *Crunch*. "Yes, it *is* good," he said, looking surprised.

I took a bite, and then my brother. *Crunch, crunch*. It was more than good; it was delicious. Raw celery has a slight sparkle, a zingy taste that you don't get in cooked celery. When Mrs. Gleason came around with the relish tray, we each took another stalk of celery, except my brother. He took two.

There was only one problem: long strings ran through the length of the stalk, and they got caught in my teeth. When I help my mother in the kitchen, I always pull the strings out before slicing celery.

I pulled the strings out of my stalk. *Z-z-zip, z-z-zip.* My brother followed suit. *Z-z-zip, z-z-zip.* To my left, my parents were taking care of their own stalks. *Z-z-zip, z-z-zip, z-z-zip.*

Suddenly I realized that there was dead silence except for our zipping. Looking up, I saw that the eyes of everyone in the room were on our family. Mr. and Mrs. Gleason, their daughter Meg, who was my friend, and their neighbors, the Badels—they were all staring at us as we busily pulled the strings of our celery.

That wasn't the end of it. Mrs. Gleason announced that dinner was served and invited us to the dining table. It was lavishly covered with platters of food, but we couldn't see any chairs around the table. So we helpfully carried over some dining chairs and sat down. All the other guests just stood there.

Mrs. Gleason bent down and whispered to us, "This is a buffet dinner. You help yourselves to some food and eat it in the living room."

Our family beat a retreat back to the sofa as if chased by enemy soldiers. For the rest of the evening, too mortified to go back to the dining table, I nursed a bit of potato salad on my plate.

Next day, Meg and I got on the school bus together. I wasn't sure how she would feel about me after the spectacle our family made at the party. But she was just the same as usual, and the only reference she made to the party was, "Hope you and your folks got enough to eat last night. You certainly didn't take very much. Mom never tries to figure out how much food to prepare. She just puts everything on the table and hopes for the best."

I began to relax. The Gleasons' dinner party wasn't so different from a Chinese meal after all. My mother also puts everything on the table and hopes for the best.

Meg was the first friend I had made after we came to America. I eventually got acquainted with a few other kids in school, but Meg was still the only real friend I had.

My brother didn't have any problems making friends. He spent all his time with some boys who were teaching him baseball, and in no time he could speak English much faster than I could—not better, but faster.

I worried more about making mistakes, and I spoke carefully, making sure I could say everything right before opening my mouth. At least I had a better accent than my parents, who never really got rid of their Chinese accent, even years later. My parents had both studied English in school before coming to America, but what they had studied was mostly written English, not spoken.

Father's approach to English was a scientific one. Since Chinese verbs have no tense, he was fascinated by the way English verbs changed form according to whether they were in the present, past imperfect, perfect, pluperfect, future, or future perfect tense. He was always making diagrams of verbs and their inflections, and he looked for opportunities to show off his mastery of the pluperfect and future perfect tenses, his two favorites. "I shall have finished my project by Monday," he would say smugly.

Mother's approach was to memorize lists of polite phrases that would cover all possible social situations. She was constantly muttering things like "I'm fine, thank you. And you?" Once she accidentally stepped on someone's foot, and hurriedly blurted, "Oh, that's quite all right!" Embarrassed by her slip, she resolved to do better next time. So when someone stepped on *her* foot, she cried, "You're welcome!"

In our own different ways, we made progress in learning English. But I had another worry, and that was my appearance. My brother didn't have to worry, since Mother bought him blue jeans for school, and he dressed like all the other boys. But she insisted that girls had to wear skirts. By the time she saw that Meg and the other girls were wearing jeans, it was too late. My school clothes were bought already, and we didn't have money left to buy new outfits for me. We had too many other things to buy first, like furniture, pots, and pans.

The first time I visited Meg's house, she took me upstairs to her room, and I wound up trying on her clothes. We were pretty much the same size, since Meg was shorter and thinner than average. Maybe that's how we became friends in the first place. Wearing Meg's jeans and T-shirt, I looked at myself in the mirror. I could almost pass for an American—from the back, anyway. At least the kids in school wouldn't stop and stare at me in the hallways, which was what they did when they saw me in my white blouse and navy blue skirt that went a couple of inches below the knees.

When Meg came to my house, I invited her to try on my Chinese dresses, the ones with a high collar and slits up the sides. Meg's eyes were bright as she looked at herself in the mirror. She struck several sultry poses, and we nearly fell over laughing.

The dinner party at the Gleasons' didn't stop my growing friendship with Meg. Things were getting better for me in other ways too. Mother finally bought me some jeans at the end of the month, when Father got his paycheck. She wasn't in any hurry about buying them at first, until I worked on her. This is what I did. Since we didn't have a car in those days, I often ran down to the neighborhood store to pick up things for her. The groceries cost less at a big supermarket, but the closest one was many blocks away. One day, when she ran out of flour, I offered to borrow a bike from our neighbor's son and buy a ten-pound bag of flour at the big supermarket. I mounted the boy's bike and waved to Mother. "I'll be back in five minutes!"

Before I started pedaling, I heard her voice behind me. "You can't go out in public like that! People can see all the way up to your thighs!"

"I'm sorry," I said innocently. "I thought you were in a hurry to get the flour." For dinner we were going to have pot-stickers (fried Chinese dumplings), and we needed a lot of flour.

"Couldn't you borrow a girl's bicycle?" complained Mother. "That way your skirt won't be pushed up."

"There aren't too many of those around," I said. "Almost all the

girls wear jeans while riding a bike, so they don't see any point buying a girl's bike."

We didn't eat pot-stickers that evening, and Mother was thoughtful. Next day we took the bus downtown and she bought me a pair of jeans. In the same week, my brother made the baseball team of his junior high school, Father started taking driving lessons, and Mother discovered rummage sales. We soon got all the furniture we needed, plus a dart board and a 1,000-piece jigsaw puzzle (fourteen hours later, we discovered that it was a 999-piece jigsaw puzzle). There was hope that the Lins might become a normal American family after all.

Then came our dinner at the Lakeview restaurant.

The Lakeview was an expensive restaurant, one of those places where a headwaiter dressed in tails conducted you to your seat, and the only light came from candles and flaming desserts. In one corner of the room a lady harpist played tinkling melodies.

Father wanted to celebrate, because he had just been promoted. He worked for an electronics company, and after his English started improving, his superiors decided to appoint him to a position more suited to his training. The promotion not only brought a higher salary but was also a tremendous boost to his pride.

Up to then we had eaten only in Chinese restaurants. Although my brother and I were becoming fond of hamburgers, my parents didn't care much for Western food, other than chow mein.

But this was a special occasion, and Father asked his coworkers to recommend a really elegant restaurant. So there we were at the Lakeview, stumbling after the headwaiter in the murky dining room.

At our table we were handed our menus, and they were so big that to read mine I almost had to stand up again. But why bother? It was mostly in French, anyway.

Father, being an engineer, was always systematic. He took out a pocket French dictionary. "They told me that most of the items would be in French, so I came prepared." He even had a pocket flashlight, the size of a marking pen. While Mother held the flashlight over the menu, he looked up the items that were in French.

"*Pâté en croûte*," he muttered. "Let's see . . . *pâté* is paste . . . *croûte* is crust . . . hmm . . . a paste in crust."

The waiter stood looking patient. I squirmed and died at least fifty times.

At long last Father gave up. "Why don't we just order four complete dinners at random?" he suggested.

"Isn't that risky?" asked Mother. "The French eat some rather peculiar things, I've heard."

"A Chinese can eat anything a Frenchman can eat," Father declared.

The soup arrived in a plate. How do you get soup up from a plate? I glanced at the other diners, but the ones at the nearby tables were not on their soup course, while the more distant ones were invisible in the darkness.

Fortunately my parents had studied books on Western etiquette before they came to America. "Tilt your plate," whispered my mother. "It's easier to spoon the soup up that way."

She was right. Tilting the plate did the trick. But the etiquette book didn't say anything about what you did after the soup reached your lips. As any respectable Chinese knows, the correct way to eat your soup is to slurp. This helps to cool the liquid and prevent you from burning your lips. It also shows your appreciation.

We showed our appreciation. *Shloop*, went my father. *Shloop*, went my mother. *Shloop, shloop*, went my brother, who was the hungriest.

The lady harpist stopped playing to take a rest. And in the silence, our family's consumption of soup suddenly seemed unnaturally loud. You know how it sounds on a rocky beach when the tide goes out and the water drains from all those little pools? They go *shloop, shloop, shloop*. That was the Lin family, eating soup.

At the next table a waiter was pouring water. When a large *shloop* reached him, he froze. The pitcher continued to pour, and water flooded the tabletop and into the lap of a customer. Even the customer didn't notice anything at first, being also hypnotized by the *shloop, shloop, shloop*.

It was too much. "I need to go to the toilet," I mumbled, jumping

to my feet. A waiter, sensing my urgency, quickly directed me to the ladies' room.

I splashed cold water on my burning face, and as I dried myself with a paper towel, I stared into the mirror. In this perfumed ladies' room, with its pink-and-silver wallpaper and marbled sinks, I looked completely out of place. What was I doing here? What was our family doing in the Lakeview restaurant? in America?

The door to the ladies' room opened. A woman came in and glanced curiously at me. I retreated into one of the toilet cubicles and latched the door.

Time passed—maybe half an hour, maybe an hour. Then I heard the door open again, and my mother's voice. "Are you in there? You're not sick, are you?"

There was real concern in her voice. A girl can't leave her family just because they slurp their soup. Besides, the toilet cubicle had a few drawbacks as a permanent residence. "I'm all right," I said, undoing the latch.

Mother didn't tell me how the rest of the dinner went, and I didn't want to know. In the weeks following, I managed to push the whole thing into the back of my mind, where it jumped out at me only a few times a day. Even now, I turn hot all over when I think of the Lakeview restaurant.

But by the time we had been in this country for three months, our family was definitely making progress toward becoming Americanized. I remember my parents' first PTA meeting. Father wore a neat suit and tie, and Mother put on her first pair of high heels. She stumbled only once. They met my homeroom teacher and beamed as she told them that I would make honor roll soon at the rate I was going. Of course Chinese etiquette forced Father to say that I was a very stupid girl and Mother to protest that the teacher was showing favoritism toward me. But I could tell they were both very proud.

The day came when my parents announced that they wanted to give a dinner party. We had invited Chinese friends to eat with us before, but this dinner was going to be different. In addition to a Chinese American family, we were going to invite the Gleasons.

"Gee, I can hardly wait to have dinner at your house," Meg said to me. "I just *love* Chinese food."

That was a relief. Mother was a good cook, but I wasn't sure if people who ate sour cream would also eat chicken gizzards stewed in soy sauce.

Mother decided not to take a chance with chicken gizzards. Since we had Western guests, she set the table with large dinner plates, which we never used in Chinese meals. In fact we didn't use individual plates at all, but picked up food from the platters in the middle of the table and brought it directly to our rice bowls. Following the practice of Chinese-American restaurants, Mother also placed large serving spoons on the platters.

The dinner started well. Mrs. Gleason exclaimed at the beautifully arranged dishes of food: the colorful candied fruit in the sweet-and-sour pork dish, the noodle-thin shreds of chicken meat stir-fried with tiny peas, and the glistening pink prawns in a ginger sauce.

At first I was too busy enjoying my food to notice how the guests were doing. But soon I remembered my duties. Sometimes guests were too polite to help themselves, and you had to serve them with more food.

I glanced at Meg, to see if she needed more food, and my eyes nearly popped out at the sight of her plate. It was piled with food: the sweet-and-sour meat pushed right against the chicken shreds, and the chicken sauce ran into the prawns. She had been taking food from a second dish before she finished eating her helping from the first!

405

Horrified, I turned to look at Mrs. Gleason. She was dumping rice out of her bowl and putting it on her dinner plate. Then she ladled prawns and gravy on top of the rice and mixed everything together, the way you mix sand, gravel, and cement to make concrete.

I couldn't bear to look any longer, and I turned to Mr. Gleason. He was chasing a pea around his plate. Several times he got it to the edge, but when he tried to pick it up with his chopsticks, it rolled back toward the center of the plate again. Finally, he put down his chopsticks and picked up the pea with his fingers. He really did! A grown man!

All of us, our family and the Chinese guests, stopped eating to watch the activities of the Gleasons. I wanted to giggle. Then I caught my mother's eyes on me. She frowned and shook her head slightly, and I understood the message: the Gleasons were not used to Chinese ways, and they were just coping the best they could.

For some reason I thought of celery strings.

When the main courses were finished, Mother brought out a platter of fruit. "I hope you weren't expecting a sweet dessert," she said. "Since the Chinese don't eat dessert, I didn't think to prepare any."

"Oh, I couldn't possibly eat dessert!" cried Mrs. Gleason. "I'm simply stuffed!"

Meg had different ideas. When the table was cleared, she announced that she and I were going for a walk. "I don't know about you, but I feel like dessert," she told me when we were outside. "Come on, there's a Dairy Queen down the street. I could use a big chocolate milkshake!"

Although I didn't really want anything more to eat, I insisted on paying for the milkshakes. After all, I was still hostess.

Meg got her large chocolate milkshake, and I had a small one. Even so, she was finishing hers while I was only half done. Toward the end she pulled hard on her straws and went *shloop, shloop*.

"Do you always slurp when you eat a milkshake?" I asked, before I could stop myself.

Meg grinned. "Sure. All Americans slurp."

407

Objectives
- Provide evidence from the text to demonstrate understanding.
- Read independently for a sustained period of time and paraphrase the reading.

Envision It! | Retell

Think Critically

1. Remember a time when you were unfamiliar with someone else's food or eating traditions. Compare your experience to something that happens in *The All-American Slurp*. **Text to Self**

2. When you are faced with embarrassing situations, humor helps. Find examples the author provides to show how the Lin daughter used humor to help in such situations. **Think Like an Author**

3. Compare the dinner at the Gleasons' house with the dinner at the Lins'. What were the similarities and differences between the two situations?  **Compare and Contrast**

4. Describe how the narrator changes from the beginning of the story to the end. What does she say or do to hint that she really is changing? **Inferring**

5. **Look Back and Write** What is the all-American slurp? How does it make an appropriate ending to this account of the Lin family? Write your response. Provide evidence to support your answer.

TEST PRACTICE Extended Response

Meet the Author

Lensey Namioka

Lensey Namioka was born in China and moved to the United States when she was nine years old. She remembers what it was like to be a little girl in China and what it was like to move to a new country. She says, "I wrote *The All-American Slurp* when a Chinese relative visited us in America and he vigorously slurped his soup. After I had lived in America for so many years, my attitude on table manners had changed so that I found his slurping startling. I wrote the story to illustrate the differences in manners." Ms. Namioka also writes about the history and samurai of Japan, the country of her husband. Although she studied mathematics in school, Lensey Namioka chose to become a writer. She has written more than twenty books, many of which have won awards. She lives in Seattle, Washington, and frequently speaks at schools and bookstores.

Other books by Lensey Namioka: *Half and Half* and *The Coming of the Bear*

Reading Log

Use the Reading Log in the *Reader's and Writer's Notebook* to record your independent reading.

Objectives
● Understand the key features of an invitation. ● Write an invitation.
● Choose words efficiently to avoid wordiness. ● Use commas correctly.

Let's Write It!

Key Features of an Invitation

● invites someone to an event

● includes important details

● may ask for a response

● has a greeting and a closing

**READING STREET ONLINE
GRAMMAR JAMMER
www.ReadingStreet.com**

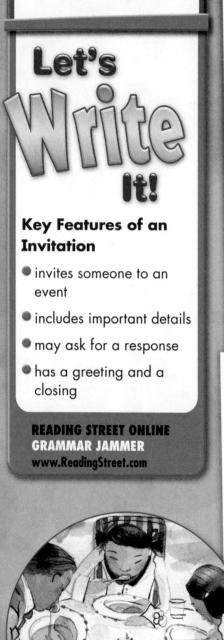

Invitation

An **invitation** is a written request for someone's attendance at an event. It includes important facts, such as the date, time, and place. The student model on the next page is an example of an invitation.

Writing Prompt Think about how the Gleasons may have invited the family for dinner in *The All-American Slurp*. Write a formal invitation to a friend, inviting him or her to a dinner party at your home.

Writer's Checklist

Remember, you should . . .

☑ begin with a greeting.

☑ include all necessary information about the event in the body of your letter.

☑ use commas in your greeting, closing, address, and date.

☑ make sure the letter is correctly punctuated.

Consuela Moreno
5200 Meadowcreek Dr.
Dallas, TX 75248

October 20, 20__

Dear Masahiko,

   Please come to a dinner party at my house on Thursday, October 30. My family and friends would enjoy meeting you. We are so pleased that you have moved to the neighborhood, and we would like to have the chance to visit with you.

   Dinner will be served at 7:00 P.M. To celebrate the season, we will be serving a fall meal, including squash soup and pumpkin pie! Dress will be casual. Please feel free to bring a guest. I hope to see you there.

   You may R.S.V.P to me at (972) 555-0666, write to the address above, or talk to me at school.

Yours Truly,
Consuela

Commas are used correctly in the address, date, and greeting.

Genre
An **invitation** requests someone's attendance at an event.

Writing Trait Word Choice
Wordiness is avoided by using language that is brief and clear.

Conventions

Commas

Remember Commas clarify meaning and tell readers when to pause. Place a comma between the city and state in an address, between the day and year in a date, and in the greetings and closings of letters.

Genre
Expository Text

• Expository text is a form of nonfiction.

• Expository text provides information and facts about people, places, events, and things.

• It may use colorful details to help explain the main ideas of what is written.

• Expository text often uses graphics and other text features such as subheads and time lines to help readers better understand the text.

• Read "The Evolution of Eating Utensils" and look for facts and details about everyday things that most people take for granted.

THE EVOLUTION OF
Eating Utensils

BY LINDA WASHINGTON

Think about the eating utensils you use every day. Have you ever wondered how they came about? Utensils have a long history.

The Knife

The knife is one of the oldest eating utensils. The first knives were made from flint, a gray stone discovered during—you guessed it—the Stone Age. A knife was handy not only for protection but also for spearing food. And, unlike a sharp stick, which could also be used for spearing, a flint knife did not break so easily.

Over time, knives became thinner and sharper as metals like bronze and iron were discovered. In early centuries, rich Egyptians, Greeks, and Romans ate with knives to avoid getting their fingers dirty. In their own way, knives became a symbol of wealth.

Prehistoric knives of flint

412

During the Middle Ages knives became more common among all people. Using two knives—one to cut with and one to carry food to the mouth—was a sign of good manners. But, as you might guess, using a sharp knife to eat with was dangerous.

Table knives like the ones you see in your family's silverware drawer or the school cafeteria came about in 1669. King Louis XIV wanted to put a stop to violence in France. He declared that all knives must have a rounded edge. Used for cutting food rather than piercing it, these safer, rounded-end knives became increasingly more common on dinner tables.

Chopsticks

Chopsticks, which originated in China, have been around for more than 5,000 years. The earliest chopsticks might have been twigs used to take hot food from a pot. These sticks kept the fingers from being burned. Chinese chopsticks were usually made from ivory, jade, or wood.

In Japan, most chopsticks were made from either wood or bamboo. And instead of two separate sticks like you see today, chopsticks were attached at one end the way tweezers are today. During the tenth century, however, the sticks were separated.

The chopsticks we use today often have a square end, to fit the hand better, as well as a rounded tip.

Chopsticks are called *kuai-zi* in Mandarin Chinese.

Let's **Think** About...

What information about the history of the knife was surprising to you?
Expository Text

413

The Fork

The first forks had only two tines. Greeks and Romans used a long-handled fork in the first century, but not to eat with. At that time, forks were used for carving and serving meat only. In the sixth century, smaller forks became more common in the Middle East. In Germany, during the eighteenth century, the fork gained more tines—rather than two, there were now four. But this four-tined fork didn't make its way to the United States until the nineteenth century.

When Catherine de Médicis of Italy married King Henry II in 1533, she brought the fork to France. Yet in France, as well as Italy, forks were not popular at first. Many people thought they were weird.

A man named Thomas Coryate claimed that he brought the fork to England. He stated in his writings that while traveling in Italy and France in 1608, he saw people using forks and decided to use one too. But back in England his friends made fun of him. They called him *ferciferus*, which meant "pitchfork handler." To this he replied, "Wait and see; one day you will each have a fork. Mark my words!" And he was right. Years later, the fork caught on among the rich, and eventually most everyone else.

Origins of Eating Utensils

prehistoric times	c. 3000 B.C.	first century A.D.	sixth century A.D.
crude knives developed	chopsticks first used	modern spoon developed	fork first used as eating utensil

Let's **Think** About...

Why is the history of the fork more varied than that of the knife?
Expository Text

Let's **Think** About...

Why did Thomas Coryate have the last laugh on his friends?
Expository Text

The Spoon

Some form of the spoon has been around since prehistoric times. Both the Greek and Latin words for *spoon* are derived from *cochlea*, meaning "a spiral-shaped snail shell." The earliest spoons were probably sticks with seashells attached to them. Later spoons were made from wood, ivory, metals, and other materials—even bone!

We have the Romans to thank for the spoon we use today. During the first century, the Romans developed two types of spoons. One had an oval bowl and a long, thin handle. The other had a round bowl. Modern spoons were modeled from these designs.

During the Middle Ages, most people used spoons made of wood, pewter, or tin. Only rich people had fancy silver spoons. That's probably why the phrase *born with a silver spoon in his mouth* means "born into a wealthy family."

The Spork

The spork is a combination fork and spoon. It has a spoon shape and short tines on the end. You've probably used a plastic one at a fast-food restaurant. The spork has been around since the 1800s, when they were made from silver or stainless steel. Large stainless steel or silver sporks are still used as serving utensils.

We can only guess what tomorrow's utensils will look like!

18th century A.D.	19th century A.D.
four-tined fork created	spork created

Let's **Think** About...

What materials were used to make early spoons? What was the very earliest spoon made of?
Expository Text

Let's **Think** About...

Reading Across Texts Which different eating utensils did families in *The All-American Slurp* probably know how to use?

Writing Across Texts If you could only use one utensil to eat with, which would you choose? Write a paragraph explaining your choice.

Vocabulary

Multiple-Meaning Words

Context Clues Some words have more than one meaning. Use the words and sentences near a multiple-meaning word—the context clues—to figure out which meaning the author intends. Look in the *Words! Vocabulary Handbook* at the back of this book for more help.

Practice It! Find the word *consumption* near the bottom of page 402 in *The All-American Slurp*. What different meanings can the word have? Which meaning makes sense in the sentence? Use a dictionary if you aren't familiar with other meanings of the word.

Fluency

Expression

When you read aloud, pay attention to how you change your voice to reflect each character's personality or feelings. You can emphasize, or stress, specific words for different impact, and you can read more slowly when you are telling something that is funny.

Practice It! With a partner, practice reading aloud page 396 from *The All-American Slurp*. Change the tone, pitch, and volume of your voice to express the emotions in the sentences and the tone of voice you think each character would use. Give feedback to your partner.

416

Listing and Speaking

When you give directions, be sure that you are very sure of how to do something. Then explain it.

Giving Directions

When you give directions, you describe how to do something. The purpose of directions is to teach others how to make an item or do an activity.

Practice It! With a partner, choose a recipe for a food you know and give him or her step-by-step directions about how to prepare, serve, and eat that food. Practice to be sure that your directions are clear. Take turns. Then give your directions to your classmates.

Tips

Listening . . .

- Listen to the speaker's messages and pay attention to any gestures.

- Ask a question if any step is unclear.

Speaking . . .

- Speak at a natural rate and enunciate clearly.

- Use notes to stay focused.

Teamwork . . .

- Consider your partner's suggestions.

- Offer to pass out copies of your partner's recipe and ask him or her to do the same with your recipe.

417

Objectives

- Listen to and interpret a speaker's message and ask questions.

Oral Vocabulary

Let's Talk About

Culture

- Express opinions about the arrival of Europeans to the Americas.
- Share what you know about the native, prehistoric peoples of Mexico and Central America.
- Ask questions about what life might have been like before the Spanish arrived.

READING STREET ONLINE
CONCEPT TALK VIDEO
www.ReadingStreet.com

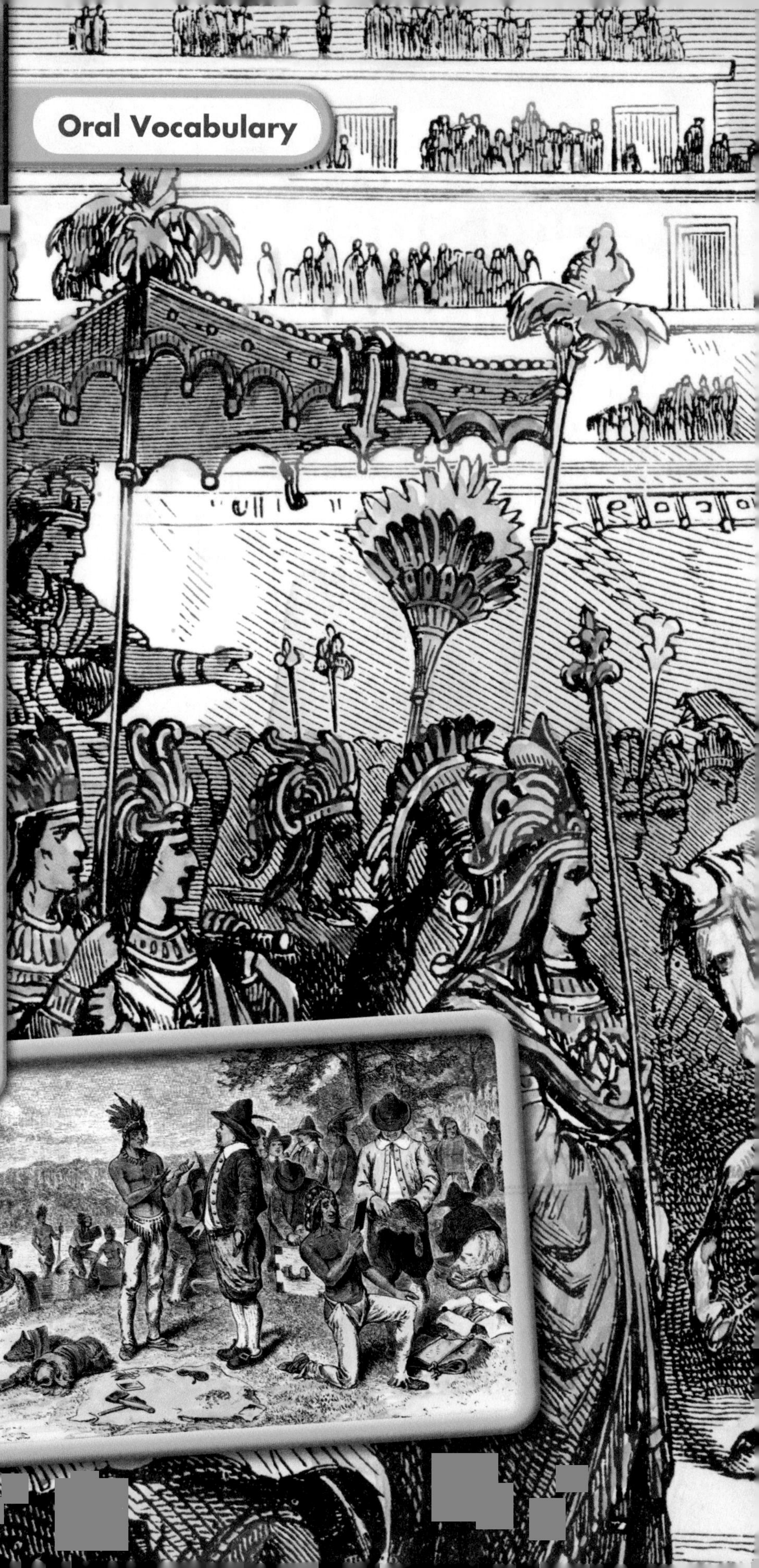

419

Objectives
- Use information from a text to infer and draw conclusions.

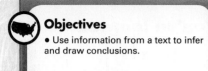

Skill

Strategy

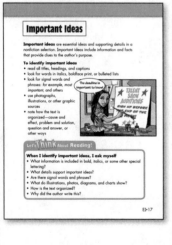

READING STREET ONLINE
ENVISION IT! ANIMATIONS
www.ReadingStreet.com

Comprehension Skill

Draw Conclusions

- When you draw a conclusion, you form a reasonable opinion about something you have read.

- Ask yourself if your conclusions are valid. Do the facts and details in the text support your conclusions? Is each conclusion valid, based on logical thinking and common sense?

- Use a graphic organizer like the one below to help you draw a conclusion about the character traits of the people who are written about in "The Conquistadores."

- Evaluate your conclusion by answering these questions: What facts or details support your conclusion? Is your conclusion based on common sense and logical thinking? Explain.

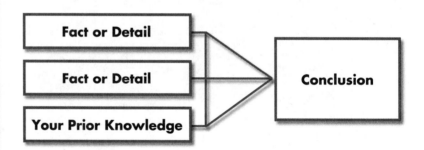

Comprehension Strategy

Important Ideas

You can better understand a selection if you look for its important ideas. The important ideas are the text's essential information, facts, and details. The title gives clues to the topic. A topic sentence tells what each paragraph is about. Reading topic sentences first can guide you to important ideas.

420

The Conquistadores

During the 1500s, Spaniards sailed to the Americas and began to explore the land they found. In time, some of them began to conquer and take control over parts of the Americas. These Spaniards were called *conquistadores,* which is the Spanish word for "conquerors." These men were arguably most interested in fighting and searching for gold.

Strategy What important idea about the conquistadores is expressed in this paragraph?

Francisco Pizarro is known for conquering the Inca people of South America. In 1531, Pizarro set sail for the center of the mighty Inca empire. He had with him 180 men and nearly 40 horses. The Incas had a much larger army, but they were fighting among themselves. Pizarro and his men made a surprise attack against the Incas and captured their leader. Later, this leader was killed by Pizarro's men, even after he gave the Spaniards a room full of gold and silver.

Skill Which of the following conclusions about Pizarro is valid?
a) He was generous.
b) He was clever.
c) He was afraid.
Think about his actions.

Sebastián de Belalcázar, another conquistador, helped Pizarro conquer the Incas. In 1534, he led a small army that attacked and occupied the valley of Quito, a former capital.

History demonstrates that most of the conquistadores were better at fighting than governing. Because of this, other Spanish leaders eventually took their places.

Skill Draw a conclusion in order to answer the following question: What do you think the conquistadores were like as rulers?

Your Turn!

❚❚ Need a Review? See the *Envision It! Handbook* for help with drawing conclusions and finding important ideas.

▶ Ready to Try It? Use what you've learned about drawing conclusions as you read *The Aztec News.*

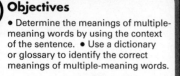

Envision It! Words to Know

campaigns

comrades

invaders

benefits

enrich

foreigners

Vocabulary Strategy for

Multiple-Meaning Words

Dictionary/Glossary Some words have more than one meaning. If the words and sentences around a multiple-meaning word do not give clues about which meaning the author is using, refer to a dictionary or glossary.

Choose one of the Words to Know that has more than one meaning and follow these steps.

1. Think about the different meanings the word can have.

2. Find the word in the glossary. Read the definitions. Think about the way the word is used in the text.

3. Decide which meaning makes sense in the sentence.

4. Reread the sentence, replacing the word with the meaning you think fits best.

5. If this meaning seems right, read on. If not, try another meaning.

Read "The End of the Aztecs." Use the glossary or a dictionary to decide which meaning fits any multiple-meaning words you find in the article.

Words to Write Reread "The End of the Aztecs." Write a summary of a battle or war that you have studied or read about. Use words from the Words to Know list.

The End of the Aztecs

During the 1500s, through exploration, Europe learned of the Americas. Europeans called this place across the ocean to the west the "New World." European people had long dreamed of finding a better route to the East, with its wealth of spices, silk, jewels, and gold. A good, quick route to the East would give the discoverer many trade benefits. Instead, adventurers sailed west and found the lands and native peoples of the Americas.

Natives such as the Aztecs of Mexico had a rich kingdom with much gold. These people had vast knowledge, including ways that would help to enrich the soil to provide good crops. They had built a huge city on a lake.

The Aztec civilization was both advanced and ingenious.

The Spanish, who sought riches, organized armies and ships and set sail. What must the proud Aztec people have thought of these pale-skinned foreigners? It is likely that the Aztec leader believed the Spanish leader was a god. The Aztecs offered valuable gifts and welcomed the Spanish. But the Spanish did not want to be comrades to the Aztecs. They came as invaders, not friends. Their campaigns against the Aztecs were bloody but success-ful. In just two years, the Aztecs were conquered and enslaved.

Your Turn!

Need a Review? For help using a dictionary and with multiple-meaning words, see *Words!*

Ready to Try It? Read *The Aztec News* on pp. 424–439.

THE AZTEC NEWS

 THE GREATEST NEWSPAPER IN CIVILIZATION

by PHILIP STEELE

Genre

Informational text is text that is based on factual information. Though *The Aztec News* is not a real newspaper, look for details that demonstrate that it is based on real information about Aztec history and culture.

SUCCESS IS OURS!

Illustrated by ANGUS McBRIDE

OUR VICTORY over the Mixtec city of Coixtlahuaca in 1458 marked the start of our triumphant rise to power under Montezuma I. A reporter from The Aztec News witnessed the final battle and sent back this report.

I AM STANDING in the center of Coixtlahuaca. All around me, the streets are filled with dead and dying Mixtecs.

The sky is thick with smoke as the Mixtec temple goes up in flames. This fire is a triumphant sign to the world that victory is ours.

Ahead of me, I can see our army's finest warriors, the Eagles and the Jaguars, rounding up captives to be sent back to our city for sacrifice.

Today's events bring to a close one of the largest campaigns we Aztecs have ever waged. There were more than 200,000 warriors in the army that left Tenochtitlán, along with 100,000 porters to carry their supplies.

I am told that the Mixtecs shook with fear as they saw row after row of our warriors marching toward them. No matter how hard the Mixtecs fought, they had no hope of defeating us.

This glorious victory will be remembered for years to come. Not only will the sacrifice of so many captives delight our gods, but the people of Coixtlahuaca must now pay a high price if they wish to be left in peace.

The Mixtecs are known throughout the land for the wealth of their traders and the fine skills of their craftworkers. The tribute payments they must send to Montezuma will fill his treasury with riches. ◪

CLASH OF STRENGTH: The Mixtecs are forced back by our Jaguar and Eagle warriors.

COUNTDOWN to CONFLICT

Illustrated by IAN THOMPSON

March 1519

Stories begin to reach Tenochtitlán from the east coast, telling of tall wooden towers floating on the sea. Reports say there are eleven of these strange ships.

April 1519

Over six hundred pale-skinned foreigners leave the ships and set up camp at Veracruz. Our spies learn that the men call themselves Spaniards. This news is taken to Montezuma II. He sends splendid gifts of gold to the Spanish leader, Hernán Cortés.

August 1519

The Spaniards burn their ships — do they plan never to leave our land? Riding on the great deer they call horses, they set off toward Tenochtitlán.

September 1519

Cortés persuades our enemies, the Tlaxcalan people, to join him as he marches through their land.

November 8, 1519

Cortés reaches Lake Texcoco, where he is greeted by Montezuma. The Spaniards and the Tlaxcalans are invited to stay in one of the palaces in our city.

November 24, 1519

Cortés tries to control Tenochtitlán by taking Montezuma hostage.

May 1520

At a religious festival, the Spaniards murder a number of our nobles. Fighting breaks out and the foreigners retreat to their palace.

June 1520

Montezuma tells us we must make peace with the Spaniards. These are not the words of a brave ruler.

Our nobles turn their backs on Montezuma and choose Cuitláhuac, his brother, as ruler.

Montezuma begs us to make peace, but we will listen to this traitor no longer. Instead, we pelt him with stones. He falls, the Spaniards carry him back to their palace, and he is never seen alive again.

SPANIARDS FLEE CITY

Illustrated by GINO D'ACHILLE

THIS GLORIOUS DAY, June 30, 1520, is one that our people will remember forever. At long last the Spanish cowards have been chased from our city——Tenochtitlán is free!

TODAY, the murderous invaders lie dead in the thousands, many of them still clinging greedily to their stolen gold.

Last night the Spanish leader made a foolish mistake. Having realized that he could not easily defeat us, Cortés decided to lead his army out of our city. And knowing that we Aztecs rarely fight at night, he waited until it was dark to escape. The gods seemed to be on his side. There was no moon, and the night was pitch-black.

The Spaniards and their Tlaxcalan allies crept through the city toward the lake, hoping to sneak across the eastern causeway to the mainland.

But they had barely reached the edge of the city when they were seen by some women fetching water from the lake.

These brave women swiftly gave the alarm, and the whole city arose to give chase.

TRAPPED AT THE GAP

As the enemy fled, our warriors took to their canoes. They planned to trap the Spaniards and Tlaxcalans at the first of the four gaps in the causeway and to attack them from the water.

Our warriors thought the enemy wouldn't be able to cross the gaps—as usual, the wooden bridges that span them had been removed to prevent anyone from entering our city at night.

But knowing this, the Spaniards had built their own bridge. Only when they came to the second gap in the causeway did they realize their mistake. The Spaniards had only one bridge, and the last of their army was still using it to cross the first gap!

By this time our warriors had reached the causeway in their canoes.

CAUSEWAY CHAOS: The enemies die in the thousands as they attempt to flee the city.

And now they let loose a deadly hail of stones, spears, and arrows. Some of the enemy were killed outright. Others were wounded and fell into the lake.

Many of the Spaniards drowned, weighed down by their heavy armor. In a desperate bid to escape, others clambered over the bodies of their dead comrades. And in this way a number of them managed to reach the mainland.

When day dawned and the bodies were counted, it became clear that as few as a third of the Spaniards and Tlaxcalans had gotten away.

Cortés must now be weeping like a cloud in the rainy season. Surely he will never dare to return to Tenochtitlán. ◪

THE PRICE OF POWER

Illustrated by LUIGI GALANTE

HAVE YOU EVER wondered what life would be like as a noble? If so, remember that life at the top isn't everything it's cracked up to be.

OF COURSE, there are many benefits to being a noble. For starters, they're seriously rich! Apart from anything else, whenever tribute payments are sent to our great ruler by conquered peoples, every noble is given a share of the goods.

And, as we all know, nobles can have two-story houses and live right in the city center.

NOBLE: Fine clothes, but is it all fun and games?

Then, there's the fact that noblemen are able to marry as many women as they want to. And they and their families are allowed to wear top-quality clothing, like long cotton or feather capes, and jewelry made from gold and precious stones.

Commoners, on the other hand, can't wear any jewelry other than clay-bead or shell necklaces and earrings. And may the gods help them if they're ever seen in anything not made out of maguey-cactus cloth!

TWO SIDES TO EVERY STORY

But there's a downside to everything, of course.

For example, if a noble is found guilty of a crime, he'll be punished far more harshly than a commoner. A commoner caught for a particular crime might be forced into slavery, but a noble might lose his life for the same offense.

Then there are your children to think of. As a noble, you'll probably send them to a calmecac school so they'll get a better choice of job when they grow up. If they study hard, they may even become a judge, a general, or a priest. But as calmecac students aren't ever allowed to visit their homes, you'll never get to see them.

The simple truth of the matter is you're better off the way you are. So count your blessings—and just be glad that you're an Aztec!

COMMONER: A simple life, but a happy one?

As a commoner, you will probably prefer your children go to a local telpochcalli school. They may have to sleep there, but at least they'll be free to come home to eat with you every day.

PUBLIC NOTICES

RUNAWAY SLAVES

Anyone caught touching a runaway slave will be forced into slavery. Only their owners may try to catch them. All slaves who escape win their freedom.

KNOW YOUR PLACE!

An increasing number of commoners have been seen wearing cotton clothes. This is a luxury allowed only to nobles. Commoners are reminded that they are forbidden to wear any clothing not woven from the fiber of the maguey cactus.

OFFENDERS WILL BE TAKEN INTO SLAVERY.

TENOCHTITLÁN, A GUIDE

Illustrated by CHRIS FORSEY

HEART OF THE CITY: The Great Temple stands at the center of Tenochtitlán——use it as a landmark and you'll never get lost.

OUR BEAUTIFUL CITY attracts visitors from all over the empire, but finding your way around can be tricky. So let *The Aztec News* help you to make the most of your stay in Tenochtitlán.

YOUR FIRST sight of our glorious island city will take your breath away—if, that is, you have any left after the long climb over the mountains that surround Lake Texcoco!

As you come down into the valley, you'll see Tenochtitlán glimmering in the distance ahead of you, like a golden jewel set in jade green water. It may not look so big from where you are now, but you'll soon discover that it's vast. Covering nearly six square miles, our city is home to more than 250,000 people.

GETTING AROUND

Once you reach the lake's edge, you have a choice. You can either paddle across the water in a dugout canoe, or you can enter the city by one of three long causeways, all of them wide enough for eight people to walk along side by side.

Once in Tenochtitlán, you can also choose to travel by canoe or walk, as the city is crisscrossed by a network of canals and streets.

But be warned, the canals can be very smelly. You might find yourself traveling next to a canoe taking sewage from the city's public toilets to enrich the soil of the chinampas—the farms at the edge of our island.

But don't let this stop you from taking a trip around the chinampas. Paddle out there some fine evening, then drift through the peaceful tunnels of leaves—it's a truly unforgettable experience!

SIGHTSEEING

Towering above the city skyline is our famous Great Temple with its twin shrines. One shrine is to Huitzilopochtli, the awesome god of the sun, war, and our nation. The other is to Tlaloc, our mighty god of rain.

Sadly, only nobles are allowed inside the Great Square, where the temple stands. But even if you aren't permitted to enter the square, you'll be able to glimpse the shrines over the high stone wall that surrounds it.

Around the outside of the square are the three royal palaces and the houses of the nobles.

But to discover how ordinary people live, head out of the city center to the busy streets that lie beyond. Here you'll find whitewashed cottages noisy with turkeys, dogs, and children.

EATING OUT

Our city is well known for its mouthwatering tortilla pancakes—buy one from a street vender.

Fresh from mountain springs, water is carried into the city by aqueducts.

SOUVENIRS

Whatever you're looking for, from the simple to the exotic, the place to go is Tlatelolco Market. To find it, just head north from the Great Square. Most traders will accept a variety of goods in exchange for their wares, but you might find it easier to take along some cocoa beans or pieces of copper instead.

FESTIVALS

If you can, go to one of our religious festivals while you're in the city—there's at least one every month. The costumes, dancing, and music at these spectacular events will make your visit to Tenochtitlán one you'll always remember! ◪

UNDER COVER

Illustrated by LUIGI GALANTE

OUR TRAVELING merchants, the pochtecas, are often envied for their great wealth. But the trade reporter of *The Aztec News* believes that their riches are well earned in view of the dangers they face.

I REMEMBER the very first time I saw the pochtecas. I was five years old. It was a hot night and I couldn't sleep, so I wandered out onto the road.

There, in the moonlight, I saw a long line of porters shuffling by, straining beneath their loads. And leading them were shadowy figures dressed in capes.

"Who are those men?" I asked my mother.

"They're pochtecas," she said, smiling. "They are the merchants who bring in marvelous things for us to buy at the market.

"They carry so much wealth with them that they travel under the cover of darkness for fear of robbers. And they store their goods in secret warehouses in the city."

My mother went on to talk of the far-off lands the pochtecas visited and of the many treasures they brought back—golden jewelry, feather capes, tortoiseshell cups, spices, cocoa beans. . . .

Of course, it wasn't surprising that I hadn't yet come across these merchants. They keep to themselves. They live in a separate part of the city and have their own temples and laws. They even have their own god— Yacatecuhtli.

But when I was a young warrior marching across the empire with the army, I often saw these merchants trading in faraway cities. And I began to realize that it's the pochtecas who help to make our city so rich. Since then, I've wondered if they do more than just buy and sell. . . .

I SPY A TRADER

I've heard people say that the pochtecas spy for our ruler in the lands they visit. We can't know this for certain, of course, but they do have the perfect cover—they speak many languages, and they do their best to blend in with other tribes.

BY THE LIGHT OF THE MOON: Three pochtecas and their porters quietly leave the city.

There's no question that many pochtecas are even richer than nobles. But then, traveling beyond the borders of the empire can be dangerous—let alone spying! Personally, I admire their courage, and I have ever since that magical night when I was a little boy.

THROWING THE PERFECT PARTY

Illustrated by ANGUS McBRIDE

WHETHER YOU'RE celebrating a birthday or doing your best to impress your friends, organizing a party can be hard work——unless, that is, you do it *The Aztec News* way.

THE GUEST LIST

Choose your guests with care. Nobles: You will want to invite men in positions of power who can help you or your family. Commoners: Ask as many people as you can afford, to show how generous you are.

THE PLACE TO PARTY

Make sure the seating areas for men and women are clearly separated. If you don't have enough space inside

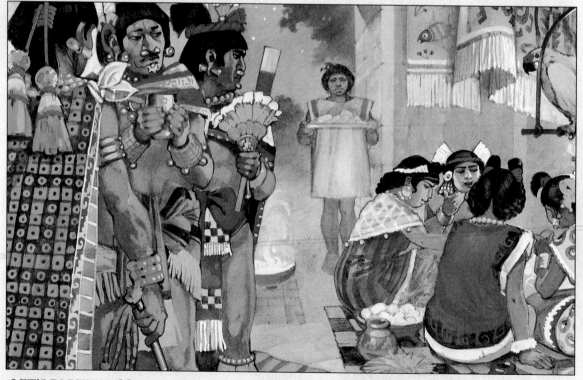

LET'S PARTY! Noble men and women gather for a feast.

your house, a courtyard will work just as well. Decorate the area with fresh flowers, incense burners, and torches for when it gets dark.

THE MENU

Bear in mind that if your guests don't like the food you give them, they can invite themselves back again the following day for another party. So really make an effort with the menu!

If you can afford it, serve specialties such as hot turkey potpies with chile and tomato sauce or lobster with avocado. And it wouldn't be much of a party without plenty of frothy hot chocolate, would it?

ENTERTAINMENT

It goes without saying that no party is complete without music and dancing. So, if you can afford to, hire some entertainers. Otherwise, invite along a few friends who are good singers or dancers.

DRESS TO IMPRESS

Everything is ready, and your guests will soon be arriving. But have you thought about what to wear? It's vital that you look your best in honor of the occasion.

Men: You'll want to wear your most brilliantly patterned cape and loincloth. If you're a noble, take the chance to show off your finest headdress and armbands and your best nose- and lip-plugs.

And ladies: Make sure that your most colorful skirt and overblouse are fresh and clean.

If you're a commoner, it's worth thinking about making a new outfit—maguey cloth does look best when it's new.

Noblewomen should add some amber or jade earrings and perhaps a gold necklace. Precious metals and stones are forbidden to commoners, of course. Instead, wear your finest clay-bead or shell necklace.

AND FINALLY...

Don't forget that as the host of the party you will be expected to give each one of your guests a suitable present at the end of the evening. 🎵

About A.D. 1100

The Aztecs leave their homeland in the north of Mexico to travel south in search of a new home.

About 1195

The Aztecs arrive in the Valley of Mexico.

1325

The city of Tenochtitlán is founded on an island in Lake Texcoco.

The first Great Temple is built by the Aztecs in thanks to their gods.

The Aztecs have to pay tribute to the ruler of Atzcapotzalco, the most powerful city on the lake.

1375

Acamapichtli, the first-known ruler of the Aztecs, comes to the throne.

1428

The Aztecs join forces with the nearby cities of Texcoco and Tlacopan, forming what is known as the Triple Alliance.

Together they conquer the city of Atzcapotzalco and dominate the Valley of Mexico.

1440

Montezuma I comes to the throne. Under his leadership the Aztec empire expands.

1486

Ahuizotl becomes ruler. During his reign the empire continues to grow.

1502

Montezuma II becomes ruler. The Aztec empire is now at its height.

1519

A fleet of Spanish ships lands on the east coast of Mexico. The Spaniards set up camp at Veracruz.

Led by Hernán Cortés, the Spanish army heads toward Tenochtitlán. It is joined by warriors of the Tlaxcalan people.

Montezuma invites the Spaniards and their allies to stay in one of the royal palaces in Tenochtitlán. Once there, they take Montezuma prisoner.

1520

Cuitláhuac, Montezuma's brother, is elected ruler. Montezuma dies, and the Spaniards flee the city.

Smallpox breaks out. Thousands die, including Cuitláhuac. Cuauhtémoc becomes the new ruler.

1521

The Spaniards and their Tlaxcalan allies return and surround Tenochtitlán. On August 13, after a siege lasting ninety-three days, the Aztecs surrender and their city is destroyed. More than 240,000 Aztecs die during the siege.

1522

Tenochtitlán is rebuilt and named Mexico City. It is declared the capital of the Spanish colony of New Spain.

Ahuizotl	*ah-wee-zotl*	**Tlaloc**	*tla-lok*
chinampa	*chee-nam-pa*	**tlamene**	*tla-may-nay*
Coixtlahuaca	*ko-eesh-tla-hwah-kah*	**Tlatelolco**	*tla-tay-lol-ko*
Huitzilopochtli	*hwee-tsee-lo-potch-tlee*	**Tlaxcalan**	*tlahsh-kah-lan*
maguey	*mah-gay*	**tortilla**	*tor-tee-ya*
Mixtec	*meesh-tek*		
Montezuma	*mon-tay-zu-ma*		
pochteca	*potch-tay-kah*		
telpochcalli	*tel-potch-kah-yee*		
Tenochtitlán	*teh-nosh-teet-lan*		
Texcoco	*tesh-ko-ko*		

Some of the names used here are modern ones, such as America or Mexico. The Aztecs would have used different names.

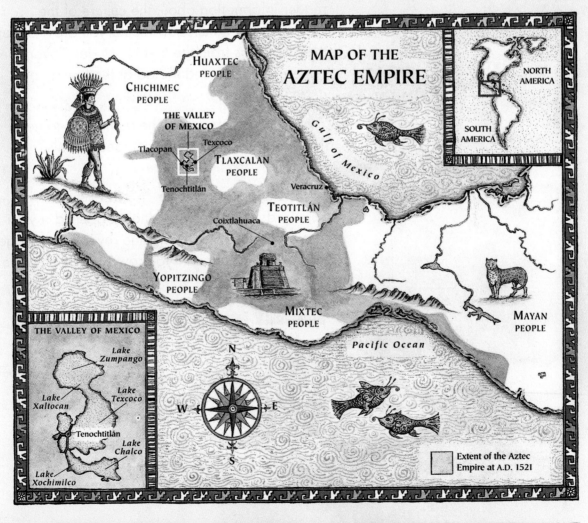

Envision It! Retell

Think Critically

1. Suppose that someone four or five hundred years from now were to write a mock newspaper about your culture today. How would the news stories resemble those in *The Aztec News*? How would they be different? **Text to Self**

2. *The Aztec News* combines information and imagination. Find statements that convey information. Then find statements that seem to spring from the author's imagination. **Think Like an Author**

3. Though we know they're not real, the advertisements in *The Aztec News* give the reader information about the culture of the Aztecs. What conclusions could you draw about the *pochtecas* from the text in "Under Cover" on pages 434–435 and the ad at the bottom of page 435? **Draw Conclusions**

4. What text features does the author use to help the reader find the important ideas in this selection? **Important Ideas**

5. Look Back and Write In 1520, the Spaniards fled the city. What happened a year later? Find the fateful outcome revealed on page 438. Write about it in your own words. Provide evidence to support your answer.

TEST PRACTICE Extended Response

440

Philip Steele

Philip Steele has published more than sixty books in Britain, where he learned about the world of publishing when he worked as an editor. When he moved to Wales to do freelance writing, he says, "I learned to speak the Welsh language, made new friends, and relaxed in some of the most beautiful scenery in the British Isles." Mr. Steele likes to travel and has backpacked across the Middle East, India, the former Soviet Union, and China. He has also spent time in the United States, Canada, Mexico, and Africa. He says these experiences have given him background material for his children's books about countries, peoples, and natural history. He says he would like to write a historical novel for younger readers "if I can ever find the time!" Mr. Steele lives in Wales with his wife and daughter.

 Other books by
Philip Steele: *Castles* and
The Best Book of Mummies

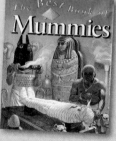

Use the Reading Log in the *Reader's and Writer's Notebook* to record your independent reading.

Objectives
- Understand the key features of a news article. • Write a news article.
- Use quotation marks correctly.
- Include important details.

Expository

News Article

A **news article** gives facts and details about an event. The student model on the next page is an example of a news article.

Writing Prompt Write a news article about an important event in your school or community, using facts and details.

Let's Write It!

Key Features of a News Article

- reports information about an event, idea, or person
- tells who, what, where, when, why
- includes direct quotations
- includes interesting information to capture a reader's attention

READING STREET ONLINE
GRAMMAR JAMMER
www.ReadingStreet.com

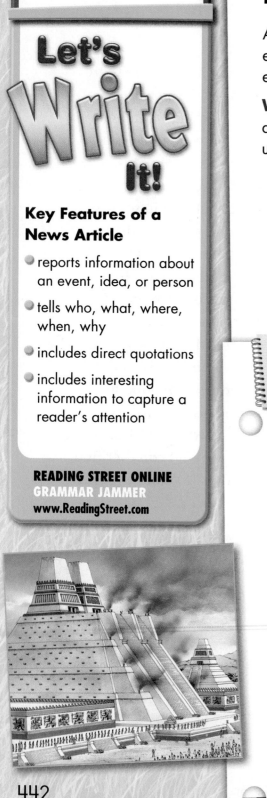

Writer's Checklist

Remember, you should ...

✓ begin with a lead paragraph that captures attention.

✓ ask the questions: Who? What? Where? When? Why?

✓ include important and interesting details.

✓ include direct quotations to make your article lively and interesting.

Mayor Visits Former Teacher's Class

On Wednesday, Mayor Richard Reboso visited Garcia Middle School. He spoke in Ms. Hong's sixth-grade class.

A Returning Student

When the mayor entered the classroom, Ms. Hong said, "Hello, Ricky!"

"Hello, Ms. Hong," Mayor Reboso said.

To this, student Billy Thompson asked, "You call our mayor 'Ricky'?"

"That's what everyone called me when I was in Ms. Hong's class," said Mayor Reboso.

An Important Lesson

Mayor Reboso turned to Ms. Hong.

"You know, Ms. Hong," he said. "You taught me a valuable lesson. You said, 'You can strive for anything you want in life, but you have to work hard.' I always wanted to be a city official, and now I am the mayor. So I wanted to come and tell your class that their hard work can pay off too."

Ms. Hong said it was an exciting day for her students.

Writing Trait Focus/Ideas
The article answers *Who? What? When? Where? Why?*

Genre
This **news article** tells facts and details about an event.

Quotation marks are used correctly.

Conventions

Quotations and Quotation Marks

Remember A **direct quotation** gives a speaker's exact words. Begin each quotation with a capital letter and enclose it in quotation marks. An **indirect quotation** is a quotation that is reworded instead of being quoted directly. It does not need quotation marks.

21st Century Skills
INTERNET GUY

Directories have large amounts of information. They organize things for you. Look for the link to the category you need. Then follow the links. Bookmark useful directories.

● Internet Web sites called online directories list links to many Web sites about a given topic.

● You can use an online directory instead of a search engine to learn about a topic.

● Directories list topics as links on their home pages. You may click on any topic link. Or you may instead choose to type in keywords and click on the Search button.

● Read "The Maya" and see how online directories can quickly yield information about these ancient people.

The Maya

The Maya, Aztec, and Inca were the largest civilizations in the lands now considered part of Latin America. The oldest of these three great civilizations, the Maya, built its empire in what is now southeastern Mexico and in Central America.

Since you have just read about the Aztecs, you might be curious about the Maya as well. You could use your Web browser to help you find an Internet online directory. Here are some of the topics you will likely find listed there.

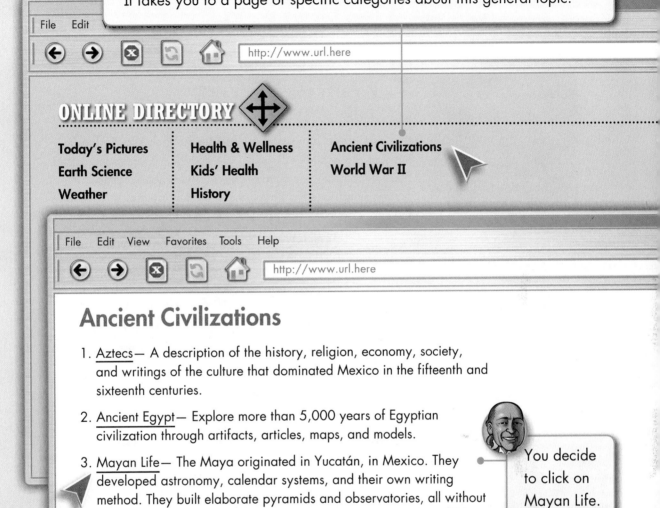

The closest general topic is Ancient Civilizations, so you click on this link. It takes you to a page of specific categories about this general topic.

File Edit View Favorites Tools Help

http://www.url.here

ONLINE DIRECTORY

Today's Pictures   Health & Wellness   Ancient Civilizations
Earth Science   Kids' Health   World War II
Weather   History

File Edit View Favorites Tools Help

http://www.url.here

Ancient Civilizations

1. Aztecs— A description of the history, religion, economy, society, and writings of the culture that dominated Mexico in the fifteenth and sixteenth centuries.

2. Ancient Egypt— Explore more than 5,000 years of Egyptian civilization through artifacts, articles, maps, and models.

3. Mayan Life— The Maya originated in Yucatán, in Mexico. They developed astronomy, calendar systems, and their own writing method. They built elaborate pyramids and observatories, all without metal tools.

4. Mesopotamia— Mesopotamia is often referred to as the "cradle of civilization" because it was the first known civilization in the world. It was located between the Tigris and Euphrates rivers in parts of what are now Turkey and Iraq.

You decide to click on Mayan Life.

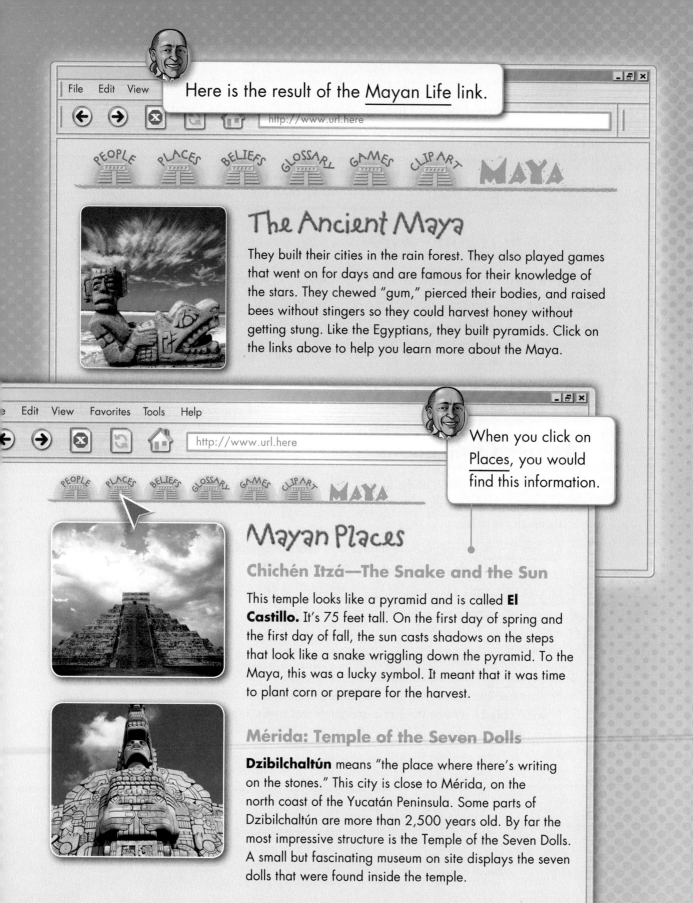

Here is the result of the Mayan Life link.

File   Edit   View

http://www.url.here

PEOPLE   PLACES   BELIEFS   GLOSSARY   GAMES   CLIP ART   MAYA

The Ancient Maya

They built their cities in the rain forest. They also played games that went on for days and are famous for their knowledge of the stars. They chewed "gum," pierced their bodies, and raised bees without stingers so they could harvest honey without getting stung. Like the Egyptians, they built pyramids. Click on the links above to help you learn more about the Maya.

e   Edit   View   Favorites   Tools   Help

http://www.url.here

When you click on Places, you would find this information.

PEOPLE   PLACES   BELIEFS   GLOSSARY   GAMES   CLIP ART   MAYA

Mayan Places

Chichén Itzá—The Snake and the Sun

This temple looks like a pyramid and is called **El Castillo.** It's 75 feet tall. On the first day of spring and the first day of fall, the sun casts shadows on the steps that look like a snake wriggling down the pyramid. To the Maya, this was a lucky symbol. It meant that it was time to plant corn or prepare for the harvest.

Mérida: Temple of the Seven Dolls

Dzibilchaltún means "the place where there's writing on the stones." This city is close to Mérida, on the north coast of the Yucatán Peninsula. Some parts of Dzibilchaltún are more than 2,500 years old. By far the most impressive structure is the Temple of the Seven Dolls. A small but fascinating museum on site displays the seven dolls that were found inside the temple.

If you clicked on <u>People</u>, you would find this information.

File   Edit   View   Favorites   Tools   Help

http://www.url.here

PEOPLE   PLACES   BELIEFS   GLOSSARY   GAMES   CLIP ART   MAYA

Mayan People

The Maya had a sense of beauty that was quite different from ours. They shaped the skulls of their newborn children by tying boards to the forehead. They admired a forehead that sloped back.

Jade earrings and jewelry box

The Maya had tattoos, pierced their bodies, and wore many different forms of jewelry. The most common was jade. Jade was worn in beads, earrings, and ear spools. It was also one of the materials that the Maya traded. The Maya also wore gold.

The Maya would put body paint on themselves for special occasions. They filed their teeth to make them pointed and put jade in the spaces. Men wore an *ex*, which is a loincloth. Women wore loose, sacklike dresses. The clothes of the priests and nobles were made with finer materials and had many shells and beads on them. For ceremonies, they wore wonderful headdresses.

Let's Learn It!

Vocabulary

Multiple-Meaning Words

Context Clues Words, phrases, and sentences around a word with more than one meaning usually give clues to the word's meaning. Use these hints to help you figure out which meaning of the word makes sense.

Practice It! Find the word *campaigns*, which is highlighted on page 426. Look it up in the glossary. What different meanings does *campaign* have? Which meaning makes sense in this sentence? *Campaign* is an example of a homonym. Learn more about multiple-meaning words in the *Words! Vocabulary Handbook* at the back of this book.

Fluency

Accuracy

Accuracy is being able to read without having to stop often to figure out words. One way to build accuracy is by skimming ahead to look for unfamiliar words or phrases. When you are sure of your reading, be sure to enunciate, or pronounce, words clearly and in a voice loud enough to be heard.

Practice It! With a partner, practice reading page 426 of *The Aztec News*. Ask your partner to make a list of the words you read incorrectly. Review the list and, if necessary, consult a dictionary for pronunciations. Reread the page. Have your partner follow the same steps by reading page 432.

Listening and Speaking

Take turns and work smoothly with others when you present a newscast to the class.

Newscast

In a newscast, TV or radio reporters tell brief news stories. The purpose of a newscast is to inform people about important events in a way that is easy to understand.

Practice It! Choose an event reported in *The Aztec News*. In a small group, take on the roles of reporters and a news anchor. Present a newscast to the class, with each reporter presenting a one-minute report on a different aspect of the event and the anchor introducing the topic, each reporter, and the wrap-up.

Tips

Listening . . .

- Look directly at each reporter.
- Consider the reporter's credibility.
- Draw conclusions about what the reporter says or doesn't say.

Speaking . . .

- Enunciate your words clearly.
- Present your most important idea first and stick to facts, not opinions.
- Face your audience and maintain eye contact.

Teamwork . . .

- Divide the topics for your reports fairly and listen to each reporter.

Oral Vocabulary

Let's Talk About

Migration

● Share what you know about the migration of people from one place to another.

● Describe some of the causes of human migration in modern times.

● Ask questions about earlier, well-known migrations of people in other parts of the world.

READING STREET ONLINE
CONCEPT TALK VIDEO
www.ReadingStreet.com

Skill

Strategy

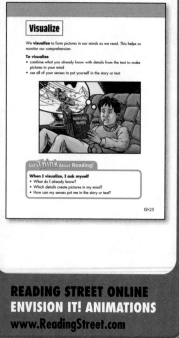

Comprehension Skill

Generalize

- A generalization is a broad statement that applies to many examples. Authors sometimes make generalizations to get across a message about a group of things or people.

- A generalization is often signaled by clue words such as *most*, *all*, *always*, or *never*.

- A generalization can be either valid or faulty. Valid generalizations are supported by examples, facts, or sound logic. Invalid generalizations cannot be supported.

- Use a graphic organizer like the one below to make a generalization about A. Philip Randolph in "Traveling Men."

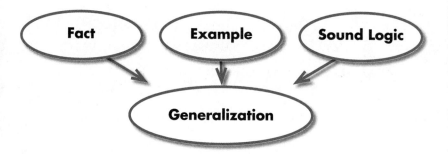

Comprehension Strategy

Visualize

Good readers look for sensory details to create pictures in their minds as they read. The sights, sounds, and smells described by an author help you to visualize what you are reading. As you read, think about the impact that sensory details and imagery have on the selection.

452

Traveling Men

Soon after the Civil War, two important events happened: slaves were freed, and the first intercontinental railroad was finished.

With the new, longer train trips, passengers needed a comfortable place to sleep on the train. Chicago businessman George Pullman claimed that his new sleeping cars offered luxury and service at affordable prices. Pullman hired former slaves, who did an excellent job working as porters on these luxury sleeping cars.

It was work the former slaves were glad to get. It gave them a steady job and respect in the neighborhood, where they were known as "traveling men."

However, their jobs were far from fair. Hours were long, pay was low, and porters could be fired for no reason. As time progressed, younger porters began to see that they deserved much better treatment. However, the Pullman company refused to make changes.

Because of the refusal, the porters formed a union in 1925 called the Brotherhood of Sleeping Car Porters, led by A. Philip Randolph. It took twelve long years of struggle, but the union finally won better pay and working conditions. And Randolph became a hero of the modern Civil Rights movement.

Skill The Emancipation Proclamation was signed in 1863. The Civil War ended in 1865. The railroad was completed in 1869. What generalization about the United States can you make from these examples?

Strategy How can visualizing help you understand what it was like to work as a sleeping-car porter? Which words and phrases help you?

Skill Would it be a valid generalization to say that all porters wanted to join a union and fight for better treatment and wages? Explain your thinking.

SLEEPING CAR

Your Turn!

⏸ **Need a Review?** See the *Envision It! Handbook* for help with generalizing and visualizing.

▶ **Ready to Try It?** Use what you've learned about generalizing as you read *Where Opportunity Awaits*.

Envision It! | Words to Know

burden

rural

urban

conformed

leisure

maintenance

sufficient

Vocabulary Strategy for

Synonyms

Context Clues When you find a word you do not know, look at words near the unfamiliar word. Often the author will provide clues to help you figure out the word's meaning. One kind of clue is a synonym, a word with the same or almost the same meaning as another word.

Choose one of the Words to Know and follow these steps.

1. Read the words and sentences near the unfamiliar word. The author may give you a synonym of the word that can help you predict the word's meaning. Authors sometimes use synonyms in their writing to help define more difficult words.

2. Look for a synonym of the unfamiliar word. Substitute the synonym in place of the word. Does this meaning make sense in the sentence?

3. If not, read on. The larger context may make the meaning clear.

4. If you still cannot find the definition of the unfamiliar word, use the glossary or a dictionary.

Read "Country Versus City." Use synonyms to help you figure out the meanings of unfamiliar words.

Words to Write Reread "Country Versus City." Look at the picture in the selection and describe it. Use as many words from the Words to Know list as you can.

Country Versus City

The twentieth century was a time of great change in the United States. In this time, America began the change from a more rural country to one that had larger and larger urban populations. In the early 1900s, most Americans lived on small farms in the country. But in large cities, industry was growing. However, world wars placed a burden, or hardship, on supplies of everything. The nation began to build more factories, and production of goods was stepped up. People were needed to work in the factories, so many people who had worked in smaller rural areas moved to urban centers, where the jobs were.

Some of these migrants had troubles. For example, an influx of workers could mean there was not sufficient, or enough, housing. Families crowded into small apartments. They were not responsible for the maintenance, or upkeep, of the apartments. Even so, the building owner might not make needed repairs. Life in the city meant changes in lifestyle. For example, what people did with their leisure, or free, time changed. Cities offered more action but less space.

As the century wore on and America became richer and more productive, urban populations became more sophisticated. Their interests conformed to, or matched up with, the opportunities they had come to know—better libraries, theaters, and other social and educational resources.

Your Turn!

⏸ Need a Review? For help using context clues with synonyms, see *Words!*

▶ Ready to Try It? Read *Where Opportunity Awaits* on pp. 456–463.

Where Opportunity Awaits

by James R. Grossman
paintings by Jacob Lawrence

Genre

Expository text tells the nature of a true event. In addition to what you will read, notice the visual information that helps to inform you about the Great Migration.

Question of the Week
How can migration affect a culture?

Painting by Jacob Lawrence. "The Migration of the Negro, Panel no. 3,"
1940–41. Casein tempera on hardboard, 12 x 18 in. Acquired 1942,
The Phillips Collection, Washington, D.C.

Painting by Jacob Lawrence. "The Migration of the Negro, Panel no. 1," 1940–194
Casein tempera on hardboard, 12 x 18 in. Acquired 1942, The Phillips Collection,
Washington, D.C.

THE THOMAS FAMILY ARRIVED IN CHICAGO IN THE SPRING
of 1917. Like thousands of other black Southerners moving north,
they first had to find a home.

For a week, they pounded the
pavements of the city's South Side. Mr.
and Mrs. Thomas, their 19-year-old
daughter, and 17-year-old son eventually
crowded into a five-room apartment—it
was cramped but probably larger than
the farmhouse they had left behind
in Alabama.

Their second task was to find work.
The men went to the stockyards, and the
women earned money doing laundry.

Painting by Jacob Lawrence. "In the North the African
American had more educational opportunities." Panel 58
from The Migration Series, 1940–1941. Tempera on gesso
composition board, 12 x 18 in. Gift of Mrs. David M. Levy,
The Museum of Modern Art, NY.

Optimistic about the future, the teenagers spent their evenings at night school, hoping to improve on the grade-school education they had earned in a rural Southern schoolhouse. In their free time, the family explored the leisure activities available on Chicago's South Side, carrying picnics into the park and venturing into theaters and ice cream parlors.

THE THOMASES WERE PART OF THE FIRST GREAT MIGRATION—the collective journeys of a half-million black Southerners to Northern cities between 1916 and 1919. By 1918, migration chains that linked South to North enabled thousands of Southerners to choose destinations where they had friends or relatives to offer a welcoming hand. A native of Abbeville, South Carolina, for example, could move to Philadelphia without worrying about where she might sleep the first night in town. From Hattiesburg, Mississippi, a newcomer could easily find the Hattiesburg Barber Shop in Chicago and be directed to the appropriate boarding house. In most cases, these patterns conformed largely to patterns established by railroad routes. North and South Carolinians went to New York, Philadelphia, and other Eastern Seaboard cities. Pittsburgh's African American newcomers were likely to hail from Alabama, Georgia, or Kentucky. From Mississippi, Louisiana, Tennessee, and parts of Georgia and Alabama, people headed for Chicago. Because of the influence of *The Chicago Defender* newspaper and the long tentacles of the Illinois Central Railroad, Chicago was an especially popular destination.

"To Let" signs such as this one in Pittsburgh, Pennsylvania, were often difficult to find as the numbers of migrants increased.

The "chains" allowed prospective migrants to make arrangements before leaving home. "Let me know what day you expect to leave and over what road, and if I don't meet you I will have someone there to

Painting by Jacob Lawrence. "Tombstones," 1942.
Gouache on paper, 28¾ x 20½ in. Whitney Museum of
American Art, NY. Purchase 43.14.

meet you and look after you until I see you," one woman wrote from Chicago to a member of her former church in Mississippi. These kinds of community and family contacts had tied Southern cities to their hinterlands for decades; they now extended north. A thin strand even stretched west from Texas and Oklahoma to the West Coast.

Because these migrants arrived during a wartime housing shortage, most encountered difficulty finding a place to live. Usually, a black Northerner in 1920 was likely to have at least several white neighbors within a few blocks. But by 1930, that likelihood had diminished considerably, with African Americans segregated into ghettoes.

HETTOES, HOWEVER, WERE NOT NECESSARILY SLUMS. PROPERTY values have not always declined as neighborhoods shift from "white" to "black." During the Great Migration and throughout much of the 1900s, the process was complicated. As Southerners—most of them poor and unaccustomed to urban life—moved into the least expensive and oldest neighborhoods, established residents tended to seek better housing in less crowded districts. But housing discrimination meant that black neighborhoods could expand only slowly, and only at their edges.

Black Northerners generally paid more than whites would pay for similar living space. At the same time, black workers earned less than their white counterparts. Hence, African Americans spent a very high percentage of their income on shelter. In some cases, this left homeowners without sufficient funds to maintain their houses adequately. In New York City's Harlem, rents generally commanded nearly half of the earnings of African

American residents. Naturally, this placed a considerable burden on family resources. In addition, because there was a constant need for housing, landlords collected rents more diligently than they maintained their buildings.

Tenants who demanded proper maintenance (and many did) could usually be replaced with newcomers who knew little about what to expect or who took what they could get because they had few choices. Gradually, the turnover of residents and the deterioration of buildings due to overcrowding and shoddy construction methods took its toll on the surrounding block. As a result, the neighborhood declined.

DURING WORLD WAR I AND AT TIMES DURING THE 1920s, black newcomers found places to work in Northern cities much more easily than they found places to live. In fact, the first Great Migration was stimulated by the opening of thousands of new railroad jobs.

By 1917, African Americans were also working in heavy industry across the Northeast and Midwest. Most of the jobs in steel mills, auto plants, packinghouses, and rubber factories could be learned quickly. It was far more difficult for many migrants from the South to adapt to a different approach to time. They were not, however, the only ones who faced this difficulty. Rural workers around the world had faced the same difficulty when introduced to industrial employment.

In the rural South, just as in other agricultural societies, the calendar and the weather determined the work pace. One planter described cotton cultivation as "a

The first Great Migration was stimulated by the opening of thousands of railroad jobs.

461

Painting by Jacob Lawrence. "The Migration of the Negro, Panel no. 17," 1940–1941. Casein tempera on hardboard, 12 x 18 in. Acquired 1942, The Phillips Collection, Washington, D.C.

This painting comments on the sharecropping system that left many African Americans in poverty.

series of spurts rather than a daily grind." In those areas where Southern workers did not have to sustain a regular pace—railroad-tie layers, dock hands, construction gangs, for example—a work song set the rhythm. These songs were flexible. A song leader, who set the tempo, could change the pace.

By the 1910s, most workers in Northern factories were punching time clocks. Arrive ten minutes late, and your pay was docked one hour. On the "disassembly lines" of the packinghouses, conveyor belts moved animal carcasses from worker to worker, each of whom would make a single cut. Tardiness or absence could disrupt the whole process. Once a line began moving, a newcomer had no control over the pace of work.

Women sorting peanuts in a Chicago factory in 1928

462

WHAT DID NOT REQUIRE adjustment, however, was hard work. "I will & can do eny kind of worke," declared one man just before heading north from his Florida home. Men with farm experience were accustomed to a workday that began at dawn and ended at sundown. Black women, responsible in both rural and urban settings for household labor as well as for producing income, began their work earlier and ended later. "I came here to Philadelphia because people said it was better," recalled Ella Lee of her early years in Philadelphia, "so much better living in the North than it was in the South. But so far as I am concerned you have got to work like a dog to have anything anywhere you go."

Painting by Jacob Lawrence. "Home Chores," 1945. Gouache and graphite on paper, 29½ x 29¹⁄₁₆ in. The Nelson-Atkins Museum of Art, Kansas City, MO. Anonymous gift, F69-6.

The difference for most migrants—the reason why most not only stayed but also encouraged their friends and relatives to join them—was that the hard work produced rewards during the war years and in the 1920s. In interviews and in letters back home, migrants spoke enthusiastically of sending their children to school, voting, sitting where they pleased on streetcars, and countless other accomplishments. Although black women in the North were pushed out of industry and into domestic employment after World War I, even domestic service paid better in the North than in the South. Black men retained their industrial footholds, putting more cash in their pay envelopes and looking forward to the possibility of promotions down the road.

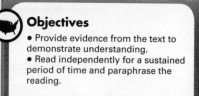

Objectives
• Provide evidence from the text to demonstrate understanding.
• Read independently for a sustained period of time and paraphrase the reading.

Envision It! Retell

Think Critically

1. Suppose your family, living in the South, is trying to decide whether or not to join the Great Migration. Make two lists, one labeled *Advantages* and the other, *Disadvantages*. What do you decide? **Text to World**

2. True to his title, the author presents advantages of the Great Migration. What about the disadvantages? Find examples. Then decide how the author manages to convey a balanced view. **Think Like an Author**

3. Make two generalizations about the experiences of those who moved North during the Great Migration. Support your generalizations with information from the text. **Generalize**

4. The Jacob Lawrence paintings shown in *Where Opportunity Awaits* portray the lives of African Americans during this time. How does this art help you visualize the experiences of those who were struggling then? **Visualize**

5. **Look Back and Write** What were "migration chains" (pages 459–460)? Write an explanation and give an example. Provide evidence to support your answer.

TEST PRACTICE | Extended Response

Meet the Author and the Illustrator

James R. Grossman and Jacob Lawrence

James R. Grossman has researched and written books about the African Americans who journeyed from the South to the North in the first half of the twentieth century. He believes that we can learn "the meaning and boundaries of American citizenship and opportunity" from that Great Migration. Dr. Grossman graduated from Cornell University and received his doctorate from the University of California, Berkeley. He is vice-president for Research and Education at the Newberry Library, Chicago, and is a senior lecturer in the Department of History at the University of Chicago.

Other books: *The Great Migration: An American Story* (paintings by Jacob Lawrence) and *Story Painter: The Life of Jacob Lawrence* by John Duggleby

Jacob Lawrence, America's best-known African American painter, defined the Great Migration in a series of sixty paintings that are recognized for their bold images and vivid colors. Mr. Lawrence began the series in 1940, when he was 22, and finished it the next year. "I painted the panels all at once, color by color, so they share the same palette," he said. The series was a major success and introduced Mr. Lawrence as a serious painter to prestigious museums. Born in Atlantic City, New Jersey, Mr. Lawrence grew up and continued to live and paint in Harlem, where he married Gwendolyn Knight, a fellow artist. He died in 2000 in Seattle, Washington.

Use the Reading Log in the *Reader's and Writer's Notebook* to record your independent reading.

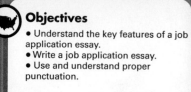

Objectives
- Understand the key features of a job application essay.
- Write a job application essay.
- Use and understand proper punctuation.

Let's Write It!

Key Features of a Job Application Essay

- tells why the writer would be the best person for a job

- uses reasons, facts, and examples to make a point

- has an opening that gets to the point quickly or grabs one's attention

- stays on topic

**READING STREET ONLINE
GRAMMAR JAMMER
www.ReadingStreet.com**

Job Application Essay

A **job application essay** responds to specific job requirements and explains why the writer would be a strong candidate for the job. The student model on the next page is an example of a job application essay.

Writing Prompt Think about a job you'd like to have. Now write a short essay explaining why you are a good candidate for the job.

Writer's Checklist

Remember, you should ...

✓ make the reader aware of your qualifications up front.

✓ select precise and persuasive words and phrases that help move your main idea forward.

✓ give examples to help support your claim.

✓ use correct punctuation.

Why I Will Be an Excellent Dog Sitter

I have read your advertisement for a dog sitter; my interest, experience, and skills make me the best choice for the job.

I care for two dogs, three cats, and a lizard of my own. Also, I take home classroom pets from my school—including a gerbil—to care for throughout the summer months.

Care I have given includes: walking dogs, playing with them, bathing them, and making sure they have plenty of food and water. I know the commitment it takes to make sure that a pet is fed, groomed, exercised, and treated with kindness and respect.

I am also a member of my school's "Friends of the Animals" club. We raise money for endangered species and disappearing habitats. I expect to be active in this club throughout my time at school.

Because of these reasons, I feel I am the best candidate to be hired as a dog sitter.

Genre A **job application essay** tells how the writer meets requirements for a job. It can also be written in letter form.

Writing Trait Word Choice Precise words and transitions help the writer stay on topic.

Punctuation is used correctly.

Conventions

Punctuation

Remember Correct **punctuation** helps make your meaning clear to readers. Punctuation should be correct in all types of written communication. Be certain to use colons, hyphens, semicolons, and dashes correctly.

Social Studies in Reading

Genre
Expository Text

● Expository text is a form of nonfiction.

● Expository text tells and explains facts and information about the nature of people, animals, events, and things. It may contain vivid details.

● Photographs and other text features such as captions and decorative typefaces help readers follow and understand the subject they are reading about.

● Read "Coming Over" and see how it is an example of expository text. Does the author make you want to read more about this important American subject? If so, how?

Coming Over

by Russell Freedman

BETWEEN 1880 AND 1920, TWENTY-three million immigrants arrived in the United States. They came mainly from impoverished towns and villages in southern and eastern Europe. The one thing they had in common was a fervent belief that in America, life would be better. Most of these immigrants were poor, and many immigrant families arrived penniless. Often the father came first, found work, and sent for his family later.

Immigrants usually crossed the Atlantic as steerage passengers. Reached by steep, slippery stairways, the steerage lay deep down in the hold of the ship. It was occupied by passengers paying the lowest fare.

Let's **Think** About...

What are three important facts that the author relates in the first paragraph?
Expository Text

Men, women, and children were packed into dark, foul-smelling compartments. They slept in narrow bunks stacked three high. They had no showers, no lounges, and no dining rooms. Food served from huge kettles was dished into dinner pails provided by the steamship company. Because steerage conditions were crowded and uncomfortable, passengers spent as much time as possible up on deck.

THE GREAT MAJORITY OF IMMIGRANTS landed in New York City, at America's busiest port. Edward Corsi, who later became United States Commissioner of Immigration, was a ten-year-old Italian immigrant when he sailed into New York Harbor in 1907. He wrote, "My first impressions of the New World will always remain etched in my memory, particularly that hazy October morning when I first saw Ellis Island. The steamer *Florida*, fourteen days out of Naples, filled to capacity with sixteen hundred natives of Italy, had weathered one of the worst storms in our captain's memory; and glad we were, both children and grown-ups, to leave the open sea and come at last through the Narrows into the Bay.

"My mother, my stepfather, my brother Giuseppe, and my two sisters, Liberta and Helvetia, . . . looked with wonder on this miraculous land of our dreams.

". . . Passengers all about us were crowding against the rail. Jabbered conversation, sharp cries, laughs and cheers— a steadily rising din filled the air. Mothers and fathers lifted up babies so that they too could see, off to the left, the Statue of Liberty. . . ."

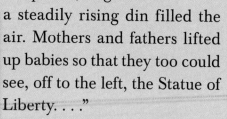

An Italian woman and her children arrive at Ellis Island, 1905.

Let's **Think** About...

How do the direct quotes from a 1907 immigrant add interest to this selection?
Expository Text

New arrivals wait in long lines in the Great Inspection Hall at Ellis Island.

Immigrant child being examined by a city health officer, 1911

Let's **Think** About...

What do the photographs on this page suggest about how immigrants might have felt at Ellis Island?
Expository Text

B UT THE JOURNEY WAS NOT YET OVER. Before they could be admitted to the United States, immigrants had to pass through Ellis Island, which became the nation's chief immigrant-processing center in 1892. There they would be questioned and examined. Those who could not pass all the exams would be detained; some would be sent back to Europe. And so their arrival in America was filled with great anxiety. Among the immigrants Ellis Island was known as Heartbreak Island.

When their ship docked at a Hudson River pier, the immigrants had numbered identity tags pinned to their clothing. Then they were herded onto special ferryboats that carried them to Ellis Island. Officials hurried them along, shouting, "Quick! Run! Hurry!" in half a dozen languages.

Let's **Think** About...

Why does the author tell readers that Ellis Island was called "Heartbreak Island"?
Expository Text

Filing into an enormous inspection hall, the immigrants formed long lines separated by iron railings that made the hall look like a great maze.

First the immigrants were examined by two doctors of the United States Health Service. One doctor looked for physical and mental abnormalities. When a case aroused suspicion, the immigrant received a chalk mark on the right shoulder for further inspection: *L* for lameness, *H* for heart, *X* for mental defects, and so on.

471

The second doctor watched for contagious and infectious diseases. He looked especially for infections of the scalp and at the eyelids for symptoms of trachoma, a blinding disease. Since trachoma caused more than half of all medical detentions, this doctor was greatly feared. He stood directly in the immigrant's path. With a swift movement, he would grab the immigrant's eyelid, pull it up, and peer beneath it. If all was well, the immigrant was passed on.

Those who failed to get past both doctors had to undergo a more thorough medical exam. The others moved on to the registration clerk, who questioned them with the aid of an interpreter: What is your name? Your nationality? Your occupation? Can you read and write? Have you ever been in prison? How much money do you have with you? Where are you going?

Some immigrants were so flustered that they could not answer. They were allowed to sit and rest and try again. About one immigrant out of every five or six was detained for additional examinations or questioning.

Most immigrants made it through Ellis Island in about one day. Carrying all their worldly possessions, they waited on the dock for the ferry that would take them to Manhattan, a mile away. Some of them still faced long journeys overland before they reached their final destinations. Others would head directly for the teeming immigrant neighborhoods of New York City. But no matter where they went, they all hoped to find the same thing: a better life for themselves and their children.

Let's **Think** About...

Where did immigrants go after facing the examinations and questions of Ellis Island?

Expository Text

472

Let's **Think** About...

What does the photograph on this page tell you about the immigrant experience?
Expository Text

Let's **Think** About...

Reading Across Texts Migrants from the South in *Where Opportunity Awaits* and immigrants from Europe both faced challenges in their moves. What were some of the challenges?

Writing Across Texts Make lists of the challenges faced by each group.

473

Objectives
• Read aloud grade-level texts with appropriate phrasing. • Determine the meanings of unfamiliar words by using the context of the sentence.
• Listen to and interpret a speaker's messages and ask questions.
• Prepare and conduct an interview.

Let's Learn It!

Vocabulary

Synonyms

Context Clues Synonyms are words that mean the same or nearly the same thing. Sometimes a writer uses a synonym to introduce a more difficult word that is more precise in that sentence. If you cannot figure out a synonym from context, you may use a dictionary to check its meaning.

Practice It! Read the sentences below. As you work to figure out the meaning of each word, use the synonyms for *elapsed* and *detest*.

• So much time had *elapsed*, or passed, I could barely remember our old town.

• No one could *detest* soccer as much as I do; I dislike it more than any other sport.

Fluency

Appropriate Phrasing

When you use appropriate phrasing, you group together words and ideas that are related so that what you are reading makes sense. Use punctuation as your guide: pause at commas; pause longer at dashes, semicolons, and colons; and stop at periods, question marks, and exclamation points.

Practice It! With a partner, practice reading aloud page 463 of *Where Opportunity Awaits*. As you read, try to use appropriate phrasing and the cues of punctuation to show emotions of Ella Lee and the man. Use phrasing to show the reasons that families continued to move to the North.

Listening and Speaking

Get Ready For High School

When conducting an interview, prepare questions, be polite, and listen carefully to your subject.

Interview

In an interview, one person asks another person questions. The purpose of an interview is to find out what the person being interviewed, the subject, knows or thinks about something. The interviewer usually follows a list of questions in order to keep the interview on track. He or she may respond to the subject's answers and change the topic slightly if that makes sense.

Practice It! With a partner, practice an interview you will conduct with a family member or neighbor who has moved from another city or country. Write down questions that ask your subject facts about his or her move, such as when it was, from where, and why.

Tips

An interviewer should . . .

- Prepare questions and share them with the interview's subject, the interviewee.
- Put the interviewee at ease by being polite and following the written questions in order.
- Listen carefully to the interviewee's responses.

An interviewee should . . .

- Answer questions in enough detail to satisfy the interviewer.
- Look the interviewer in the eye.
- Speak clearly, in a voice that can be heard by the interviewer and a recorder, if one is being used.

Poetry

- **Narrative poems** tell stories. Long, traditional narrative poems use regular **rhyme** and rhythm, but shorter stories may be told in different poetic forms.

- Whatever its form, a narrative poem has the features of a story and includes a plot, characters, and a theme.

- The story a narrative poem tells may be based on a famous or a personal historic event.

- Read the poems on these two pages. What story does each poem tell?

Borders

by Arnold Adoff

Great Grandma Ida came from a small village
in Poland
    on the Russian border
    to America,
    on a ship that sailed
    for weeks,
    on the rough Atlantic
        Ocean:

to make a new place for her self;
to work in a factory; to find her father;
to find a man
    from a German town on the Polish
        border

to marry; to have and raise a daughter
    who would find and marry
    a man from a Russian town
        on the Polish
        border.

And in 1935 they would have a baby boy
        in a New York City hospital
Who is daddy now to
    me.

My Bird Day

by Janet S. Wong

When my grandfather says *birthday*
in his Chinese accent,
it sounds like "bird day,"
which is closer to truth—
for us, anyway.

At my birthday parties
we never have
paper streamers,
piñatas in trees,
balloons taped up
on the wall.
We decorate with platters
of peking duck,
soy sauce chicken and squab
in lettuce cups.
Food is all
that matters.

Other Chinese families
might do things
differently,
but my grandfather,
whose name is Duck,
thinks it's good
luck to make
a bird day
special.

Happy Bird day!

Let's **Think** About...

Why can "Borders" be considered a narrative poem?

Let's **Think** About...

What does "My Bird Day" tell you about Chinese culture?

477

The Colors Live

by Mary O'Neill

The Colors live
Between black and white
In a land that we
Know best by sight.
But knowing best
Isn't everything,
For colors dance
And colors sing,
And colors laugh
And colors cry—
Turn off the light

And colors die,
And they make you feel
Every feeling there is
From the grumpiest grump
To the fizziest fizz.
And you and you and I
Know well
Each has a taste
And each has a smell
And each has a wonderful
Story to tell. . . .

The New Colossus

by Emma Lazarus

Not like the brazen giant of Greek fame,
With conquering limbs astride from land to land;
Here at our sea-washed sunset gates shall stand
A mighty woman with a torch, whose flame
Is the imprisoned lightning, and her name
Mother of Exiles. From her beacon-hand
Glows world-wide welcome; her mild eyes command
The air-bridged harbor that twin-cities frame.
"Keep, ancient lands, your storied pomp!" cries she
With silent lips. "Give me your tired, your poor,
Your huddled masses yearning to breathe free,
The wretched refuse of your teeming shore.
Send these, the homeless, tempest-tossed to me—
I lift my lamp beside the golden door!"

Glossary

How to Use This Glossary

This glossary can help you understand and pronounce the highlighted words in this book. The entries in this glossary are in alphabetical order. There are guide words at the top of each page to show you the first and last words on the page. A pronunciation key is at the bottom of the following page. Remember, if you can't find the word you are looking for, ask for help or check a dictionary.

The entry word is in dark type. It shows how the word is spelled and how the word is divided into syllables.

The pronunciation is in parentheses. It also shows which syllables are stressed.

Part-of-speech labels show the function or functions of an entry word and any listed form of that word.

con·quer (kong′kər), *V.* to overcome; get the better of: *conquer a bad habit.* ❑ *V.* **con·quered, con·quer·ing, con·querors.**

Sometimes, irregular and other special forms will be shown to help you use the word correctly.

The definition and example sentence show you what the word means and how it is used.

Aa

ac·cess (ak′ses), **1.** *N.* right to approach, enter, or use; admittance: *All students have access to the library during the afternoon.* **2.** *V.* to make information available by putting into or retrieving from a computer memory: *Please access that list of names.* ❑ *V.* **ac·cessed, ac·ces·sing.**

ac·cus·tomed (ə kus′təmd), **1.** *ADJ.* usual; customary: *By Monday I was well again and was back in my accustomed seat in class.* **2.** accustomed to; used to; in the habit of: *I am accustomed to getting up early.*

ar·chi·tec·ture (är′kə tek′chər), *N.* style or special manner of building: *Greek architecture made much use of columns.*

au·thor·i·ty (ə thôr′ə tē), *N.* power to enforce obedience; right to command or act: *Parents have authority over their children.*

Bb

ben·e·fit (ben′ə fit), **1.** *N.* anything that is for the good of someone or something; advantage: *Good roads are of great benefit to travelers.* **2.** *V.* to do good to; be good for: *Rest will benefit a sick person.* ❑ *V.* **ben·e·fits, ben·e·fit·ed, ben·e·fit·ing.**

bond·age (bon′dij), *N.* condition of being held against your will under the control or influence of some person or thing; lack of freedom; slavery.

bur·den (bėrd′n), *N.* something carried; load of things, care, work, duty, or sorrow: *Everyone in my family shares the burden of housework.*

Cc

cam·paign (kam pān′), *N.* **1.** in a war, a series of related military operations that are aimed at some special purpose: *In order to capture the enemy's most important city, the general planned one of the largest campaigns of the war.* **2.** series of connected activities to do or get something: *Our town had a campaign to raise money for a new hospital. Every four years there is a campaign for President of the United States.* ❑ *N. PL.* **cam·paigns.**

cap·tive (kap′tiv), *ADJ.* kept in confinement; held against your will: *captive animals.*

char·ac·ter·is·tic (kar/ik tə ris/tik), *ADJ.* distinguishing one person or thing from others; special: *Bananas have their own characteristic smell.* ❏ *ADV.* **char·ac·ter·is·ti·cal·ly.**

com·mis·sioned (kə mish/ənd), *ADJ.* military officer holding the rank of second lieutenant or above in the U.S. Army, Air Force, or Marine Corps, or of ensign or above in the U.S. Navy.

com·pan·ion·ship (kəm pan/yən ship), *N.* friendly feeling among companions; fellowship.

com·rade (kom/rad), *N.* **1.** a close companion and friend. **2.** fellow worker; partner. ❏ *N. PL.* **com·rades.**

con·form (kən fôrm/), *V.* **1.** to agree with: *They agreed to conform to the rules.* **2.** be the same as: *Uniforms let people conform to the same appearance.* ❏ *V.* **con·formed, con·form·ing.**

con·quer (kong/kər), *V.* to overcome; get the better of: *conquer a bad habit.* ❏ *V.* **con·quered, con·quer·ing.**

con·se·quence (kon/sə kwens), *N.* a result or effect: *The consequence of the fall was a broken leg.* *PL.* **con·se·quen·ces.**

con·vert (kən vèrt/), *V.* to turn to another for a particular use or purpose; change: *The generators at the dam convert water power into electricity.* ❏ *V.* **con·vert·ed, con·vert·ing.**

cor·rode (kə rōd/), *V.* to wear or eat away gradually: *Acid caused the pipes to corrode.* ❏ *V.* **cor·rod·ed, cor·rod·ing.**

Dd

de·cline (di klīn/), *N.* process of losing power, strength, wealth, beauty, etc.; growing worse: *Lack of money led to a decline in the condition of the school.*

de·moc·ra·cy (di mok/rə sē), *N.* government that is run by the people who live under it. In a democracy, the people rule either directly through meetings that all may attend, such as the town meetings in New England, or indirectly through the election of representatives to attend to the business of government. ❏ *N. PL.* **de·moc·ra·cies.** (*Democracy* comes from Greek words meaning "people" and "rule.")

dense (dens), *ADJ.* closely packed together; thick: *In the densest fog it is difficult to see your hand held out in front of your face.* ❏ *ADJ.* **dens·er, dens·est.** ❏ *ADV.* **dense·ly.**

des·ti·ny (des/tə nē), *N.* what becomes of someone or something; your fate or fortune: *It was George Washington's destiny to become the first President of the United States.* ❏ *N. PL.* **des·ti·nies.**

de·vise (di vīz/), *V.* to think out; plan or contrive; invent: *She needed to devise a way of raising furniture up to her treehouse.* ❏ *V.* **de·vised, dev·is·ing.**

dis·grace (dis grās/), *V.* to cause loss of honor or respect; to bring shame upon: *The embezzler disgraced her family.* ❏ *V.* **dis·graced, dis·grac·ing.**

Ee

earth·en (èr/thən), *ADJ.* **1.** made of ground, soil, or earth. **2.** made of baked clay: *earthenware dishes.*

an earthen house-1

a in *hat*	èr in *term*	ô in *order*	ch in *child*	ə = a in *about*
ā in *age*	i in *it*	oi in *oil*	ng in *long*	ə = e in *taken*
â in *care*	ī in *ice*	ou in *out*	sh in *she*	ə = i in *pencil*
ä in *far*	o in *hot*	u in *cup*	th in *thin*	ə = o in *lemon*
e in *let*	ō in *open*	ù in *put*	ᴛʜ in *then*	ə = u in *circus*
ē in *equal*	ò in *all*	ü in *rule*	zh in *measure*	

eave • hatch

eave (ēv), *N.* **1.** the projecting lower level. **2.** the lower level of a roof that sticks out over the side of a building: *They clean leaves out of the eaves every fall.* ❑ *N. PL.* **eaves.**

ef·fi·cien·cy (ə fish′ən sē) *N.* ability to produce the effect wanted without waste of time, energy, etc.: *The skilled carpenter worked with great efficiency.*

e·go (ē′gō), *N.* **1.** sense of worth; self-esteem: *Their criticism punctured my ego.* **2.** conceit; self-importance. ❑ *PL.* **e·gos.** (*Ego* comes from a Latin word meaning "I": *People with a lot of ego tend to say "I" a lot.*)

e·mis·sions (i mish′əns), *N.* substances discharged into the air from a smokestack or automobile engine: *The car's emissions left a plume of blue smoke over the road, so the driver got a ticket.*

em·pire (em′pīr), *N.* group of countries or states under one ruler or government: *The Roman Empire consisted of many separate territories and different peoples.*

en·coun·ter (en koun′tər), *v.* **1.** to meet as an enemy; meet in a fight or battle: *He knew he would encounter the enemy in direct combat.* **2.** to meet unexpectedly. ❑ *V.* **en·coun·tered, en·coun·ter·ing.**

en·gulf (en gulf′), *V.* to swallow up; overwhelm: *A wave engulfed the small boat.* ❑ *V.* **en·gulfed, en·gulf·ing.**

en·rich (en rich′), *V.* to make rich or richer: *Using compost will enrich the soil of your garden.* ❑ *V.* **en·riched, en·rich·ing.**

ex·ist·ence (eg zis′təns), *N.* **1.** condition of being: *Dinosaurs disappeared from existence millions of years ago.* **2.** occurrence: *The news media reported the existence of many new cases of influenza across the country.*

ex·panse (ek spans′), *N.* open or unbroken stretch; wide, spreading surface: *The Pacific Ocean is a vast expanse of water.*

ex·pe·di·tion (ek′spə dish′ən), *N.* journey for some special purpose, such as exploration, scientific study, or military purposes.

ex·ploit (ek sploit′), *V.* to make use of: *The men wanted to exploit the mine for its minerals.* ❑ *V.* **ex·ploit·ed, ex·ploit·ing.**

ex·tract (ek strakt′), *V.* to pull out or draw out, usually with some effort: *extract iron from the earth.* ❑ *V.* **ex·tract·ed, ex·tract·ing.**

Ff

fer·o·cious (fə rō′shəs), *ADJ* **1.** very cruel; savage; fierce: *The bear's ferocious growl was terrifying.* **2.** intense: *a ferocious headache.* ❑ *ADV.* **fer·o·cious·ly.**

fore·cast·er (fôr′kast′ər), *N.* person who predicts or tells what is coming, particularly the weather: *The forecasters predicted record high temperatures for the weekend.* ❑ *N. PL.* **fore·cast·ers.**

fo·reign·er (fôr′ə nər), *N.* person from another country; alien. ❑ *N. PL.* **fo·reign·ers.**

for·mer (fôr′mər), *ADJ.* **1.** earlier; past: *In former times, cooking was done in fireplaces instead of stoves.* **2.** the first of two: *Offered ice cream or pie, everyone chose the former.* *ADV.* **for·mer·ly.**

former

Gg

gen·e·rate (jen′ə rāt′), *V.* to cause to be; bring into being; produce: *The political candidate generated a great deal of enthusiasm among voters.* ❑ *V.* **gen·e·rat·ed, gen·e·rat·ing.**

Hh

hatch¹ (hach), *N.* **1.** an opening in a ship's deck or in the floor or roof of a building, etc.; hatchway: *They climbed down the hatch to get into the submersible.* **2.** the trapdoor covering such an opening: *The hatches were closed tightly during the storm.* ❑ *N. PL.* **hatch·es.**

hatch² (hach), *V.* **1.** to come out of an egg: *The chicks hatched this morning.* **2.** to plan something secretly: *The spies hatched a scheme to steal government secrets.* *V.* **hatch·es, hatched, hatch·ing.**

hoard (hôrd), **1.** *N.* what is saved and stored away; things stored: *They have a hoard of candy.* **2.** *V.* to save and store away: *The wealthy man hoarded his money.* *V.* **hoard·ed, hoard·ing.**

home·stead·er (hōm′sted′ər), *N.* a person who owns and lives on land granted by the U.S. government. ❏ *N. PL.* **home·stead·ers.**

Ii

i·de·al (ī dē′əl), *ADJ.* just as you would wish; perfect: *A warm, sunny day is ideal for a picnic.*

in·cu·ba·tor (ing′kyə bā′tər *or* in′kyə bā′tər), *N.* **1.** box or chamber for hatching eggs by keeping them warm and properly supplied with moisture and oxygen. **2.** a system for nurturing something by using proper care and attention: *a business incubator.*

in·su·late (in′sə lāt), *V.* **1.** to keep something from losing electricity, heat, or sound by lining or surrounding it with a material that does not conduct the kind of energy involved: *Telephone wires are often insulated by a covering of rubber.* **2.** to set apart; isolate: *Celebrities are often insulated from contact with common people.* ❏ *V.* **in·su·lat·ed, in·su·lat·ing.**

in·trep·id (in trep′id), *ADJ.* very brave; fearless; courageous: *She is an intrepid adventurer.* ❏ *ADV.* **in·trep·id·ly.**

in·vad·er (in vād′ər), *N.* person who enters with force or as an enemy: *The invaders conquered the country.* ❏ *N. PL.* **in·vad·ers.**

i·so·la·tion (ī′sə lā shən), *N.* the state of being separated from others, of being alone.

Ll

lance (lans), *N.* a long, wooden spear with a sharp iron or steel head: *The knight carried a lance as he rode into battle.*

lei·sure (lē′zher *or* lezh′ər), *ADJ.* free; not busy: *leisure hours after work.*

lush (lush), *ADJ.* having thick growth; covered with growing things: *The hillside was lush with spring flowers.*

lush

Mm

main·te·nance (mān′tə nəns), *N.* act or process of keeping in good repair.

mis·for·tune (mis fôr′chən), *N.* bad luck: *She had the misfortune to break her arm.*

mois·ture (mois′chər), *N.* slight wetness; water or other liquid suspended in very small drops in the air or spread on a surface: *Dew is moisture that collects at night on the grass.*

my·thol·o·gy (mi thol′ə jē), *N.* a group of legends or stories about a particular country or person: *Greek mythology tells stories that people still read and learn from.*

Nn

nav·i·ga·tor (nav′ə gā′tər), *N.* person in charge of finding the position and course of a ship, aircraft, or expedition.

Oo

ob·sta·cle (ob′stə kəl), *N.* something that prevents or stops progress; hindrance: *The fallen tree was an obstacle to traffic.*

or·deal (ôr dēl′), *N.* a severe test or experience: *I dreaded the ordeal of waiting in line for tickets.*

ore (ôr), *N.* rock containing enough of a metal or metals to make mining profitable. After it is mined, ore must be treated to extract the metal.

out·burst (out′bèrst′), *N.* act of bursting forth: *There was an outburst of laughter when the clown stumbled over his shoe.* ❑ *N. PL.* **out·bursts.**

Pp

per·cent·age (pər sen′tij), *N.* allowance, commission, discount, etc., figured by percent, or hundredths of the entire amount: *Their percentage of the profits was ten percent.*

pres·ence (prez′ns), *N.* **1.** condition of being present in a place: *I just learned of her presence in the city.* **2.** appearance; bearing: *The singer had a fantastic stage presence.*

prim·i·tive (prim′ə tiv), *ADJ.* very simple, such as people had early in history: *A primitive way of making fire is by rubbing two sticks together.* ❑ *ADV.* **prim·i·tive·ly.**

pro·claim (prə klām′ *or* prō klām′), *V.* to make known publicly and officially; declare publicly: *The congresswoman proclaimed that she would run for reelection.* ❑ *V.* **pro·claimed, pro·claim·ing.**

pro·gress (prog′res), *N.* an advance or growth; development; improvement: *the progress of science, showing rapid progress in your studies.*

pro·mote (prə mōt′), **1.** *V.* to raise in rank, condition, or importance: *Pupils who pass the test will be promoted to the next higher grade.* **2.** *V.* to further the sale of something by advertising. ❑ *V.* **pro·mot·ed, pro·mot·ing.**

pro·pul·sion (prə pul′shən *or* prō pul′shən), *N.* **1.** act of driving forward or onward. **2.** a propelling force: *the propulsion of jet engines.*

pro·vi·sions (prə vizh′əns *or* prō vizh′əns), *N. PL.* a supply of food and drinks: *After a long winter, the settlers were low on provisions.*

Qq

quest (kwest), *N.* expedition by knights in search of something: *There are many stories about the quests of King Arthur's knights.* ❑ *N. PL.* **quests.**

Rr

rel·ish (rel′ish), *N.* **1.** a pleasant taste; good flavor: *Hunger gives relish to simple food.* **2.** a side dish, often of fresh vegetables, to add flavor to food: *Olives, celery, and carrots were on the relish tray.*

re·new (ri nü′), *V.* make like new; restore: *The rain renewed the greenness of the fields.* ❑ *V.* **re·newed, re·new·ing.**

re·nowned (ri nound′), *ADJ.* famous: *Dr. Jonas Salk is renowned for finding a cure for polio.*

re·pro·duce (rē′prə düs′), *V.* to make a copy of: *to reproduce a photograph.* ❑ *V.* **re·pro·duced, re·pro·duc·ing.**

re·sound (ri zound′), *V.* be much talked about: *They knew that the fame of the first flight across the Atlantic would resound all over the world.* ❑ *V.* **re·sound·ed, re·sound·ing.**

re·treat (ri trēt′), **1.** *N.* act of moving back or withdrawing: *The army's retreat was orderly.* **2.** *N.* a retirement or period of retirement by a group of people for religious exercises, meditation, etc.: *The monks conducted a retreat in the mountains.*

re·volt·ing (ri vōl′ting), *ADJ.* disgusting; repulsive: *a revolting odor.*

rur·al (rür′əl), *ADJ.* in the country; belonging to the country; like that of the country: *a rural school, rural roads.* ❑ *ADV.* **rur·al·ly.**

rural

Ss

sanc·tu·ar·y (sangk′chü er′ē), *N.* place of refuge or protection: *Wildlife sanctuaries help ensure animals' safety.* ❑ *N. PL.* **sanc·tu·ar·ies.**

set·tle·ment (set′l mənt), *N.* group of buildings and the people living in them: *The prairie settlement was a day's ride from the next town.*

silt (silt), *N.* very fine particles of dirt carried by moving water and deposited as sediment: *The harbor is being choked with silt.*

squire (skwir), *N.* (in the Middle Ages) a young man of noble family who attended a knight until he himself was made a knight; attendant.

stim·u·lat·ing (stim′yə lāt ing), *ADJ.* lively; engaging: *The stimulating conversation made the party interesting.*

sub·mer·si·ble (səb mèr′sə bəl), **1.** *N.* a submarine. **2.** *ADJ.* able to be put under water or submerged: *The rubber duck was not submersible.*

suf·fi·cient (sə fish′ənt), *ADJ.* as much as is needed; enough: *sufficient proof.* ❑ *ADV.* **suf·fi·cient·ly.**

sus·tain·a·ble (sə stān′ə bəl), *ADJ.* of, relating to, or being a method of harvesting or using a resource so that the resource is not depleted or permanently damaged: *The architect designed a house that uses sustainable techniques for its heat.* ❑ *ADV.* **sus·tain·ab·ly.**

Tt

ten·tac·le (ten′tə kəl), *N.* a long, slender, flexible growth on the head or around the mouth of an animal, used to touch, hold, or move; feeler: *Both an octopus and a squid have tentacles.* ❑ *N. PL.* **ten·tac·les.**

toll[1] (tōl), **1.** *V.* to sound with single strokes that are slowly and regularly repeated: *a bell's toll.* **2.** *N.* something paid, lost, suffered, etc.: *Accidents take a heavy toll of human lives.* ❑ *V.* **tolled, tol·ling.**

toll[2] (tōl), *N.* tax or fee paid for some right or privilege: *We pay a toll when we use the bridge.*

tor·ment (tôr′ment), *N.* a cause of very great pain: *A bad burn can be a torment.*

trans·mit (tran smit′ *or* tranz mit′), *V.* to send out signals by means of electromagnetic waves or by wire: *Some radio station is transmitting every hour of the day.* ❑ *V.* **trans·mit·ted, trans·mit·ting.**

tur·bine (tėr′bən *or* tėr′bīn), *N.* engine containing a wheel with paddles or blades, caused to rotate by the pressure of rapidly flowing air, water, or steam: *Those wind turbines turn generators that produce electric power for the town.* ❑ *N. PL.* **tur·bines.**

Uu

un·ac·com·pa·nied (un′ə kum′pə nēd), *ADJ.* not accompanied; alone.

u·ni·son (yü′nə sən), *N.* agreement: *The marchers' feet moved in unison. We spoke in unison.*

ur·ban (ėr′bən), *ADJ.* typical of cities: *urban life.*

urban

Vv

ven·ture (ven′chər), *V.* to dare to come or go: *We ventured out on the thin ice and fell through.* ❑ *V.* **ven·tured, ven·tur·ing.**

ver·i·fy (ver′ə fī), *V.* to prove to be true; confirm: *The witness's account of the accident would verify the driver's report.* ❑ *V.* **ver·i·fied, ver·i·fy·ing.**

Ww

wilt (wilt), *V.* **1.** to become limp and bend down; wither: *Flowers and plants wilt when they don't get enough water.* **2.** to lose strength, vigor, assurance, etc.: *The performers wilted after their three-hour concert.* ❑ *V.* **wilt·ed, wilt·ing.**

Unit 4

Into the Ice

English	Spanish
conquer	conquistar*
destiny	destino*
expedition	expedición*
insulated	aislados
isolation	aislamiento
navigator	navegador *
provisions	provisiones*
verify	verificar*

The Chimpanzees I Love

English	Spanish
captive	en cautiverio
companionship	compañía*
existence	existencia*
ordeal	experiencia terrible
primitive	primitiva*
sanctuaries	santuarios*
stimulating	estimulantes*

Black Frontiers

English	Spanish
bondage	esclavitud
commissioned	comisionados*
earthen	de tierra
encounter	enfrentar
homesteaders	nuevos colonos
settlement	asentamiento

* English/Spanish cognate: A **cognate** is a word that is similar in two languages and has the same meaning in both languages.

Deep-Sea Danger

English	Spanish
ego	ego*
hatch	trampilla
intrepid	intrépido*
propulsion	propulsión*
silt	cieno
submersible	sumergible*
tentacles	tentáculos*

Inventing the Future: A Photobiography of Thomas Alva Edison

English	Spanish
converts	convierte*
devise	concebir
efficiency	eficiencia*
generated	generaba*
percentage	porcentaje*
proclaimed	proclamaron*
reproduce	reproducir*
transmitted	transmitía*

Unit 5

The View from Saturday

English	Spanish
accustomed	acostumbrados*
decline	no aceptar
former	anterior
presence	presencia*
unaccompanied	solo

Harvesting Hope: The Story of Cesar Chavez

English	Spanish
access	acceso*
authority	autoridad*
lush	exuberante
obstacle	obstáculo*
toll	estragos
torment	tormentos*
wilt	marchitarse

Word List English/Spanish

The River That Went to the Sky: A Story from Malawi

English	Spanish
densest	más tupido
eaves	aleros (techo de árboles)
expanse	gran área
moisture	humedad
ventured	aventuraban*

Gold

English	Spanish
characteristic	característico*
corrode	se corroen*
engulfed	sumida
exploit	explotar*
extract	extraer
hoard	botín

Greensburg Goes Green

English	Spanish
consequences	consecuencias*
emissions	emisiones*
ferocious	feroz*
forecasters	pronosticadores
incubator	incubadora*
sustainable	sostenible*
turbines	turbinas*

Unit 6

Don Quixote and the Windmills

English	Spanish
lance	lanza*
misfortune	desventura
quests	búsquedas
renewed	renovado
renowned	célebres
resound	resonarán
squire	escudero

Ancient Greece

English	Spanish
architecture	arquitectura*
democracy	democracia*
empire	imperio*
ideal	ideal*
mythology	mitología*

The All-American Slurp

English	Spanish
disgraced	deshonramos
progress	progreso*
promoted	promovido
relish	aperitivos
retreat	retirarse
revolting	repugnante
unison	al unísono

The Aztec News

English	Spanish
benefits	beneficios*
campaigns	campañas*
comrades	compañeros
enrich	enriquecer
foreigners	extranjeros
invaders	invasores

Where Opportunity Awaits

English	Spanish
burden	carga
conformed	conformaron*
leisure	libertad
maintenance	mantenimiento*
rural	rural*
sufficient	suficiente*
urban	urbano*

Acknowledgments

Text

Grateful acknowledgment is made to the following for copyrighted material:

Alfred A. Knopf, a division of Random House, Inc.

"The Dream Keeper" edited by Arnold Rampersad with David Roessel, Assoc, Copyright © 1994 by The Estate of Langston Hughes, from *The Collected Poems Of Langston Hughes* by Langston Hughes. Edited by Arnold Rampersad with David Roessel, Associated Editor, Copyright © 1994 by The Estate of Langston Hughes. "Dreams" edited by Arnold Rampersad with David Roessel, Assoc, Copyright © 1994 by The Estate of Langston Hughes, from *The Collected Poems Of Langston Hughes* by Langston Hughes. Edited by Arnold Rampersad with David Roessel, Associated Editor, Copyright © 1994 by The Estate of Langston Hughes. "Pecos Bill" from *American Tall Tales* by Mary Pope Osborne. Copyright © 1991 by Mary Pope Osborne. Illustrations copyright © 1991 by Michael McCurdy. "Youth" edited by Arnold Rampersad with David Roessel, Assoc, Copyright © 1994 by The Estate of Langston Hughes, from *The Collected Poems Of Langston Hughes* by Langston Hughes. Edited by Arnold Rampersad with David Roessel, Associated Editor, Copyright © 1994 by The Estate of Langston Hughes. Used by permission of Alfred A. Knopf, a division of Random House, Inc.

Andrew Wylie Agency & Simon & Schuster Books for Young Readers, an imprint of Simon & Schuster Children's Publishing Division

From *Black Frontiers* by Lillian Schlissel. Copyright © 1995 by Lillian Schlissel. Used by permission of the Andrew Wylie Agency and Simon & Schuster Books for Young Readers, an imprint of Simon & Schuster Children's Publishing Division.

Atheneum Books for Young Readers, an imprint of Simon & Schuster Children's Publishing Division

From *The View from Saturday* by E.L. Konigsburg. Copyright © 1996 E.L. Konigsburg. Used with the permission of Atheneum Books for Young Readers, an imprint of Simon & Schuster Children's Publishing Division.

Candlewick Press, Inc. on behalf of Walker Books Ltd.

The Aztec News. Text © 1997 by Philip Steele. Illustrations © 1997 by Walker Books Ltd. Reproduced by permission of the publisher, Candlewick Press, Inc., Cambridge, MA, on behalf of Walker Books Ltd, London.

Capstone Press

From *Ancient Greece* by Kim covert. © 2004 by Capstone Press. Used by permission of Capstone Press. All rights reserved.

Cobblestone Publishing, a division of Carus Publishing Company

"Going Ape Over Language" by Natalie M. Rosinsky from *Oddysey's October 2001 Issue: Passionate About Primates.* Copyright © 2001, Cobblestone Publishing, 30 Grove Street, Suite C, Peterborough, NH 03458. All rights reserved. Used by permission of Carus Publishing Company.

Columbia University Press

"Gold Rush" from the *COLUMBIA ENCYCLOPEDIA 6th EDITION* found at www.enclyopedia.com. Used by permission of Columbia University Press.

Dutton Children's Books, A Member of Penguin Group (USA) Inc.

"Coming Over" by Russell Freedman from *Immigrant Kids.* Copyright © 1980 by Russell Freedman. "Science Fair Project" by Carol Diggory Shields from *Almost Late To School And More School Poems.* Copyright © 2003 by Caorl Diggory Shields, text. Used by permission of Dutton Children's Books, A Division of Penguin Young Readers Group, A Member ofPenguin Group (USA) Inc., 345 Hudson Street, New York, NY 10014. All rights reserved.

Farrar, Straus and Giroux, LLC

"Don Quixote and the Windmills" a retelling by Eric A. Kimmel from *The Ingenious Hidalog Don Quixote de la Mancha* by Miguel de Cervantes Saavedra, pictures by Leonard Everett Fisher. Retelling copyright © 2004 by Shearwater Books. Used by permission of Farrar, Straus and Giroux, LLC.

HarperCollins Children's Books, a division of HarperCollins Publishers

"For the Earth Day Contest" by Jeanette Neff from *We The People* by Bobbi Katz. Text Copyright © 2000 by Bobbi Katz. Illustrated by Nina Crews. Used by permission of HarperCollins Publishers.

HarperCollins Publishers

"Borders" from *All the Colors of the Race* by Arnold Adoff. Text © 1982 by Arnold Adoff. "Farmworkers" from *Gathering The Sun* by Alma Flor Ada and illustrated by Simon Silva. Text Copyright © 1997 by Alam Flor Ada. Used with permission of the HarperCollins Publishers.

HarperCollins Publishers & Curtis Brown, Ltd.

Copyright © 1997 by Ann Turner. "Seeds" now appears in *Mississippi Mud: Three Prairie Journals,* published by HarperCollins. Used by permission of Curtis Brown, Ltd.

Holiday House, Inc.

From *How to Survive in Antarctica* by Lucy Jane Bledsoe. Text and photograph copyright © 2006 by Lucy Jane Bledsoe. All rights reserved. Used by permission of Holiday House, Inc.

Houghton Mifflin Harcourt Publishing Company

Harvesting Hope: The Story of Cesar Chavez by Kathleen Krull, illustrated by Yuri Morales. Text copyright © 2003 by Kathleen Krull. Illustrations copyright © 2003 by Yuri Morales. From *Into the Ice: The Story of Arctic Exploration* by Lynn Curlee. © 1998 by Lynn Curlee. Reproduced by permission of Houghton Mifflin

Illustrations

Acknowledgments

Photographs

Every effort has been made to secure permission and provide appropriate credit for photographic material. The publisher deeply regrets any omission and pledges to correct errors called to its attention in subsequent editions.

Unless otherwise acknowledged, all photographs are the property of Pearson Education, Inc.

Photo locators denoted as follows: Top (T), Center (C), Bottom (B), Left (L), Right (R), Background (Bkgd)

18 ©Greg Ryan/Alamy Images; 20 (B) ©david tipling/Alamy, (Bkgd) ©Gordon Wiltsie/Getty Images; 21 ©Jon Arnold Images Ltd/Alamy Images; 24 (B) ©Alaska Stock LLC/Alamy Images, (C) ©Bates Littlehales/Getty Images, (T) ©Galen Rowell/Corbis; 44 ©Danita Delimont/Alamy Images; 46 ©Danita Delimont/Alamy Images; 50 ©Nick Hanna/Alamy Images; 51 (T) ©Corbis Premium RF/Alamy, (B) ©FLPA/Alamy Images; 54 (T) ©imagebroker/Alamy Images, (B) ©Roy Morsch/PhotoLibrary Group, Inc., (C) Photos to Go/PhotoLibrary; 56 (Bkgd) ©Michael Neugebauer; 59 (Bkgd) ©Hugo Van Lawick/NGS Image Collection; 60 (TL) ©Randy Wells/Corbis, (TR) ©Tetsuro Matsuzawa; 61 (TR) ©Gerry Ellis/Minden Pictures, (TL) ©Michael Nichols/NGS Image Collection; 62 (BR, BL) ©Michael Nichols/NGS Image Collection; 64 (Bkgd) ©Kristin Mosher/Danita Delimont, Agent; 67 (Bkgd) ©Michael Nichols/NGS Image Collection; 68 (TL) ©Michael Neugebauer; 82 (Bkgd) ©Lowell Georgia/Corbis, (C) Corbis; 83 (B) ©Greg Ryan/Alamy; 86 (T) ©Alison Wright/Corbis, (B) ©philipus/Alamy, (C) Corbis; 88 (Bkgd) ©LC. S611.016. Nitrate negative, ca. 1911–1915. Erwin E. Smith Collection of the Library of Congress on Deposit at the Amon Carter Museum, Fort Worth, Texas/Amon Carter Museum, Fort Worth, Texas; 90 (R) Corbis; 91 (C) ©J.C. Coovert/Library of Congress; 92 (Bkgd) ©David Muench/Corbis, (TR) Corbis; 93 (BL) ©Nebraska State Historical Society Photograph Collections/Nebraska State Historical Society, (BR) ©Peter deLory/Getty Images; 94 (TR) ©Courtesy of/Kansas State Historical Society, (R) ©David Muench/Corbis; 95 (TL, B) ©Courtesy of/Kansas State Historical Society; 96 (TC) ©Nebraska State Historical Society Photograph Collections/Nebraska State Historical Society, (Bkgd) Baseball Hall of Fame Library, Cooperstown, NY; 97 (BR) ©Nebraska State Historical Society Photograph Collections/Nebraska State Historical Society; 98 (TR) ©Records of the U.S. House of Representatives/National Archives; 99 (B) ©Henry A. Schmidt Collection, image#000-179-0728/Center for Southwest Research, General Library, University of New Mexico, (TL) ©Use of Tenth Cavalry insignia does not constitute endorsement by the U.S. Army; 100 (CR) ©Underwood & Underwood/Corbis, (TR) Corbis; 101 (BR) Corbis; 110 (Bkgd) ©Ralph White/Corbis, (T) GRIN/NASA;

111 ©Michael Patrick O'Neill/Alamy Images; 114 (B) ©age fotostock/SuperStock, (C) ©Ralph White/Corbis, (T) ©Sereda Nikolay Ivanovich/Shutterstock; 115 (Bkgd) ©Paul Thompson/©Danita Delimont, Agent, (BR) ©Stephen Frink/Getty Images, (T) ©Frank Greenaway/Courtesy of the Weymouth Sea Life Center/©DK Images; 136 Getty Images; 138 (B) ©Al Giddings, (T) Jupiter Images; 139 (TR) Getty Images; 142 (Bkgd) ©Underwood & Underwood/Corbis, (B) Photos to Go/Photolibrary; 143 Jupiter Images; 146 (C) ©Frazer Harrison/Getty Images, (C) ©Helge Pedersen/Alamy Images, (B) ©Hill Street Studios/Getty Images, (T) Getty Images; 149 (C) SuperStock; 150 (TL) From the Collections of The Henry Ford; 151 (CR) Bettmann/Corbis; 152 (TL, CL, BL) Edison National Historic Site/National Park Service/U.S. Department of the Interior; 153 (BC) Edison National Historic Site/National Park Service/U.S. Department of the Interior;

154 (T) From the Collections of The Henry Ford; 155 (BC) Edison National Historic Site/National Park Service/U.S. Department of the Interior; 156 (C) From the Collections of The Henry Ford; 159 (C) ©Mathew B. Brady/Corbis; 160 (TC) Edison National Historic Site/National Park Service/U.S. Department of the Interior; 161 (BL) Schenectady Museum, (CR) The Granger Collection, NY, (TR) Thomas A. Edison Papers at Rutgers, the State University of New Jersey/Thomas A. Edison Papers at Rutgers, the State University of New Jersey; 162 (C) Schenectady Museum; Hall of Electrical History Foundation/Corbis; 163 (TR) Edison National Historic Site/National Park Service/U.S. Department of the Interior; 164 (TL) ©Breton Littlehales/Courtesy George Eastman House; 165 (BR) Edison National Historic Site/National Park Service/U.S. Department of the Interior, (TC) From the Collections of The Henry Ford; 170 (TR) Western Reserve Historical Society; 171 (BR) Schenectady Museum; Hall of Electrical History Foundation/Corbis; 172 (TR) Hulton-Deutsch Collection/Corbis; 180 ©Anthony Dunn/Alamy Images; 182 (B) ©Ariel Skelley/Corbis, (Bkgd) ©Jose Luis Pelaez Inc./Getty Images; 183 ©Chris Ryan/Getty Images; 185 ©DK Images; 186 (C) ©Bo Zaunders/Corbis, (T) ©Walter B. McKenzie/Getty Images, (B) Jupiter Images; 214 (Bkgd) ©Bettmann/Corbis, (B) ©David Taylor/Alamy Images; 215 ©Bettmann/Corbis; 218 (B) ©Nigel Cattlin/Alamy Images, (T) ©SB Photography/Alamy, (C) Getty Images; 240 (C) ©Ilene MacDonald/Alamy, (Bkgd) ©Phil Degginger/Alamy Images; 241 Jupiter Images; 243 (Bkgd) ©DK Images, (TR) ©Rick Gayle/Corbis; 244 (T) ©Jerome Scholler/Shutterstock, (C, B) Jupiter Images; 245 ©Frans Lanting/Corbis; 264 (Bkgd) ©Bryan F. Peterson/Corbis; 265 (B) Photolibrary Group, Inc., (T) Photos to Go/Photolibrary; 268 (C) ©canadabrian/Alamy, (T) ©John Boud/Alamy, (B) Jupiter Images; 270 (Bkgd) Digital Vision; 272 (BL) © Elio Ciol/

WORDS!

Vocabulary Handbook

Antonyms

Synonyms

Base Words/Root Words

Prefixes

Suffixes

Context Clues

Related Words

Word Origins: Roots

Multiple-Meaning Words

Dictionary

Thesaurus

Antonyms

An antonym is a word that has the opposite meaning of another word. *Day* is an antonym for *night*.

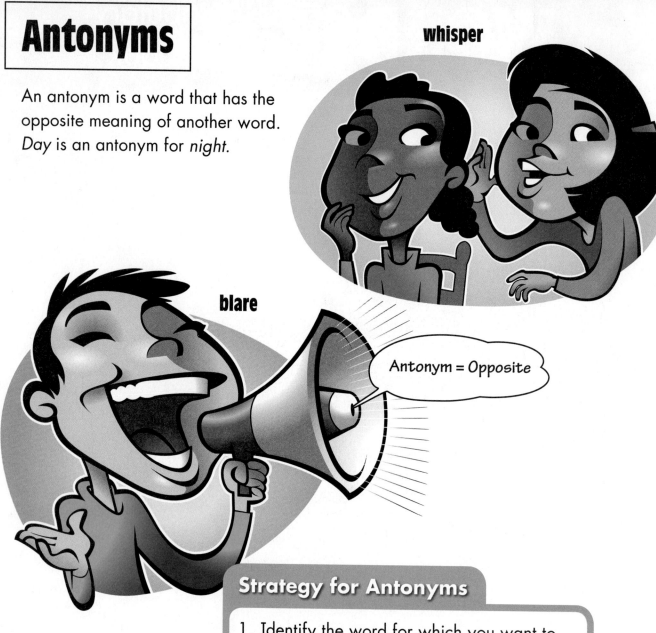

whisper

blare

Antonym = Opposite

Strategy for Antonyms

1. Identify the word for which you want to find an antonym.
2. Think of other words or phrases that have the opposite meaning.
3. Use a thesaurus to help you find antonyms.
4. Use a dictionary to check antonyms' meanings so that you use the word that best communicates your ideas.

Synonyms

Synonyms are two or more words that have the same meaning or nearly the same meaning.

display

Synonym = Same

show

Strategy for Synonyms

1. Identify the word for which you want to find a synonym.
2. Think of other words or phrases that have the same, or almost the same, meaning.
3. Use a thesaurus to help you find more synonyms, and make a list.
4. Use a dictionary to find the word that best communicates your ideas.

Base Words/Root Words

A base word, also called a root word, is a word that can't be broken into smaller words.

unlock

Lock is the base word.

lock

Strategy for Base Words

1. Look for a base word in the unknown word.
2. Determine the meaning of the base word.
3. Guess the meaning of the unknown word. Does it make sense in the sentence?
4. Check your guess in a dictionary.

Prefixes

A prefix is a word part added onto the front of a base word to form a new word.

cap

uncap

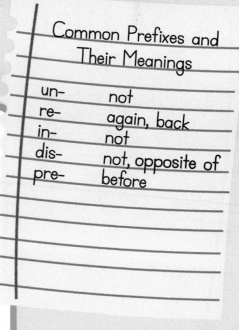

Strategy for Prefixes

1. Look at the unknown word and identify the prefix.
2. What does the base word mean? If you're not sure, check a dictionary.
3. Use what you know about the base word and the prefix to figure out the meaning of the unknown word.
4. Use a dictionary to check your guess.

Common Prefixes and Their Meanings

Prefix	Meaning
un–	not
re–	again, back
in–	not
dis–	not, opposite of
pre–	before

Suffixes

A suffix is a word part added to the end of a base word to form a new word.

coat

coatless

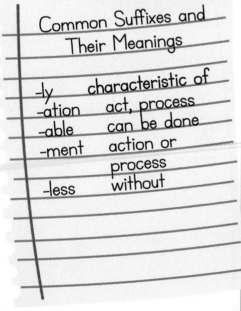

Common Suffixes and Their Meanings

-ly	characteristic of
-ation	act, process
-able	can be done
-ment	action or process
-less	without

Strategy for Suffixes

1. Look at the unknown word and identify the suffix.
2. What does the base word mean? If you're not sure, check a dictionary.
3. Use what you know about the base word and the suffix to figure out the meaning of the unknown word.
4. Use a dictionary to check your guess.

Context Clues

Context clues are the words and sentences found around an unknown word that may help you figure out a word's meaning.

My mother and I bought some delicious fruit today. We bought bananas, grapes, apples, and my favorite—kiwis!

SALE

Strategy for Context Clues

1. Look for clues in the words and phrases around the unknown word.
2. Take a guess at the word's meaning. Does it make sense in the sentence?
3. Use a dictionary to check your guess.

Related Words

Related words are words that all have the same base word.

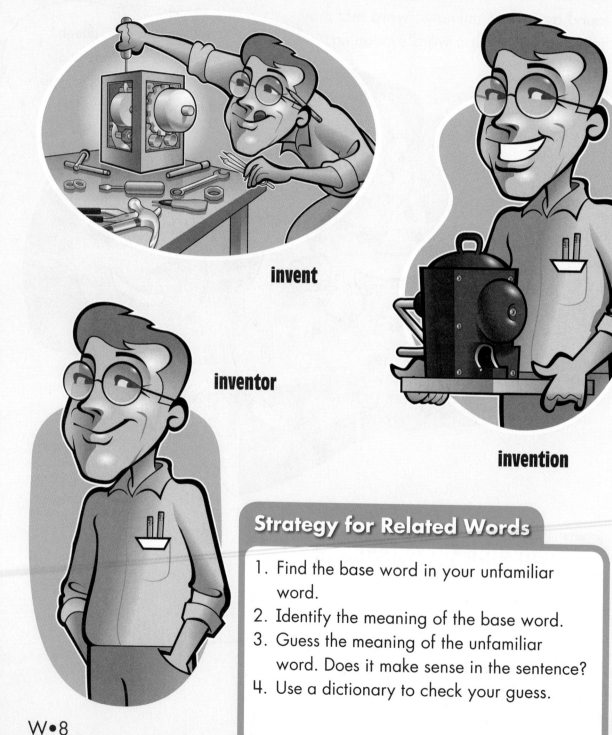

invent

inventor

invention

Strategy for Related Words

1. Find the base word in your unfamiliar word.
2. Identify the meaning of the base word.
3. Guess the meaning of the unfamiliar word. Does it make sense in the sentence?
4. Use a dictionary to check your guess.

Word Origins: Roots

Many English words contain
Greek and Latin roots.

microscope

dentist

submarine

Latin Roots

dent	tooth
dict	to say; to speak
scrib	to write
sub	under; below
tract	to pull
vis	to see

Greek Roots

auto	self
bio	life
micro	very small
ology	the study of
phon	sound; voice
scope	see
tele	far

Strategy for Roots

1. Using what you know about roots, guess the meaning of the unknown word.
2. Does your guess make sense in the sentence?
3. Use a dictionary to check your guess.

Multiple-Meaning Words

Multiple-meaning words are words that have different meanings depending on how they are used. Homographs, homonyms, and homophones are all multiple-meaning words.

Homographs

Homographs are words that are spelled the same but have different meanings and are sometimes pronounced differently.

bow

bow

Some Common Homographs

bass
close
contract
lead
live
present

Strategy for Homographs

1. Read the words and phrases near the homograph.
2. Think about the homograph's different meanings and decide which one makes the most sense in the sentence.
3. Reread the sentence with your guess to see if it makes sense.
4. Check your guess in a dictionary.

Homonyms

Homonyms are words that are pronounced the same and have the same spelling, but their meanings are different.

row

row

Some Common
Homonyms

pen
duck
mail
ear
bank
bark

Strategy for Homonyms

1. Read the words and phrases near the homonym.
2. Think about the homonym's different meanings and decide which one makes the most sense.
3. Reread the sentence with your guess to see if it makes sense.
4. Use a dictionary to check your guess.

Homophones

Homophones are words that are pronounced the same way but have different spellings and meanings.

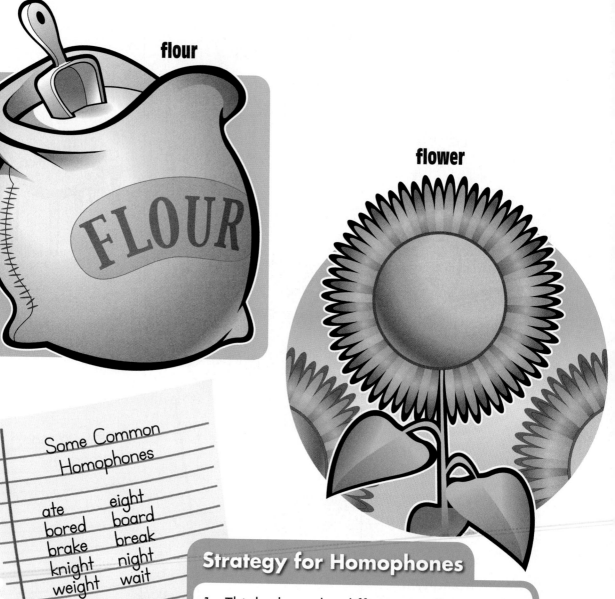

flour

flower

Some Common Homophones

ate	eight
bored	board
brake	break
knight	night
weight	wait

Strategy for Homophones

1. Think about the different spellings and meanings of the homophone.
2. Check a dictionary for the definitions of the words.
3. Use the word that best fits your purpose.

This chart can help you remember the differences between homographs, homonyms, and homophones.

Understanding Homographs, Homonyms, and Homophones

	Pronunciation	Spelling	Meaning
Homographs	may be the same or different	same	different
Homonyms	same	same	different
Homophones	same	different	different

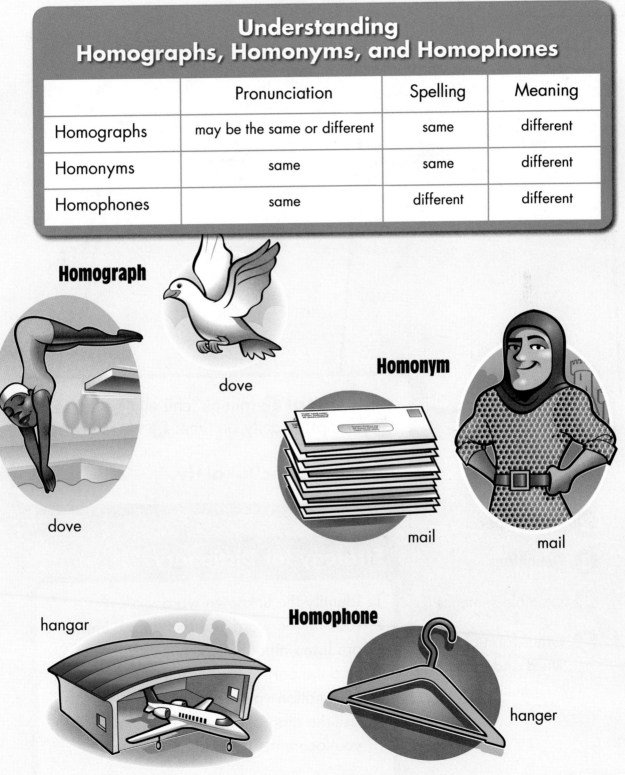

Homograph

dove

dove

Homonym

mail

mail

Homophone

hangar

hanger

Dictionary

A dictionary is a reference book that lists words alphabetically. It can be used to look up pronunciation, parts of speech, definitions, and spelling of words.

> **punc•tu•al** ❶ (pungk' chü əl),❷ *ADJECTIVE.*
> ❸ prompt; exactly on time: ❹ *He is always punctual.*
> ❺ ✳ *ADVERB* **punc'tu•al•ly.**

❶ Pronunciation

❷ Part of speech

❸ Definitions

❹ Example sentence

❺ Other form of the word and its part of speech

Strategy for Dictionary

1. Identify the unknown word.
2. Look up the word in a dictionary. Entries are listed alphabetically.
3. Find the part of the entry that has the information you are looking for.
4. Use the diagram above as a guide to help you locate the information you want.

Thesaurus

A thesaurus is a book of synonyms. A thesaurus may also list antonyms for many words.

cute
adjective
attractive, appealing, amusing, charming, adorable, enchanting.
ANTONYMS: plain, ugly

Strategy for Thesaurus

1. Look up the word in a thesaurus. Entries are listed alphabetically.
2. Locate the synonyms and any antonyms for your word.
3. Use a dictionary to help you choose the word with the exact meaning you want.